HE
2754
.B8
A3
1991

Brown, Charles P., b.
  1879.

Brownie the boomer.

$24.00

DATE			

Brownie the Boomer

Brownie the Boomer

The Life of Charles P. Brown, an American Railroader

Edited by H. Roger Grant

 NORTHERN ILLINOIS UNIVERSITY PRESS
DeKalb
1991

For my mentors at Simpson College:

R. William Helfrich

Joseph W. Walt

Introduction and Notes © 1991 by the Northern Illinois University Press.
Text © 1930 by Charles P. Brown, renewed 1958 by Josephine (Mrs. Charles) Brown.
Our attempts to locate the heirs of Charles and Josehine Brown have failed. If anyone can
offer further information, please contact the managing editor of the Press.

∞ Published by the Northern Illinois University Press, DeKalb, Illinois 60115
Manfactured in the United States of America. All casebound books published by the Press
are printed on acid-free paper and Smyth sewn.
Design by Julia Fauci

Library of Congress Cataloging-in-Publication Data

Brown, Charles P., b. 1879.
    Brownie the boomer : the life of Charles P. Brown, an American railroader / edited
by H. Roger Grant.
    p.   cm.
    Includes bibliographical references and index.
    ISBN 0-87580-146-3 (alk. paper)
    1. Brown Charles P., b. 1879.   2. Railroads—United States—Employees—Biography.
3. Seasonal labor—United States—Biography.
I. Grant, H. Roger, 1943–   . II. Title.
HE2754.B8A3   1991
385'.092—dc20   90-26731
[B]   CIP

Title Page Art: *The Pleasant Part of a Brakeman's Life* (A. B. Frost, 1888)

Contents

Acknowledgments

Occasionally historians make wonderful discoveries. In this respect I have been fortunate. In the early 1970s, for example, I helped to uncover the diary of a remarkable Iowa farmer who thoughtfully chronicled his troubled life in the 1930s. This massive document later became *Years of Struggle: The Farm Diary of Elmer G. Powers, 1931–1936* (Ames: Iowa State University Press, 1976), coedited with L. Edward Purcell. While recently preparing a collection of reminiscences of railroad travel, I noticed in Donovan L. Hofsommer's *Railroads of the Trans-Mississippi West: A Selected Bibliography of Books* (Plainview, Texas: Llano Estacado Museum, 1976, p. 72) reference to a volume with a catchy title: *Brownie the Boomer: The Life of Chas. P. Brown as a Boomer Railroad Man.* Not knowing what to expect, I requested a copy through inter-library loan from the University of California at Los Angeles, the only OCLC-network library, except for the Library of Congress, to list one. Soon after it arrived, I began to read Charles Brown's saga of railroading at the turn of the century. I found his story captivating, and, after a few dozen pages, I realized that this was a forgotten gem: Brown, more than others, describes clearly and in a readable fashion the workaday life of a bygone breed, the railroad "boomer." I knew that his obscure book—at the time I failed to appreciate its rareness—deserved to be read by a large audience. I subsequently learned of an earlier version of Brown's autobiography. Once I obtained it—only the Library of Congress had one available—I embarked upon my editing.

The process of piecing together Brown's life and adding explanatory notes has been both challenging and rewarding. A host of individuals showed remarkable sensitivity to my needs. I wish to thank Boris Blick, Keith L. Bryant, Jr., Daniel Nelson, and David C. Riede, colleagues at The University of Akron; Cynthia Birt, Whittier Public Library, Whittier, California; Emily Clark, Chicago Historical Society, Chicago, Illinois; Ronald L. F. Davis, California State University, Northridge, California; Don L. Hofsommer, St. Cloud State University, St. Cloud, Minnesota; Mary Lincoln, Northern Illinois University Press, DeKalb, Illinois; Connie Menninger, Kansas State Historical Society, Topeka, Kansas; Edward Parker, State Historical Society of Missouri, Columbia, Missouri; Andrea Paul, Nebraska State Historical Society, Lincoln, Nebraska; Robert C. Post, Smithsonian Institution, Washington, D.C.; Sally C. Proshek, The Huntington Library, San Marino, California; Jacqueline J. Pryor, Railway & Locomotive Historical Society Archives, Sacramento, California; Don Snoddy, Union Pacific Museum, Omaha, Nebraska, Ellen Schwartz, California State Railroad Museum, Sacramento, California; Jean B. Thompson, Crawfordsville District Public Library, Crawfordsville, Indiana; John H. White, Jr., Smithsonian Institution, Washington, D.C.; W. Thomas White, James Jerome Hill Reference Library, St. Paul, Minnesota; and William L. Withuhn, Smithsonian Institution, Washington, D.C. Jere R. Baker, Napa, California; C. Susan Chester, M.D., Brecksville, Ohio; William D. Edson, Potomac, Maryland; William Jackson, Whittier, California; Gregory W. Maxwell, St. Louis, Missouri; Charles C. Shannon, Arlington Heights, Illinois; and Fred A. Stindt, Kelseyville, California, also assisted me. Once more, my wife, Martha Farrington Grant, proved to be a helpful critic. My typists, Mia S. O'Connor and especially Edie Richeson, made the "Brownie" project something special.

H. Roger Grant

Introduction

H. Roger Grant

The story of a "common" person is not always so common. Admittedly, scores of scholars in recent years have attempted to examine the past from the "bottom up," that is by exploring the lives of lesser-known and usually inarticulate Americans, whether weavers, carpenters, laundry workers, or household servants. But few historians have looked closely at railroad workers, especially the thousands who roamed the country during the late nineteenth and early twentieth centuries. These are the so- called boomers, men who failed to secure a permanent job with one company, either by choice or circumstance.[1]

Unquestionably, boomers, these "men in motion," helped to build and operate an ever-expanding network of steel rails. Railroads during this time not only supplemented or replaced established forms of transportation but also introduced modern transportation where none had existed. Trackage ballooned from 52,922 miles in 1870 to 240,831 miles in 1910, a whopping increase of 455.07 percent. Carriers were often so desperate for manpower that they hired large numbers of temporary employees for construction and maintenance jobs. Before World War I the Great Northern Railway, for one, engaged more than 5,000 Japanese laborers in addition to thousands of others, including many eastern and southern Europeans, to do its seasonal unskilled or semiskilled work.[2] Workers' tasks involved grading rights-of-way, installing ties and rails, and ballasting, tamping, and aligning track. Railroads also employed thousands of trainmen, enginemen, and telegraphers—skilled personnel—on a short-term basis. When traffic soared, for instance during the grain and livestock rushes, companies needed these men badly. A retired official of the Chicago & North Western Railway recalls that as late as the 1930s his road still hired scores of "extra" switchmen to handle seasonal shipments of range cattle and sheep from parts of the Great Plains to eastern destinations. "We had to have those boomer switchmen. We simply could not get the cars moved without them. . . . [W]e regularly hauled a stock train out of Wyoming every hour on Fridays."[3]

Specific figures on the number of boomer railroaders are impossible to determine, but, as suggested, they were significant. Since the job turnover was often rapid, especially for those engaged in construction and maintenance, railroad recordkeeping was often incomplete. Companies did not count accurately the many boomers who came and went in short order. If contractors and subcontractors hired workers, then the railroads usually made no attempt to maintain employment figures. Moreover, admitted the corporate secretary of the Chicago Great Western Railroad in 1912: "Our company . . . like others, has not kept good count of transients. . . . Trainmasters, Roadmasters and Superintendents care about recording activities of men who expect to remain in the company's employ. . . . [T]imesheets and payroll records show [boomers'] presence, but the annual statement [of the work force] is the number of men employed at the end of the year."[4] The latter, of course, would not reflect seasonal help. Not surprisingly, state labor bureaus' annual reports are likewise flawed. They are too low because they relied on the railroads' own figures. Federal census returns and data, too, are not particularly useful.

Undeniably a common phenomenon in railroading, boomers existed for a variety of reasons. Those who lacked skills were hired for their brawn; after all, the industry before dieselization and modern mechanization was enormously labor-intensive. Those who possessed skills—commonly members of the running trades—offered talents that railroads also required. Since carriers needed boomers, they typically overlooked an individual's less-than-perfect record. Some men jumped from job to job because of drinking problems or other service violations. Some, too, became boomers due to strikes or political agitation; "black-listed" workers could, and often did, easily change their identity, and employment then generally followed. Others may have had unhappy domestic lives and therefore they wanted to be on the move. Yet Charles P. Brown, in his remarkable autobiography, explains why "booming," particularly among operating men, flourished for several generations.

> . . . when [Union Pacific] cut the board . . . and layed [sic] all of us extra
> men off, of course we had to leave . . . and go some place else looking

for work, and this thing of traveling around looking for a job, is what makes a boomer out of a fellow, and that is the reason that the boomer never stays any place on any one job long enough to get promoted, but keeps jumping around over the country from place to place, and working as a brakeman, switchman or a fireman, on different railroads where business is good, and when business falls off where he is working, so that he can't make any money on the extra board, in most cases if he don't get layed [sic] off, he bunches [quits] the job on his own accord, and . . . beats it to some other part of the country and gets a new job on another railroad and sticks through the rush until things get too dull, then he is on his way again, looking for new adventures and a chance to have a heck of a good time, if there is a good time to be had. So this is the life of the boomer, who is a happy-go-lucky, not caring-a-hang sort of cuss, here today, and there tomorrow, not giving a dang where he is. . . .[5]

Brown correctly implies that some individuals quit or "bunched" their jobs and relocated so as to gain periods of free time. Transportation workers before the 1940s generally did not earn vacation days, and so they had either to "lay off" without pay or to change jobs in order to get a respite from their work. "To have a heck of a good time," probably meant finding a new position.

Although moving about with some frequency, boomers, as a group, possessed considerable skills. Freeman H. Hubbard, an astute observer of these individuals, believes that "the boomer, man for man, was a more capable car hand, throttle artist, fireman, switchman, telegraph operator . . . than the more conservative home guard." The reason, most of all, for the boomers' prowess centered on their vast experiences with hectic schedules. They understood how to handle those ubiquitous seasonal rushes, whether it be grain, sugarcane, or oranges. "The regular men, used to easy, take-your-time gait, were suddenly heaved into a madhouse of car movement," contends Hubbard. "When work is done under unaccustomed pressure, mistakes are more likely to be made, and accidents more frequent. . . . The boomer, on the other hand, had just left one high-pressured rush and from this one would go on to another. Constantly working under those conditions, he had become inured to them, and they were his natural pace."[6]

Boomers often shared other common characteristics. Most were unattached young males in their twenties or early thirties. "[T]he boomers are young single guys, who would rather boom around over the country," observes Brown. "[W]here on the other hand, most of the old heads are married men with families who have settled down in some railroad division point, and are using good judgment in trying to hold their jobs as long as they can, for many of them are past the age limit, and would have a hard time to make connections with another railroad job. . . ."[7] As Brown suggests, most boomers probably enjoyed the adventures of movement or at least accepted that lifestyle. Similarly, a sizable number of these boomer trainmen had been hoboes before they took railroad jobs. Recalled a vagabond telegrapher-station agent in the 1950s, "I knew lots of boomer fellows on the Western pikes who once had been 'boes. . . . They still could travel around but there [sic] financial positions were much stronger after having railroad jobs."[8] Most boomers also lacked much formal education, and railroading was frequently their first steady wage-earning experience beyond agriculture or odd jobs.

Boomers, though, knew no occupational bounds. While they were commonly found in the railroad industry during the late nineteenth and early twentieth centuries, transiency seemed a prominent feature of working-class life. Indeed, this held true for both the skilled and the unskilled. Some professionals, too, moved with considerable frequency. Teaching and preaching, for example, were nomadic occupations. Often responding to changing market conditions, these drifting souls traveled the nation, especially during times of severe economic dislocation. This tramping, to some extent, can be associated with the age of the worker. As one historian of carpenters during the late nineteenth century concludes, "Many carpenters in their twenties took to the road before they settled down."[9] Thus "boomerism" might be considered a function of the male life cycle, irrespective of a person's talents or economic status.

Boomer railroaders dwindled rapidly in the 1920s and 1930s. Railroad jobs, for one thing, declined dramatically during this time. Carriers in 1920 employed 2,076,000 individuals; in 1930 1,517,000; and in 1938 only 950,000. "A railroad job was hard to land after the War [World War I]."[10] While continuing to require some seasonal employees, companies tended to rely on regular personnel. For skilled trainmen and enginemen some midwestern roads used farmers who held seniority rights on divisions with erratic traffic patterns. Just as Brown notes that boomers were rare in the East at the turn of the century—in his case the New York Central—carriers in the Middle West and West after World War I resembled eastern roads. These lines, with worker approval, encouraged men to stay on the "extra board" and to earn seniority rights. "A goodly number [of boomers]," remembers one railroad official, "gave up traveling and became regular employees."[11] Also, by the 1930s pension plans and other fringe benefits and the depressed economy encouraged railroaders to end their booming. Others left railroading and perhaps wandered the countryside doing something else.

The demise of the boomer troubled few. Carriers found no noticeable labor shortages, particularly in light of their increased mechanization and policies of retrenchment. Railroad workers themselves typically viewed their wandering brothers with little enthusiasm, perhaps because of boomers' tendencies to drink excessively and, of course, to move freely. On several occasions Brown reveals this disfavor: for example, as a Terminal Railroad Association of St. Louis conductor told him, "[W]ell how in the blankity blank heck did you expect me to know that you had worked for the Terminal before, that is the trouble with you boomers, you work everywhere for a short time, but you don't stay any place very long at a time. . . ."[12] Brown might not have wanted to mention one reason for the boomers' short stays: "All he had to do when things went wrong, when the car he was switching fell off the dock or when he failed to deliver a train order, was to roll up his toothbrush and a couple of shirts into a bundle and hop the next outbound freight, change his name, and go on railroading elsewhere, leaving the regular employees to face the music."[13]

Charles P. Brown (1879–19??) came from a transient background. His father was a boomer brakeman in Missouri, Kansas, Indian Territory and Indiana before his death in a railway accident. As Brown recalls, "[M]y father was of a roving disposition."[14] Perhaps this spirit of wanderlust was hereditary. Unquestionably, Brown himself preferred a rootless existence to a more static one. His early life included a plethora of odd jobs and short-term wage-earning experiences, and he continued this tramping tradition by moving both from railroad to railroad and also from job to job while still with one company. By the time of his forced retirement at the age of thirty-four, Brown had "hired out" to thirteen railroads in the East, Middle West, and West, including twice with the same three roads.[15] And he had worked as a fireman, brakeman, switchman, and briefly as an engineer, demonstrating vividly an interchangeability among running jobs.

Brown's love for travel and adventure led him to write and then to rewrite his autobiography. Although he lacked much schooling and admits that he "never wrote anything before,"[16] he, nevertheless, uses his considerable natural talents and his strong desire to recreate, if only on paper, his former career. Brown's poignant statement, "I get so homesick at times for the railroad and everything that goes with it, that I don't know hardly what to do with myself,"[17] reveals an unhappiness with his subsequent life. The loss of both feet in a switching accident, which restricted his movements but probably did not shorten his life, compelled him to change occupations. As a result, Brown became an elevator operator as early as 1922 in Los Angeles, California. The boring nature of this job undoubtedly gave him ample opportunity to reflect on his past adventures, and so, in 1928, he began to pen his thoughts of happier times. It is conceivable, though, that Brown dictated his autobiography (perhaps his wife or a friend had stenographic skills), for in places it has that structure. Proper names, for example, are often spelled phonetically. However he accomplished it, within a year he had completed a massive manuscript, *The Life Story of Chas. P. Brown As a Boomer Railroad Man*. He then took it to a large, nearby commercial printer, the Western Printing Corporation, located in Whittier, California.[18]

Details of Brown's publishing activities are few. He likely paid Western about $2,250 for 500 copies of the 450-page soft-back book.[19] But a year later, Brown had this company produce an abridged version, called, *Brownie the Boomer: The Life Story of Chas. P. Brown As A Boomer Railroad Man*. Why he did so is a puzzle. A possible explanation may be that he wanted a tighter and hence more salable volume. The 1930 edition, which numbered 271 pages, deleted detail and minor chunks of his life. He left out, for example, a 20-page description of a trip that he made from his mother's home in Illinois to Arkansas in 1899. Possibly this press run exceeded 500 copies, although the cost of a thousand at the standard price of five dollars per page would have been a substantial and perhaps an irrecoverable investment. Brown's accident-settlement money, income from his elevator job, and the possible earnings or wealth of his wife, Josephine, whom he likely married about 1930, may have underwritten this venture. Since seemingly so few copies of either edition have survived, sales must have been slow, and the undertaking must surely been a financial disappointment, even a disaster. Or, as some authors who publish their own books have done, Brown may have given his autobiography away to friends and others interested in railroading.

Like most members of the working class, Brown left few traces. Not only are details about his publishing ventures obscure, but little of his life can be readily documented. Brown's constant movements make him impossible to locate in the federal manuscript censuses of 1900 and 1910. (Returns for 1890 were destroyed in 1921, and later ones remain closed.) This is likewise true for those states that conducted their own enumerations, often at mid-decade.

Furthermore, railroad personnel records lack completeness. Since the Interstate Commerce Commission requires companies to retain employee files for only five years after a termination, carriers have ordinarily discarded such materials. After all, the volume of paper was enormous; in 1910, for example, the nation's railroad work force stood at nearly 1,700,000 and increased steadily until 1920. Some companies, however, kept personnel records for longer periods, but frequent corporate mergers since the 1960s have hastened the process of their destruction. Brown worked for many of these "fallen flags," including the Clover Leaf, Frisco, and Wabash; and personnel papers from these firms have vanished. For carriers that remain, most notably the Union Pacific and Santa Fe, appropriate records are limited. The Union Pacific disposed of all its personnel documents from its operating department, largely because of the staggering quantity. Even the company's "Personal Injury Registers" remain only partially intact; those from the Wyoming Division for July 1912 to April 1919 are "missing." This record group would have noted Brown's nearly fatal accident outside Superior, Wyoming, in December 1913.[20] Fortunately, some materials that pertain to Brown's career on the Santa Fe survive. Payroll records for December 1909 indicate that he worked on the Arizona Division and received $69.90 that month after deductions of $31.95 for "Board and Miscellaneous Collections" and "Hospital Collections."[21]

One aspect of Brown's railroad career is chronicled in an obscure place. During this time, railroad brotherhoods published monthly journals containing statements of claims for death or disability insurance payments. Indeed, such protection was a vital function of these unions. The March 1914 issue of *The Brotherhood of Locomotive Firemen and Enginemen's Magazine,* published in Columbus, Ohio, indicates that Brown, member of the Silver Mountain Lodge in Needles, California, filed a petition on January 22, 1914, for $1,000, for "Amputation of foot." Although he also belonged to the trainmen's brotherhood, its journal, *The Railroad Trainman,* failed to note any insurance claims.[22]

Even after Brown sank his roots, little can be found. City directories for Los Angeles, his adopted hometown, confirm his arrival there by 1916, first as a renter at 176 South Rio and then in the early 1920s at 325 East 9th. About 1925 he bought a house at 1418 McBride Avenue, in a low-income neighborhood and remained there through 1932.[23] Then record of Brown disappears. California's Department of Public Health cannot provide a death certificate; he likely left the state. All that is known is that Brown died prior to 1957.[24]

While historical data that mention Brown's life are meager, an examination of his writings reveal few discernible errors, and these are, without exception, minor. Parts of his narrative, fortunately, can be corroborated. Furthermore, the experiences that he describes ring true; nothing sounds farfetched. This is not surprising if Brown is taken at his word. As he wrote in his preface: "I believe that the details of my story run as true to life as I can remember them, as any other person who might try to write the memories and story of their life."[25] What is remarkable is that Brown recalled so much specific information—locomotive numbers, distances between stations, names of acquaintances and the like. These are particulars that most people quickly forget. Brown may have consulted a journal that he had kept or used letters that he had written to his family. Still, his memory seems to have been exceptional.

The richness of detail in both versions gives a vivid portrait of Brown. While no photograph of him is available, a mental image emerges: he called himself "strong and husky,"[26] and he indicated that he was somewhat short of stature, standing less than five feet eight inches. As for personality, Brown appears to have been gregarious, with a keen sense of humor, and a loyal friend and union member. He undoubtedly believed that his word was his bond. Similarly, he seems modest; he never cast himself in his writings as a heroic figure. And, of course, he was a free spirit, who "bummed" for a time and willingly bunched a railroad job to have a chance for fresh adventures. Perhaps this rootlessness and the considerable pleasure that he received from life made him enormously patriotic. "I am an American, this is my country, and Old Glory is my flag, and to me the greatest flag that waves over the land and sea."[27] While appropriately nationalistic, he, nevertheless, held some common prejudices. In his writings, African Americans are "coons" and "big smokes"; Eastern and Southern Europeans are "bohunks" and "wops"; and American Indians, Jews, and Mexicans command little respect. Brown also exhibited signs of being superstitious and having a sense of fatalism, especially while at work. He also enjoyed small pleasures, which was fortunate because Brown never had much money. He found delight in church gatherings (regardless of denomination), dances, and visits with his mother and younger brother, Tom, also a boomer railroader. Collectively, then, Brown's physical and emotional make-up resembled that of many of his contemporaries; he was not a bizarre figure. Brown was unusual in that he wrote about his railroad life in considerable detail; only a handful of his peers did so.[28]

The autobiography of Charles P. Brown offers numerous insights into the lives of a segment of the working class at the turn-of-the-century. Brown apparently did not realize that, when he discusses his railroading career, his nostalgia is not just for his youth, but for a disappearing way-of-life. His pre-railroading journeys as a hobo indicate how tens of thousands of people once traveled in search of employment and adventure. Brown carefully describes the culture of "bo" life. Often the individuals who "hit the road" exhibited kind and generous qualities; a code of honor prevailed. Yet a treacherous side existed. Some vagabonds, mainly the professional "yeggs," robbed, even killed fellow hoboes. Those "knights of the road" who had earned harvest money were at high risk; the low-life yeggs literally "harvested the harvestors." Railroad train crews, too, might treat unauthorized riders badly, whether extracting illicit "bo money" or physically abusing them.[29]

Once Brown "decided to go railroading," his narration includes descriptions of how crew members performed their daily duties. In this broad context he talks of many things: operating procedures, work rules, wages, personalities, hardships, and dangers. He tells, for example, how accidents happened and indicates that defective or poorly maintained equipment, not worker negligence, frequently contributed to injury or death. Railroads were exceedingly dangerous places: accidents that involved operating personnel had become a serious national problem by 1910. In 1895, 1,811 workers died and 25,696 were injured; in 1900 the figures rose to 2,550 and 39,639; in 1910 they stood at 3,383 and 95,671 respectively, and in 1913, the year of Brown's accident, the numbers were 3,715 employees dead and 171,417 injured. The threat of death or crippling injury at work was always near, lending strength to the ties that bound operating railroaders together. Indeed, Brown reveals that a strong esprit de corps existed, as reflected by the presence of supportive brotherhoods. Generally, these union men helped each other, and their organizations provided much-needed economic benefits.

While brotherhoods somewhat lessened the difficulties and uncertainties of railroading, the work was nevertheless demanding. "Featherbedding" or make-work was largely unknown during Brown's time. As a fireman, for instance, he cleaned hot ash-pans and shoveled coal for hours; as a brakeman and switchman, he climbed moving cars and walked along their tops in all types of weather, exposing himself to constant danger. But important technological changes occurred during the formative years of the century, and they usually meant improved and safer working conditions. Brown, as a fireman, seemed especially pleased with the appearance of state-of-the-art oil-burning steam locomotives on the Santa Fe, once he learned how to fire them effectively.

Brown possessed the necessary qualities to be a good boomer railroader. Without question he understood and liked things mechanical. Early in his life he tinkered with farming equipment and then worked in a machine shop. He used these skills in railroading, especially when he entered engine service. Also of value was Brown's resourcefulness. Helping his hard-pressed mother, enduring his years in an orphanage, and then living on his own led him to develop and refine a "streetwise" sense. Brown knew how to cope with the uncertainties of the workplace. Even his habits helped him to survive. Although he enjoyed alcohol, there is no indication that he faced disciplinary action for violating "Rule G." And he did not smoke or chew tobacco. Moreover, his personal hygiene was good: he washed and bathed whenever possible; he took pride in his appearance, especially his clothing; and he remained free from the social diseases of his day, for he continually passed examinations made by railroad physicians.

One contribution that Brown makes to understanding operating railroaders involves his feeling about class distinctions. He repeatedly considers himself to be part of the masses. While examples abound, one vividly conveys his sentiment. Recalling Union Pacific executives riding their posh business car, Brown reflects, "[W]hen I think of reading all of that bunk and bull, about the poor, hard working, and self-sacrificing officials, it gives me a pain in the neck, for if some of [them] . . . would only get out once and do their laps with the train and engine crews in trying to get a drag of freight over the road on some nice, dark, cold, stormy night, with a fierce blizzard raging, instead of being wheeled over the division in a nice, comfortable private car coupled onto the rear of a fast passenger train, with a bunch of yes boys to do their bidding, they would know what the words (hard-work and struggling) really meant." He adds, "Yes, I have seen some of those hard climbing boys going over the division in their private cars on that man killing job known as a tour of inspection."[30]

Brown, though, never saw the world as "us" versus "them." He expressed respect (perhaps it was habit) toward officials when he repeatedly identified them as "Mr." These were minor officers who knew him as an operating person and he knew them. Later, when Brown encountered the Industrial Workers of the World, the "Wobblies," while picking hops in northern California, he showed neither support nor interest; he was not about to align himself with the most militant and class-conscious of early twentieth century unions. Brown did not consider hops harvesting as particularly exploitive, and he liked the festive nature of after-work activities, especially the company-sponsored dances. His loyalty, of course, went to the much more docile railway brotherhoods. Their emphasis on self-help rather than the "one big union" appealed to him. Brown also seemed consciously to avoid strikes. Although not opposed to such job actions—he clearly detested "scabs"—his care-free spirit conceivably prompted him to leave a job if labor conflict was brewing. That appears to have been the case in a minor labor skirmish in Granger, Wyoming, for "I used this trouble for an excuse to quit, . . . my boomer blood that I had inherited from my father, predominated within me. . . ."[31] Beckoning adventures were too strong for Brown to become embroiled in a labor-management dispute.

The working-class railroaders had an expressive language of their own. Today, words and expressions like "shack," "to bunch a job," and "on the cathop" have virtually disappeared. Brown's prose reveals both the speech patters of his colleagues and their mostly forgotten slang and jargon. Yet, he avoids the ever-present vulgarities in that nearly all-male environment. "Dang," "heck," and "scissorbill" are his strongest words; custom surely precluded his use of other expletives in print.

Considerable editorial changes and additions are part of this republication of *Brownie the Boomer*. Portions of the first chapter have been deleted; most of this material deals with boyhood experiences. Additional short passages have also been removed. Still, several sections, mostly descriptive paragraphs, from his original version have been added, and they are identified with appropriate footnotes. Extensive explanatory notes have been included to clarify various persons, places, terms, and events. A variety of illustrations have been employed to help visualize Brown's many workplaces; neither the 1929 nor 1930 book contains pictures. An index has also been added. Finally, improper grammar and spelling have generally not been corrected, although some punctuation and obvious typographical errors have been altered to permit smoother reading.

Brownie
the
Boomer

*N*ow I want to ask my readers to excuse the very noticeable lack of grammar and construction of my story, for I had a very poor chance to even get a common school education.

And up to the time that I started to write this story, and memories of my life, I never wrote anything before.

And I could not use proper grammar if I wanted to, for it would not fit into this story, for up-to-date grammar is not used in the lingo of the railroadman's everday slang.

So I am telling this story in my own simple way, or rather in the language of the common everyday railroad working man.

And I want to state herein, that I believe that the details of my story run as true to life as I can remember them, as any other person who might try to write the memories and story of their life.

I am dedicating this story to the railroad men of the United States and Canada.

Chas. P. Brown

Chapter I

I was born on the ninth day of Feb. 1879, in the little town of Lamar, Missouri.[1] My ancestors on my father's side were Irish, and on my mother's side they were English and Holland Dutch, and from what I was told, they dated back for several generations in this country.

My father was a railroad man of the old school or a carhand as the old timers would say, back in the good old days of the handbrakes and the link and pin couplers.[2]

My mother was raised on a farm in Missouri, and about the first thing that I can remember, is one time when she took me on a visit out to the farm to see her people, and of course they all made quite a fuss over me, for up to that time I was the only grandchild of that line.

And the next that I remember, we were living in Wichita, Kans.[3] And as my father was of a roving disposition, he got a family-pass from Wichita to Crawfordsville, Ind.,[4] and as soon as we got settled there, he went to work as a brakeman for the old IB&W railroad,[5] which is now part of the Big Four System. And after working there for a while, he quit that job and went over to Lafayette, Ind.,[6] and went to work on the Monon Route,[7] running from Lafayette down thru Crawfordsville and to Bloomington, Ind.[8]

But my mother and us kids stayed in Crawfordsville, and of course we lived right beside the Monon tracks, and could see my father when he passed through in the daytime, and to save us from buying fuel to heat our home, he would always throw big lumps of coal for us when his train went by our house.

Now back in those days railroad men got very poor wages, and after my father paid his board and room, he had very little left to send home to my mother, so it was up to me to get out and hustle to help my mother make a living.[9]

So things went along like that until one day in February, 1889, when the railroad company sent my mother a message notifying her that my father had been killed. The report stated that somewhere between Crawfordsville and Bloomington, Ind, that the train had broken in two, (which happened quite often in those days with the old link and pin couplers) and that my father had got knocked off the top of his train by a low bridge while setting up the handbrakes in an effort to stop the train.[10]

Well, after my father got killed, the railroad company did not pay my mother any money, except what wages he had coming to him up to the time of his death. So my mother was left a widow with us five children to look out for, and she was doing the best that she could with what little that I could give her, when one day about a month after my father's death there were two officials drove up to the old shack in which we were now living and they told my mother that they had an order from the court to take us children from her and put us in the Orphans Home, which was located about two miles from town on a little twenty acre farm.[11]

So there was nothing left for her to do but give us up, and I remember we all had a big cry before they took us kids away, but the officers told my mother that they would help her to get a job and that she could come out to the Home to see us on Sundays.

So we kids were taken to the Orphans Home, and my mother got a job as a cook and all around housemaid in a private home, and worked for the enormous sum of three dollars a week and board and room, and on Sundays she would walk that two miles out to the Home to see us kids, and she would always bring us kids candy and fruit and such things when she came.

Now I was just ten years old when they took me to the Home, and up until that time I had never seen the inside of a school-house, so Mrs. Hiner, the matron in charge of the Home, started me right into school, as there were two months left yet before the school closed.

And when I finished those two last months of school, it was then springtime, and all of us larger kids at the home had to work in the garden and truck patches, hoeing weeds, and besides this work, we each and every one, boys and girls alike, had regular duties assigned to us to do every day.

Some boys fed the horses and cleaned out the stables, some milked the cows, while others slopped the pigs and fed the chickens.

And the girls had to work in the house, helping the cook with the meals, waiting on the tables in the dining room, and washing the dishes, and doing many other things.

Now the food that they gave us to eat was plain, but good and wholesome, and on Thanksgiving Day, Christmas, and New Year, they always gave us nice big dinners.

I remember that we did not get a regular supper on Sunday evenings, but instead we each one were given a big piece of pie or cake, and we kids used this pie and cake in the place of money among ourselves, for that was the only medium of exchange that we had to carry on trade with, and when a boy had something to sell or trade, he would sell to the highest bidder for cake or pie which was to be paid to him for two or more Sundays on the installment plan until the article was all paid for.

Now they had a man working there as overseer of the farm by the name of Frank Stout, and after I had been there about two years, in age and size, I was the topcutter over all the rest of the kids, so I became Frank's right hand man, and worked with him in the fields, driving the horses for him when he plowed the corn and truck-patches.

Now one of the rules at the home, was when they wanted the children to assemble in the big playroom for any occasion, they would ring a bell that they had there for that purpose, and when the kids would hear the bell ring, they would go into the playroom and line up around the walls and wait to see what it was all about.

So, one Sunday afternoon in the latter part of April, 1891 (I remember that I was just passed the age of twelve years old), we had all been assembled in the playroom and were waiting to see what it was all about, when Auntie Hiner came into the room accompanied by a weasel-faced old woman, and Auntie Hiner told us that this dear lady wanted to take a boy home with her to raise, as she wanted company for herself and daughter.

So old Rain-in-the-face walked down the line giving us all the onceover, and when she got to me she stopped, and after looking over me and sizing me up, she turned to Auntie Hiner, and says, this boy will do, I will take him.

Well, after Auntie and the old woman had left the room, my two brothers and two sisters gathered around me and we all began to cry, for they hated to see me go, and of course I hated to go and leave them, for they were all younger than I was.

But alas, there was no hope for me, for the order had been given, and I had to go and leave my little brothers and sisters, for it was the law, and the law had to be obeyed regardless of all the suffering, pain and unhappiness it caused to the parties who were concerned.

So after they had got my clothes ready, and I had bid everybody a tearful goodbye, we started for the old woman's home, which was about seven miles north of Crawfordsville, where we arrived about supper time. The woman and her old maid daughter lived alone in a two-story frame house which was located on the east end of the old woman's farm.

Well, after we had eaten our supper, the old woman and her daughter asked me many questions about the Orphans Home, after which the old woman showed me upstairs to what was to be my room and I went to bed, but I could not go to sleep right away for thinking of my brothers and sisters that I had left behind in the home and I wondered if they were thinking of me too as I was thinking of them, and I also thought of what a surprise my mother was going to get the next time she came out to the home and found me gone.

Well, the next morning after we had finished our breakfast, she took me out and showed me around and told me what my duties were going to be. I was to feed and care for the one old horse, slop and feed the hogs, and keep the weeds hoed and pulled out of the garden and truck patch, but there was not much for me to do, for the old woman rented all of her farm out to other farmers except right around the house, barn and the orchard.

And, I'll tell the world that I was one lonesome kid around there all by myself, and no other kids to play with. But I had to make the best of it, and sometimes I would play in the big barn and climb up all around in the big hayloft, and look for barn swallows' nests which they built by carrying mud and daubing it to the rafters under the roof.

Well, about the middle of May, or after I had been there around about three weeks, one day I was playing down at the lower end of the orchard trying to shoot birds with a bow and arrow that I had made for myself when up jumped a rabbit and started to run down through a big field toward a woodpasture, but after he run for a few hundred feet he stopped, so I climbed over the rail fence and started to run after him, but before I got to him he jumped up and run again and I soon lost sight of him, but I went on down across the field and climbed over the fence into the woodpasture, and Oh, boy, what a happy hunting ground I had found.

I saw a big red fox squirrel setting on a stump, and another one playing on the ground near by, and I also discovered a nice little creek running down through the woods, and I could see some small fish swimming in the clear water, and down by the water's edge I saw some coon tracks in the mud. Gee, but I sure was happy playing up and down the creek, and rambling all around through the woods, and the time had slipped by so fast that it was quite late before I realized it, so I started for the house, and it was almost dark when I got there, and the old woman and her daughter had the chores all done up and supper was ready when I came into the house.

So the old woman let out a roar, and wanted to know where I had been all afternoon? And what did I mean by hiding out so that she and her daughter had to do up my chores for me? but I told her that I did not hide out, for I had chased a rabbit down across the field into the woods and everything was so new and strange to me, and I had saw some squirrels, and lots of birds, and some fish swimming in the creek and everything, that I did not notice it was getting so late, then she said, well, don't ever let me catch you goin down to them air woods agin, for I want you to stay here close to the house so when I need you, I will know where to find you.

So I eat my supper and went up to bed, and I was tickled pink to think that I had got off so easy, but some time away in the night, I thought that I was having a bad dream, and I finally woke up, for my mouth felt like it was on fire, and I looked all around, but I could not see or hear anything, for it was dark and quiet, and gee, I wondered what had happened to me, for my mouth and throat was burning like heck, and I began to think that the old house was haunted and the spooks had been working on me, so I flopped down in bed and covered up my head, and finally went to sleep wondering what would happen next.

Well, the next morning while we were eating our breakfast, I noticed the old woman and her daughter kept exchanging sly glances at each other, and finally the old woman said to her daughter, he did not even wake up when I gave him the dose. So right there I smelled a long-tailed rat, and I put two and two together and figured it out in my own mind that the old wildcat had been the spook that had slipped into my room during the night while I was asleep and gave me the hot shot, but she did not know that it had awakened me later. Well, right then I made up my mind to always be on my guard after that when the old woman was sore on me.

So one nice day a short time after that, I sneaked off and went down to the woodpasture again, but I met with a little hard luck this trip, for I got mixed up with an old buck sheep. It so happened that after I had been rambling around through the woods for a while, I came upon a drove of sheep, and while I was busy watching the little lambs running, jumping and playing around, I did not see the old buck stealing up on me from behind until it was too late, and before I could get out of his way he took a run and jump and smacked me a good sock in the back and knocked me flat. Gee whillickers, I thought I had got hit by a locomotive, and while he was backing off to give me another bump, I jumped up and run to a big stump near by and scrambled up on it just in time, for he was right after me. Well, he had me treed up that stump all right, while he kept walking around it with his neck bowed just dying to get another whack at me, but I was not coming down off that stump as long as he was hanging around there, so finally he gave up the idea and strolled off and joined the rest of the sheep, and then I jumped down on the ground and ran as fast as I could until I reached the fence and climbed over into the field and started for the house, and in the meantime the old woman had been looking for me, and when I got there she was waiting for me as she wanted me for something and was unable to find me, where in the world have you been? I have been looking all over the place for you, she roared at me, as I came up. I suppose you was down in the woods agin playing with the squirrels and rabbits.

So I told her yes I had been playing in the woods and an old buck sheep had butted me down while I was watching the little lambs play, and then she says, what did I tell you about goin down to them air woods agin? Well young man, you'll git a hot dose tonight that yu'll not fergit til your dyin day. Well, that wise crack from her put me wise to what the old tiger cat had on her mind, for it seemed like this old nut had funny little notions all her own as to how a boy should be punished.

And that night when I went to bed I thought I would fool the old girl by locking my door, so that the old hotshot artist could not get in, and I laughed to myself to think what a surprise she was going to get when she found the door locked. But she was game and come right back at me, for the next morning when I got up and was ready to go downstairs I could not open my bedroom door at first, for she had fastened it from the outside. I had locked her out and the sly old fox had locked me in, so she thought, but I took hold of the doorknob and put one foot against the door jamb, then I gave a good yank and the door came open, and then I saw a rope tied to the doorknob on the outside which reached across the hall and into her daughter's bedroom and was tied to one of the bed legs, and when I pulled my door open the rope had pulled the girl's bed out of the corner toward the middle of the room. Well, it was too funny for anything, and I snickered to myself as I went down the stairs and into the kitchen, but just as soon as I got to the kitchen I saw her daughter grab the water bucket and go out to the pump to get some water, and then the old warhoss galloped over and locked the door and I knew right then that the war was just starting, for I could see that the enemy was maneuvering for an attack, and just at this moment I spied a strong looking switch on top of the cupboard, and as I thought that she was going after it, I tried to beat a hasty retreat through the locked door, and while I was fumbling with the key trying to unlock the door, she rushes me from behind and clamps a half-nelson on me with her left arm around my neck and under my chin, but instead of having the switch, she had a teacup in her right hand and was trying to get it to my mouth, so I let loose of the door and began to struggle to get away from her, but she hung on like a pup at a root, and kept saying, drink it or I will throw it in your face, and just then I broke her hold on me and she slammed the whole works into my face and eyes. Now, I don't know what it was, but it almost blinded me for a few moments, then she grabbed the switch off the cupboard and began to rain blows over my head and face, and I threw up my arms to protect my face as I could not see where I was at, but my eyes soon cleared a little bit and I made for an old muzzle-loading rifle that stood in one corner of the kitchen, and grabbing it up I pointed it at her, and I says, if you hit me again I'll shoot you, for I was mad enough right then to do anything, but she says, no you won't, tain't loaded, and she started to charge me again, but I drawed the gun up like a club and says, I will knock you over the head with it then, so right then the advantage swung into my favor, for she started to back away from me, but I kept the gun raised above my head ready to strike and I could see that she was ready to sue for peace for she says to me, now you put down the gun and I will not whip you any more, but I was not taking any chances, so I told her to break up the switch and I would put down the gun. Then she broke the switch in two and the war was over.

And her daughter who had been watching the battle through the kitchen window all of this time, was now yapping for her mother to unlock the door and let her come in, so the old warhoss went over and unlocked the door and her daughter came in with the bucket of water and filled the washpan and asked me to come and wash my face and bathe my eyes which I did, but I could not eat any breakfast, and the old woman asked me if I was going to be a good boy, and mind her after this, and I told her yes that I was, but I was only stalling for time, for I already had my mind made up to beat it just as soon as I got outside that door.

Well, after they had finished their breakfast, the girl was doing the dishes and the old woman went upstairs for something, then I put on my coat and cap and went to the door and opened it and just as soon as I got outside I was gone from there as fast as my legs could carry me, but I had not gone very far down the road before a man driving a horse to a buggy overtook me and stopping his horse, he says to me, don't you want a ride sonny? and I says yes sir, but I was afraid, and as soon as the man saw my face, he says, why ain't you that boy that old lady Parker took out of the Orphans Home to raise? and I says yes sir again, and then he says to me, it pears like she give you a whoppin from the looks of your face, and I'll bet that you are runnin off from her, but I did not say anything for I was afraid that he was going to take me back to her, but I don't blame you for running off from her, he continued, for the crazy old fool ain't fit to raise a boy no how. Then he asked me where I was going and I told him that I had started back to the Home at Crawfordsville, and then he says, all right, I am going to town so jump in and I will take you back to the home, and while we were riding along I told him the story about how everything happened.

Well, when we arrived at the Orphans Home, I was a little bit scared to go in for I did not know what they would say or do to me for running away and leaving the old woman, but the man said that he would go in with me and that gave me more courage to face them, and when Auntie Hiner saw me, she says, why Charley Brown, what on earth happened to you? (I guess I did look a little bit out of order with my eyes all puffed and bloodshot, with red welts across my face and a patch of skin peeled off of one of my ears.)

So I told her the story of how it all happened, and the man would cut in once in a while to help me out by saying something about the old woman, as he knew her well and kept insisting that she was crazy.

So they fixed a medical solution and had me bathe my eyes in it three and four times a day, and after a week or so I was all right again, but my face had all peeled off and left me with a nice new skin.

Well, I had only been back about two weeks when an old man and his son by the name of Cunningham, came and took me away again.

And these Cunninghams lived on a big farm down in the country about twenty miles southwest of Crawfordsville, and they were very rich farmers, for besides owning several hundred acres of land, and hundreds of head of livestock of different kinds, they owned and operated a big sawmill, and they also owned and operated an up-to-date threshing outfit, but they were so tight that they squeaked.

Now they told Auntie Hiner when they took me away from the Home, that if I stayed with them until I was twenty-one years old, that they would give me a horse, bridle and saddle, and one hundred dollars in money. Yea, bo, they were too big hearted for me, and after struggling through almost two years, as a general farm and an all around choreboy, for just what little I got to eat and wear and no chance to go to school, I ran away and struck out for myself as now I was passed fourteen years old.

I remember I went into another neighborhood about five miles east of there and hired out to a farmer by the name of Bloomer Myers for nine dollars a month, board, room and washing, and he furnished me a young horse to ride so that I could go places and see things. This was along in May of 1893.

Well, I worked right straight through to about the first of December, when we had the crops all gathered in, and Bloomer told me that I could stay there and go to school the rest of the winter and help do the chores for my board and room as my help would come in handy for them, for they had lots of livestock to be fed and cared for through the winter months.

Well, I sure did enjoy myself there that winter, for there were many places to go, such as Church and Sunday School on Sundays, night singing school at the church through the week, box suppers, oyster suppers, and many other kinds of doings, at the different country schoolhouses, churches and many other places around through the country.

And boy, I want to tell the world that I thought that I was leading some gay and highflying life, with a horse to ride and go places, real store clothes to wear and money to spend. Hot diggity dog!

Well, when the first of March came, I had to quit school and go back to work again for wages on the farm. I was now fifteen years old and had grown to be a pretty husky kid for my age. This was in the spring of 1894, and Bloomer had hired another farm hand to work with me, and I remember that our first work through the months of March and April, was that of cutting the summer's supply of cook-wood and we also had to cut down big oak trees and split rails which we used to repair the rail fences with around over the farm. And, like our great Lincoln, I have mauled and split rails a many a day, and I used to be able to swing a pretty mean ax and also a cross-cut saw.

Well, nothing unusual happened throughout that summer, but just the general routine of work that is characteristic of all country farms, and after the corn was all gathered into the cribs late that fall, I started to school again, and went until the Christmas holidays, for in the meantime on one of my visits to the Home, I had found out that my mother had got married again, and was living in a little town by the name of Knightstown, Indiana,[12] about thirty miles east of Indianapolis and I had wrote to her and had planned to make a visit with her during the holidays.

So I went to Crawfordsville and took a train on the Big Four System for Indianapolis,[13] where I had to change to the Pennsylvania Lines, and it so happened that I had to lay over there four hours between trains, and in the meantime I got to talking with a train newsboy about his job, and I asked him if he thought that I could get a job on the trains as a newsboy.

So he said if I wanted to go with him, he would take me over to the Union News Company's office and I could talk to the manager about a job, which I did, and the manager said yes, that he could use me if I wanted to buy a blue uniform and one of the company's uniform caps and that I would also have to put up ten dollars security for the train box full of stock.

Well, I told him that I would think the matter over and would be back in about a week and let him know what I would do, so I went on over to Knightstown and paid my mother and step-father a visit and I told them that I had a chance to go to work on the passenger trains as a newsboy, and that I was going to take the job, for my mind was already made up to become a railroad man when I got old enough, and that by working as a train newsboy was a good way to get started to learn the business.

So when I got back to Indianapolis, I went to the Union News Company's office and told the manager that I would take the job, and after I bought my uniform and got all lined up, I was assigned to a run on the P.&E. division of the Big Four System running from Indianapolis to Springfield, Ohio.[14]

Now, us boys were not paid wages, but we worked for a twenty percent commission on everything that we sold for the company, but the news butcher that don't sell nothing but straight company stock all of the time, is a dumbbell, and I think that I am safe in saying that all train news butchers, after they have been in the game for a while, gets wise to themselves and carry a side line of their own.

For I carried a complete stock of my own which I bought cheap and sold at news company prices. I remember that us boys used to go to a cigarmaker there in Indianapolis and buy cigars, fifty in a box for one cent apiece, and peddle them out for five cents apiece, but as I never chewed or smoked in my whole life, I don't know a good cigar from a bad one, but from some of the wise cracks that I used to hear the men make in the smoking-car after they tried to smoke one of my cigars, I was inclined to think that those old cabbage-ropes were pretty bad.

But the wise cracks from those guys did not mean anything in my young life, for I was out to get the jack and that was just one of my ways of getting it.

Well, in the meantime my mother and stepfather had moved over into Illinois, and were living in a little town by the name of Hoopeston,[15] and one day in the latter part of September, 1895, I received a letter from my mother and stepfather and they wanted me to come over there to Hoopeston, and work for my stepfather in his tin and plumbing-shop that he had just opened up.

And as I was only just making a kid living as a news boy, I quit the news company and beat it over to Hoopeston, but as my stepfather had not worked up much trade as yet, he could not afford to pay me wages, so as this part of Illinois was a great corn belt, I went out into the country and got a job of shucking corn for a farmer by the name of Ed Strader, for which I got paid two cents a bushel for the corn that I cribbed, and after we finished up at Ed's place, I went over to his brother-in-law's place and helped him finish up, and by this time it was getting real winter, for we were having plenty of snow already, but there was another farmer came to me who wanted me to come over to his place and help him finish up, as his man had quit him on account of the bad weather, and because his corn was very badly blown down in some places, but as I did not crave shucking blown down corn when there was snow on the ground, I did not care much about going, but he told me if I would come and stick until his corn was all cribbed, that he would pay me three cents a bushel, so I went over and stuck through to the end, but yea, bo, never again, for it was some job, and he was right when he said it was blown down, for some places it was flat on the ground, and I had to dig it out of the snow, and I did not blame his man for quitting such a job.

Well, I remember that we finished up just before the Christmas-Holidays, and after I figured up my total for the three places, I had cribbed just a little over three thousand bushels of corn that season, and we had to weigh it in at the rate of seventy-five pounds to the bushel, for the farmers all had big wagon-scales in that part of the country on their farms.

Well, after I got all through shucking corn, I went back to Hoopes-ton and stayed at home with my mother and stepfather the rest of that winter, and in the meantime, I had met up with a young fellow by the name of Pat Kelly, and we soon became pals.

Now Pat was working in a foundry learning the molder's trade, and in connection with this foundry there was a big machine-shop, and I started in to learn the machinist-trade, and I worked there up into the summer of 1898,[16] when Pat and I quit our jobs and enlisted in a volunteer company for the Spanish-American War, but as peace was declared before we got to go, Pat and I did not go back to our old jobs, for we had made up our minds to take a hobo trip up through the long-straw country of the northwest, as we were peeved because we did not get to go to war and help lick the Spaniards.[17]

Chapter II

Now, I remember it was in the latter part of July [1898], and the weather was hot and dry, when one day Pat and I hopped a freight train on the C.&E.I.[1] and beat our way to Chicago. (Beating your way means stealing a ride on a train without paying any railroad fare.) Well, when Pat and I got to Chicago it was in the night time and we went to a cheap rooming house for men only, on State Street, and got us a bed, that is, we each got a little cell-like room with a very narrow cot in it to sleep on. Now the partitions of these little rooms were just a little higher than a man's head and the whole works was covered with heavy wire netting.

I remember that Pat and I almost backed out when we saw this layout, for we thought that we had busted into some kind of jail or other, but as we had paid our money, we had to make the best of it for we were pretty short as it was, so we piled onto the cots and went to sleep and they were not so bad after all.

Now these sleeping places are known to the roving classes of working men as flop houses, and you will find them in all big cities where there is many homeless working men, and they are a pretty good thing for the men at that.

Well, the next day Pat and I walked around and took a look at the town, for it was the first time that either one of us had been in Chicago before, and we wanted to see all we could before proceeding on our journey.

I remember we went up on top of the Masonic Temple[2] and took a look at Lake Michigan, and boy, as it was the first big body of water that I had ever seen, it sure gave me a thrill. Then we went out to Lincoln Park and gave things the once over, and from there we went over to Ferris Wheel Park[3] right near there, and took a ride on the old Ferris wheel which was one of the great attractions at the Chicago World's Fair in 1893. Then we took in a show, after which we went back to the flop house and slept in our little cells.

Now, Buffalo Bill's Wild West Show[4] was playing a stand in Chicago at that time, so the next afternoon Pat and I went out to see the show, and boy, it sure was some show, no foolin. I will never forget the impression that Buffalo Bill made on me when he rode out on his beautiful horse with his gold and silver trimmed trappings, buckskin suit, big white sombrero, and hair plaited, silver bitted bridle, and gold and silver mounted saddle.

And then there were Anna Oakley[5] and Johnnie Baker,[6] who were crack shots with rifle and pistol. Also cowboys, Indians and Mexicans, saying nothing about all the foreigners from Europe and other countries. Gee, it was the most spectacular sight that I had ever seen in my whole life. There was a sham battle fought between the American Indians and the U.S. cavalry troops, representing General Custer's last fight.

Well, after the show was over, Pat and I took a street car and rode out to the Chicago, Milwaukee and St. Paul railroad yards[7], where we caught a freight train and beat it for Milwaukee, where we arrived early the next morning.

And after eating some breakfast, we went to the Old Soldiers Home,[8] and slept on the grass all of that day, in the Soldiers Home Park. And that evening just about dark, we grabbed another C.M.&St.P. freight train headed west for LaCrosse, Wisconsin.[9] (Now I will explain here that Pat and I were headed for Fargo, North Dakota, to make the great wheat harvest.) And there were lots of other fellows, both young and old traveling the side door pullman route,[10] headed for the great Northwest to make a stake in the harvest. (Making a stake means that a fellow will work on a job long enough to make himself some money to carry him over while he is traveling to some other part of the country that suits him better.)

Well, after riding all night and most of next day, we pulled into LaCrosse a little city located on the east bank of the Mississippi River in Wisconsin, and it was a division point for the C.M.&St. Paul road, and also the C.B.&Q.[11]

Well, Pat and I did not stick around there only long enough to wash up and get something to eat, then we walked across the river on a wagon bridge and waited for a train on the west side (as the

C.M.&St.P. crossed the river there over into Minnesota, where it followed the west bank of the river up to St. Paul), for it was easier to catch a train over there, as the yard bulls (railroad police) were inclined to be hostile to the hoboes in the railroad yards of LaCrosse. And the railroad shacks [brakemen] were out for the money, and if they caught you hiding on their trains it was either dig up or unload (meaning pay or get off). So that evening a little after dark, a long freight train made up of empty boxcars (known to railroad men as a drag of empties) came across the river and headed for St. Paul, the next division point north of there, so Pat and I grabbed her and climbed into an empty boxcar with several hoboes.

I remember that Pat and I were setting over in one corner of the car trying to get some shut eye, . . . when one of the brakemen stuck his lantern in through the small end door, and when he saw us in there he climbed through the door and dropped down inside of the car (and he was one of them tough, hard-boiled babies too, believe me). So he held his lantern above his head (which railroad men do, as they can see much better in a dark boxcar) and says to us men, where all of you bums goin' and what are you ridin' on, and some sap over in a far corner of the car makes a wise crack that he is ridin' on this here boxcar, and that crack sort of riled the old boomer brakeman, so he walked over and took a look at the wiseacre, and says, say listen bo, don't try to get funny with me, cause I am bad medicine my self. Then he turns around and says to the rest of us, come on all of you yeggs and line up here, I wanta see whatcha got. So we all went over to where he was, and he says to the yegg that he had bawled out, what have ya got, and the guy told him that he did not have anything, so the shack says, will you stand a frisk (meaning would he let the brakeman search him), and the fellow said no, then the shack told him to stand over by the door, so he sifted us out and the fellows that gave him some money, he let them ride, but the rest of us that did not dig up had to unload.

Well, as the train was not going very fast it was easy to get back on again, which we did, for it is hard to keep men off of a long drag of empties after night when it is so dark, so after playing hide and seek with the train crew all night, Pat and I rode the train into the St. Paul yards the next morning.

And after we got some breakfast, we took a street car and rode over to Minneapolis, where we went to a flop house and slept all day. And that evening after we got up and ate some supper, we went out to the Northern Pacific yards[12] and caught a train headed west.

And after dodging the train crew all night we rode into a little town called Staples, Minn.,[13] which was the next division point west.

So Pat and I went over to a little restaurant near the yards where we washed up and got a good breakfast of ham and eggs and plenty of coffee, after which we went back to the yards, just in time to catch a train pulling out for Fargo, the next division point west of there, and I remember that we climbed up on a flatcar loaded with a new traction engine[14] and that there were many other men setting along the sides of the car with their feet hanging over the edge. So pretty soon along came the head brakeman (and he was a foxy old boomer too), and he says to the men, hello there boys, I suppose you are all going out to the wheat harvest, yes; well now be careful don't get hurt, and all of you boys with your feet hanging over there, watch out for them cattle guard fences that they don't catch your feet and drag you off while going by, then he says who is going to give me a chaw of terbacker, and one of the big Swedes setting alongside of me offered him a chew of Copenhagen out of his snuffbox, but someone had passed his plugcut up to the old boy by this time and he took a chaw as he called it, then he says, well boys, I have got to be moseying along but before I go, I will pass my hat around and take up the collection, so throw in what you can and help me out, for I am working extra at the present time and am not making much money.

Well he had us all so bulled up by this time, that we would have given him a French kiss on both cheeks if he had of asked us to, for everybody dropped something in his hat as he passed it around.

Well, we rode all the rest of that day, and some time before midnight we pulled into Fargo,[15] and Pat and I had reached our journey's end for the time being anyway, for this was the place that we had started out for, so we went to a cheap rooming house and got us a bed and hit the hay between the sheets, for this was the second time that we had slept in a bed since we left Chicago.

Now the little town of Fargo is located in the Redriver Valley on the west bank of the Redriver, and the Redriver Valley in North Dakota and Minnesota, is known to be one of the greatest wheat growing districts in the world, and there were hundreds of men flocking into Fargo, for this was the distributing point for the great wheat fields, and boy, I never saw so much growing wheat before nor since.

Well as near as I can remember, it was around about the third or fourth of August, 1898, when Pat and I reached Fargo, and the wheat was a little too green to cut as yet, so the farmers were not taking on any help just then, and the outcome of it was, there was a small army of hobo wheat harvest hands waiting for the big works to start, and the most of them were living just outside of the town in hobo camps along the river banks. Now in the slang of the hobo, these camps are known as the jungles, and you will always find them located where the men can get fire-wood and water.

Now as Pat and I had taken up with two other boys,[16] we all four went out into the jungles and made us a camp, and we each one would throw in some money and make up a jackpot, then a couple of us would go into the town and buy some groceries, and bring them back to the jungles and cook up a big can of mulligan-stew, for we done all of our cooking and eating in the jungles. We only eat two meals a day, but oh, boy, they sure did taste good. No doubt you wonder what we used for cooking utensils in the jungles. Well in all hobo jungle camps, there is all sorts of tin cans, ranging from the well known tomato can, up to the big five gallon square oil cans, and the hoboes cut the tops out of these different cans, and use them to cook with, and they also use the big oil cans to boil up with (boil and wash their clothes). We used to take one of the big square cans and cut it off about two inches from the bottom and use it (that is the bottom part) to fry bacon and eggs and potatoes in, just like a skillet or a frying pan, and we would use the one gallon fruit cans to boil food in, and the small tomato cans to drink our coffee out of.

Now after a guy has bummed around over the country long enough to get wise to himself, after he cooks a meal in a jungle camp, he will always wash up the cans and frying pans that he has used and leave them in good order for the next fellow, for that is the code of the hoboes in the jungles, especially among the old time hoboes.

And you can always tell when a gay cat has been in camp, for he leaves the cans all dirty and scattered every which way. (A gay cat is a green horn who has not hoboed long enough yet, to get wise to the ways of the road.) And if one of these guys comes around where some old seasoned hoboes are cooking up a feed, the old timers will all begin to hiss, and holler scat, for they can tell by his looks and actions that he is a gay cat, and they don't want him around, but some times on the other hand if they are a gang of professional yeggs, they might invite the gay cat to have some feed with them, for in many cases they can use a green horn in their business as a lookout, or a stool-pigeon to bring them information as to the lay of a store, postoffice, or any other place in a small town that they have planned on robbing.

[21]

There is a big difference between the working stiff that lives in the jungles, and hoboes around over the country, beating his way from place to place while looking for work, and the regular professional hobo yegg, that won't work at all, but lives by plying his trade as a thief and a robber.

He and his brother yeggs will lay around in the jungles outside of a small town or city, while they scheme and plan to rob some post-office, or crack the safe in some store or small bank, and railroad men in the train service soon became able to tell the difference between the two classes, for the hobo working man in most cases is very frank, and will talk and answer questions, for he has nothing to conceal, while on the other hand, the hobo yegg is a hard-boiled, surly cuss that keeps his trap shut, and you will most always find him keeping off to himself when riding in a boxcar where there are other hoboes, for he does not care to mix with anybody except his own kind.

Well, to get back to my story, as I said before, we four boys done our cooking and eating in the jungles, for the days were hot, but the nights were pretty cool, so instead of sleeping by camp fires in the jungles, like many other hoboes did, we would go out into the Northern Pacific train yards where they had many boxcars stored, waiting to be used in the wheat rush, and sleep in a boxcar on a bed of straw that we would fix up for ourselves.

We would take off our shoes and coats, and spread the coats over the upper part of our bodies, covering up our chests, shoulders and head, so that our warm breath would keep us warm, for that is the best way to keep warm when you have only got your coat to cover yourself with.

Well, after we had laid around Fargo for about a week, we four boys made up our minds to beat it up to Grand Forks, N.D., which was the next division point north of Fargo on a branch line of the Great Northern.[17]

Now I will explain at this time that the railroads up in that part of the country at this season of the year are in the same fix as the farmers, for they have to hire the floating element of railroad men (known as boomers) to help handle and move their trains during the big wheat rush, just the same as the farmers have to hire the floating hobo working men known as working stiffs, to help them harvest the wheat.

Now these boomer railroad men (sometimes called boomer rails) go up into that part of the country to make a stake while the wheat rush is on, for they go jumping around over the country working for first one railroad and then another whenever business is good, and many of them are kept on the go for they have violated rule "G" so often that they in many cases have got such bum records that they have to work under a flag and phoney references. (Rule "G" in the book of rules, says that a man cannot, and must not use intoxicating liquors. And working under a flag, with phoney references, means that a boomer is working under another name, and has sprung false service letters on the railroad officials.) But when business is good and the railroads have a rush of some kind and their yards are blocked and they need experienced men to move their trains, they will forget all about the boomers bad faults and will almost give him a French kiss on both cheeks until the rush is over for they know that these men are all around railroad men, and can hit the ball and play the game wherever they put them, but just as soon as the rush is over and they do not need them any longer, they start cutting the board and laying them off, and just because they have to go chasing around over the country looking for another job, the companies blame them for being boomers. I will never be able to understand why railroad companies always hate a boomer like a rattlesnake when business is slack and they don't need him, but this is a well known fact in the railroad world.

Well, to get back to my story, there were many boomers come up to this part of the country, to make a stake through the wheat rush, and by picking up bo money from the harvest hands that rode their trains, and as they was out after all the jack that they could get, they sure was hostile, and it was dig up or hit the grit.

Now us boys had made it up among ourselves, that if the train crews were hostile, and chased us off, that instead of us all trying to stick together we would each and every one look out for himself, and if we did get separated we would go on and wait for each other in Grand Forks.[18]

So one night we grabbed a train of empty boxcars headed north on the G. N. but the shacks were trying to keep everybody off that did not come across with a piece of change, and I got separated from the rest of the boys, but as I figured that they were on the train some place, I stayed on thinking that I would meet them somewhere further up the line, so I rode out about thirty miles from Fargo to a storage yard at a little place called Alton Junction,[19] where the crew set their train out, and then returned to Fargo light (with just the engine and caboose).

And as it was just breaking day, I went over to the jungles and waited for the rest of the boys, but after laying there all day and they did not show up, I figured it out to myself that they had not made the train out of Fargo, as I had done. So that evening I grabbed a southbound train and beat it back to Fargo, and the next day while I was looking for them, I met some fellows that we had talked with a few days before, and one of them told me that he was pretty sure that he saw them in one of the Employment offices the day before where they were shipping men out to Montana, on a railroad grading job for the N. P. railroad.

Well, I could not figure out why they would ship out on a job in Montana, when we came up there to make a stake in the harvest. But, nevertheless, after what that fellow told me, instead of going up to Grand Forks, and waiting for them as we had agreed to do, I went to the employment office and asked the shipping clerk there if he had shipped three guys out on a grading job in Montana the day before, and he told me that he had, so that settled everything with me right there, for I was sure that those three fellows were my pals, and I made up my mind to ship out on the same job if it could be done. So I asked the clerk if he needed any more men on that job and he said yes, that he did, and that the job was a skinner job, and paid thirty dollars a month and found. Then he asked me if I was a mule skinner? and I told him no, that in fact I did not know what a mule skinner was (for I was a gay cat at that time, and had not got wise to myself yet). Then he says, can you handle horses? did you ever drive a team? and I says, sure I can drive horses, I was raised on a farm. Well that was O.K. with him, for every man that he shipped out was another dollar for his office, as the railroad company carried the men out to the job free.

So he booked me up for that evening, and I, along with several other mule skinners, that were shipping out to different jobs along the line, were loaded into the smoking car of a west bound passenger train on the Northern Pacific, and started on our way to the wild and wooly west.

I remember that it was over a five hundred mile ride for me, and I could not get over the idea of riding five hundred miles on a passenger train for one dollar. So after riding all night and the most of the next day, I was let off at the grading camp where my job was at, and believe me it was a desolate looking place if I ever saw one. The camp consisted of a few tents and a large corral where they kept the horses, and there was some old dump wagons, small slip scrapers,[20] and a lot of other junk lying around, and the camp was pitched on the south bank of the Yellowstone River.

Well, I took my roll of blankets that I had bought in Fargo (for they would not ship me out without a roll of bedding) and walked over to the largest tent, which was the cooking and dining tent, and I asked the cook where the boss was at, and he told me to just stick around until quitting time and the boss would be in from the works, so I unrolled my blankets and spread them down in one corner of an empty tent and rested until supper time. And when the boss came in off the works, I went over to his tent and gave him the ticket from the employment office. Then he wrote my name down in a book, and I asked if he had three men by the names of Patrick Kelley, George Hines, and Billy Smith, so he looked in his book, but he did not have any such names there. So I thought maybe they had gotten off at some other camp, by mistake or something, for I was sure that they had shipped out.

Well, pretty soon the cook rang the supper bell and we filed into the dining tent to supper. I remember we had boiled navy beans, boiled potatoes, some kind of meat, bread and black coffee. Now, some of the old timers had me buffaloed that night by telling stories about rattlesnakes, and how they would crawl into a fellow's blankets when he had his bed on the ground on chilly nights at this time of the year. And to make things worse, it was a fact that the cook had killed a rattler in the cook tent just a few days before, that he found coiled up under a sack of spuds.

Well, as I had my bed made down on the ground, there was nothing left for me to do but sleep in it that night, but I slept very good, for I had rode so far in the smoking car that I was tired. So the next morning they got us out good and early, and after breakfast [they] . . . showed me the team that I was to drive.

Now one of these horses was an old timer at the business, but the other one was a young fiery bronco (and he was a gay cat the same as me, and when it come to this camp work, he and I both were dumbbells). So when the boss hollered all out, I climbed aboard the old boy and led the young bronc, for we had to go about a mile to where the work was being done, and when we got there, the boss told me to hitch my team to one of the small slip scrapers, and get in line and follow around just the same as the other teams were doing, and boy, I'll tell the world that it was some continuous merry-go-round too. Now, the work that we were doing was called shouldering up, that is, we were bringing up dirt and dumping it at the end of the cross-ties of the track to widen the roadbed, for at some places the dirt had been washed away so bad that the track looked like it was strung out on top of a sweet potato ridge.

Well, every time we came around there the dirt was plowed up, I would grab one of the handles of the slip and flop it over right side up, and there was a guy there who would take hold of the handles and hold the slip in such a manner that it would scoop itself full of dirt, and when we got up to the track there was another guy who would grab the handles and dump it over. The teams never stopped, but just kept going around and around.[21]

Now some time the wind would blow the dust so bad that we could hardly see, and yea, bo! we were getting a dollar a day and our chuck, and a tent to flop in, for eating dust and going around and around ten hours a day. Well too much was a plenty for me, and after ten days I told the boss that I knew when I had enough, but he tried to talk me into staying awhile longer, for he could not keep men on the job; they were coming and going all of the time, but his talk did not sound good to me. So I told him to just give me my ten dollars and I would be on my way, and he gave me an identification slip to the big contractor whose office was in Miles City[22] so that I could get my ten dollars, as my boss was just one of many little subcontractors along the line that checked all of their labor to the big contractor. So after breakfast I rolled up my bedding and tied it up with a rope and swung it over my shoulder like I had seen the other bundle stiffs do, and started hiking for Miles City, about ten miles west of there, and as the day was hot and dry I took it easy and it was along in the afternoon when I got there.

Well, the first thing that I did was to go to a Jew second-hand store and peddle my roll of bedding, for I was not going to lug those blankets around any longer. Then I looked up the office of the big contractor and showed them my identy, (as the camp followers call the identification slips) and the clerk paid me my ten dollars, after which I went to a short order restaurant and ordered a big steak and treated myself to a nice big feed.

And that night I grabbed a freight train and started on west, I did not know where I was going, but I was on my way.[23]

So I kept going until I found myself in the little city of Billings, Montana,[24] at which place I stayed for about a week, and I met a young fellow there who said that he was from Missouri, and he talked me into the notion of going back to old St. Louie as he called it, with him.

So the next night after I met him, we grabbed a freight train eastbound on the N.P. and started back, but we only got as far as a little station called Huntly,[25] for when they stopped to take water the head shack found us and told us to dig up a dollar apiece or hit the grit, and as we did not want to part company with our dollars, we hit the grit (got off) and hung around there the rest of the night hoping to catch another train, but not one came along. So the next morning we went down to the river bank (for the Yellowstone River was close by, in fact the Northern Pacific railroad follows the Yellowstone clear across the state of Montana) and started to digging old pieces of lumber out of a big pile of driftwood to build a raft with, for we had made up our minds to float down the River on a raft, instead of riding the side door pullmans, and after working about three hours or so, we had completed a sort of a make-shift raft by tying the timbers and pieces of boards together with rope and baling wire. Then we got on and we each had a pole to push and steer with, and after working our way out into the stream, the water was running very swift, and gee, the way we went down that River for a few miles was a holy fright. Oh boy, how we shot the rapids, for I am telling you she sure was running swift at many places, and by the time we struck some smooth deep water, our raft was just about a complete wreck, and when we got the thing to the shore we got off, and figured that we had better keep to the side door pullmans and hard-boiled brakemen after all, if we did not want to feed the fishes in the Yellowstone.

Well from where we landed we started hiking along the track for there was no place there to catch a train. In fact there wasn't anything there but the track and River, surrounded by a wild and desolate lot of country, so we kept on hiking eastward all the rest of that day which was Sunday, and part of that night, and I remember that I got the scare of my life a little while after dusk as we were hiking along, for I just came within a foot of stepping on a big rattlesnake which was all coiled up and ready to strike, and boy, when he cut loose with them sleigh bells of his, I just about tore up that railroad track getting away from there, and my partner was close behind me too. And from the sound of his rattles he must have been a whopper for I only got a glimpse of him in the semi-darkness before I was gone from there, and after that every time the wind would rattle a weed or anything, I was ready to jump and run. Well we hiked on and around midnight came to a place where somebody had cut some wild grass and piled it up for hay not far from the track, and when we saw that pile of hay, I says to my partner, rattlesnakes or no rattle-snakes, I am going to crawl up on top of that hay and sleep until morning.

Well when we awoke the next morning, we crawled down and brushed the hay off our clothes and went over to a section house[26] nearby, and asked the lady if she would sell us some breakfast, and she says yes, for us to come right in and set down. Then she fixed us bacon and eggs and good, hot coffee for which she charged us two bits apiece, and boy, it sure did taste good, for that was the first we had to eat since the day we left Billings. So after thanking her for her trouble, we started hiking east again along the track, and that evening just before dark we hiked into a little place called Custer Station,[27] located in the Crow Indian Reservation.

And as luck would have it, there were big shipping pens there where they loaded cattle trains for the east, and there was a big round-up of cattle there at the time loading beef cattle for shipment to the eastern markets, and the outfit that was doing the shipping, was known as the R L Bar outfit.

When a train was loaded the boss of the round-up always sent two men along with the train of cattle to look after them enroute, so the fellow that I was with went and talked to the foreman of the round-up that was doing the shipping and fixed it up with him to work his way as one of the cattlemen for his free passage over the road where he could ride in the caboose instead of having to beat his way in boxcars.

Well, when I saw all of those cattle and cowpunchers at Custer Station, I changed my mind about going back east, for here was a chance of a lifetime for me to see wild range cattle and cowpunchers in their natural element.[28] And as it was a sight that very few outsiders ever get to see, I was not going to pass up the opportunity. So I went from the shipping corrals over to the chuck wagon, where the round-up cook had his camp pitched on the south bank of the Yel-lowstone, and I must have had a hungry look on my face for the cook says, hello there kid are you hungry? and I says yes sir, I am just about starved. Then he says to me, take these two buckets and bring them full of water from the river while I fix you up a couple of sandwiches, and when I came back with the water, he had two big beef sandwiches all ready for me, and boy, I'll tell the world that when cowpunchers eat beef they have the best that there is, no foolin'.[29]

Well the next day I walked about three miles east of Custer Station and got a job as a mucker[30] in the Big Horn Tunnel which took its name from the Big Horn River that empties into the Yellowstone just east of the tunnel.

Now our camp was located at the east end of the tunnel, and there was a big camp of Crow Indians at the west end of the tunnel, and these Indians would go over to Custer's battlefield once a month where the Crow Agency was located, and each and every one would be issued money, clothes, and blankets, and when they came back, they would bring the clothes up to our camp and peddle them to us white men, and then they would buy whiskey with the money that we paid them for the clothes, for of course there were bootleggers in the Indian Reservation in those days, just the same as there is every where today.[31]

I remember we only got two dollars a day for ten hours back in those days, and we thought we were lucky, and if I remember right, I started to work there about the middle of September [1898] and I stayed there a little over two months. I remember we took our meals in a big camp dining room, erected from rough pine lumber, and our meals cost us four dollars a week, but the company had built a large bunk house for the men to sleep in but everybody had to furnish his own bedding which could be bought at the commissary.[32]

I remember along about the middle of October it began to get real winterish, for we were having cold rains and snow, and about this time I took up with a young fellow by the name of Otto Berg, from Oshkosh, Wisconsin, and at that time we were bunking in the company bunk-house, and we both got as crumy as pet coons, for the bunks were full of cooties, so Otto and I went to work and built us a dugout in the side of a hill, and then we boiled our clothes in big tin cans to kill the crums, then we went to the commissary and bought new blankets, and moved into our new home, the dugout, which we used to sleep in until we quit the job and left there along about the last of November. And boy, it sure was cold up in that part of the country by this time.

Now I will never forget the night that we left there. It was blowing and snowing, and was cold enough to freeze the tail off of a brass monkey.

I remember that I had on two suits of heavy underwear, and a heavy suit of clothes, and an overcoat, all of which I had bought off the Indians.

And I remember that there was an old man left there with Otto and I, and he was carrying his roll of blankets, so we all grabbed an east bound stock train, but there was no place to ride except up on top, so we climbed up on top of the cars and laid down, and the old man unrolled his blankets, and we tried to keep covered up with them, but the train was making pretty good time and the wind was blowing a gale, so we did not have much luck, for the blankets kept whipping in the wind like a loose sail, so I got it into my head to get in one of the cars with the cattle, and putting my thoughts into action, I climbed down and crawled in through one of the small doors of a car and got astraddle of an old steer's back. And I was holding onto an iron rod that run across the car just under the roof with my hands, and everything was fine and dandy until the old steer came to life and discovered me up there on his back. Then the fun started. Oh boy, the way he twisted, bucked, and snorted until he crowded the other cattle over far enough so he could wiggle out from under me. And all of this time I was just about busting myself trying to get back to the door, so that I could get the heck out of there, but he had got me so far away from the door that I could not reach it. And there I was, hanging onto the iron rod, and wondering what would happen next, when just then the train shot around a curve and gave the cattle a lurch causing them to sway toward my end of the car, and my old steer's body carried me close enough so that I got one of my legs through the end door which gave me a chance to get out, and boy, when I did get out, I'll tell the world that I was not cold, no foolin'.

Well I climbed back up on top of the car where the other two fellows were at and I thought that I would freeze. And I was sure glad when the train reached the next division point east, a little place called Forsyth, Montana.[33] Well we all decided that it was too cold to go any further that night, so we went into the waiting room of the small depot, where the night operator had a good hot fire going in the stove. Then the old man spread his blankets down on the floor, and we all slept there until morning, after which we went to a lunch room and ate some breakfast. Then we went over to the train yards and caught an eastbound freight out of there, but we had to dig up four bits apiece to the head brakeman to let us ride in an empty gondola (open coal car) to the next division point which was Glendive, Montana,[34] and we arrived there about midnight. Well after getting something to eat, and drinking lots of coffee, we grabbed another eastbound freight, and crawled down into the empty ice compartment of an empty refrigerator car (called a reefer by railroad men) and closed down the hatch-lid on top to keep out the wind, but it was plenty cold in there at that, and the train had not gone very far when one of the brakemen came along and raised up the lid, and wanted to know where we were going, and what we were riding on. (I will mention here that if a fellow carries a union card of some trade or other, the brakemen will always let him ride, for that is the reason that they always ask a fellow what he is riding on.) So we told the brakeman that we were going just as far as this train would take us, and he says all right it will cost you just one dollar apiece to ride to the next division point, which was Dickinson, North Dakota.[35] And we paid him the three dollars, rather than get ditched away out there on the open plains on a night like this. Now just before we pulled into Dickinson, the brakeman came over again, and told us that his crew had orders to go right on through with this train to the next division point, which was Mandan, N.D.,[36] and if we wanted to give him another three dollars, that we could stay right where we were until we got to Mandan. So we told him all right, for him to come around after the train left Dickinson and we would give him the money, for we were not sure if we would stay on or not.

Now when the train reached Dickinson along in the afternoon, it was blowing and snowing something fierce, so we got off and run over to a lunch room and got a bite to eat and drank plenty of hot coffee, then we beat it back to the yards and got in the reefer again just before the train pulled out. And pretty soon here came the brakeman again to collect three dollars which we gladly handed over to him for we wanted to get out of this part of the country as soon as we could.

Well our train pulled into Mandan the next forenoon and it was still blowing and snowing. So we crawled out of the reefer and went over to a saloon and got some drinks to warm us up, then we went into a sort of a boarding house where they were just putting dinner on the table, and washed up a bit, after which we went into the dining room and put our feet under the big long table which was loaded with a lot of good old home cooked food, and served family style, everybody helping themselves, and boy, I want to tell you that we put a feed under our belts that should have cost us a dollar apiece, but which only cost us two bits each.

Well after eating our dinner, we went back to the railroad yards and climbed into an empty boxcar to get out of the wind and snow, and we saw our old private car, the reefer, in a train that was all made up and was just about ready to pull out. And the head shack saw us over in the empty boxcar, and he came over there and wanted to know if we were headed east. So we told him yes, that we were, then he says, well I will take you over my division as far as Jamestown,[37] if you got any money. Then we told him that we would give him four bits apiece, but he said nothing doing, then he went away and left us. But when his train started to pull out he could not stand to let a dollar and a half get away from him, so he hollered over for us to come and load on, and that was just what we were waiting for. We knew we had the old shack where the hair was short so we outsmarted him. So we jumped down out of the boxcar, and run over and got on our same refrigerator car and climbed down into our private compartment as we now called it, and pretty soon the old boomer brakeman came over to collect his dollar and a half.

Well our train pulled into Jamestown some time after midnight but we did not get out, but stayed right in our old car, for after changing engines and train crews we were on our way again, but the brakeman found us, and of course we had to dig up another dollar apiece from Jamestown to Fargo where we arrived the next evening just before dark. And we had to get out and get something to eat for by this time we were pretty hungry, but we were lucky enough to catch our same old car again, leaving Fargo, and of course, we had to dig up to the brakeman to ride to the next division point which was Staples, Minn., where we arrived in the afternoon. So we climbed out of our car and went over to a restaurant to get something to eat, and while we were over there eating, the train pulled out with the old man's bedding. Well we went back to the yards, and a stock train had just pulled in. And they were changing engines and crews and were getting ready to pull right out, so we asked the head man [head brakeman] what was the chances to go to Minneapolis with him, and he says O.K. if you have got a dollar apiece, load on, so when they pulled out we grabbed her, but there was no place to ride only in between on the couplers, but as the train made good time it was not long before we pulled onto Little Falls, Minn.,[38] where they made their first stop, and as the brakeman had not come around yet to collect his three dollars fare, and as it was getting dark, we decided that we would not go any further that night so we got off and went over into town and eat our suppers. Then we went to a rooming house and went to bed, and I am sure I never before, nor since, appreciated sleeping in a nice, fresh, clean bed as I did there that night in Little Falls, Minn.

Now the next morning I went to the postoffice, and sent a money order to the amount of forty dollars on ahead to my mother so that

I would have it when I got home, and that forenoon we grabbed another train, and rode it to Minneapolis where we arrived that evening. And after eating some supper, we went to a flop-house and slept until morning, and after breakfast we went over to the depot, for the old man wanted to get some folders, so that he could dope out his route from here on, as this was the parting of the ways for us three. For the old man was headed for Hot Springs, Ark., to spend the winter, and Otto was going home to Wisconsin and he tried to talk me into going with him, but I told him nothing doing, for I was homesick to see my mother and that I was going to beat it home just as fast as I could. So that afternoon we all three went to a show together. . . .

And after the show we all went to a saloon and had some farewell drinks, and bid each other a last good bye, after which I boarded a street car for St. Paul where I caught a freight train that night on the C.B.&Q. for La Crosse, Wisconsin, and I remember the brakeman let me ride for four bits down over his division to La Crosse where we arrived the next morning a little after daylight.[39]

So I climbed out of the boxcar that I had been riding in and walked over to a restaurant right close to the railroad yards to get some breakfast, and while I was waiting for my order of ham and eggs, a big flat-foot cop came in and gave me the once over, then went out again, and the girl behind the counter says, listen kid, look out for that guy, for he is a bad bull and is always chasing hoboes off the C.B.&Q. trains, and out of the yards. So when I came out he says to me, did you get off that C.B.&Q. train that just pulled in a little while ago? and I says, yes I did, why, and he says well where are you goin? and I says to Chicago. Then he says, well, get out of town, and don't let me catch you around here agin, or I will run you in for thirty days. Then he took a swift kick at me, and says now git going', and boy, I went, for he was sure one tough bull.

Well, I hiked east on the C.M.&St.P. tracks out for about two miles from town to a railroad junction, and I stopped there in the jungles where several hoboes were lying around a camp fire waiting for a train. And they asked if I got tangled up with that hard-boiled bull downtown? and I told them that I sure did, and that he gave me the bums-rush out of town.

So along about the middle of the forenoon along comes a rattler (a freight train) and two other bums and I grabbed her. And we were riding in an empty boxcar when the brakeman found us. I remember one of these guys called himself Denver Red, and the other was

[33]

Chicago Blackie. So the shack made us dig up four bits apiece to ride to Milwaukee, where we arrived the next morning.[40] And as soon as we got out of the yards, I lost myself from Denver Red and Chicago Blackie, as I had them sized up as pretty tough birds. Then I went into a saloon and told the bartender to fix me up some kind of hot whiskey drink, as I had been riding all night, and I was almost froze and wanted to thaw out. So after throwing the drink into me, I sit down behind the stove and took a snooze for about an hour, after which I bought another drink and then I went out to the C.M.&St.P. yards, but the bulls were so hostile that I could not get near enough until after dark to catch a train for Chicago which I did just before midnight. I remember that I was riding in an empty stock car, and the wind that was blowing in off Lake Michigan was so cold and raw that I had to keep walking from one end of the car to the other to keep from almost freezing.[41] And I sure was glad when I landed in Chicago the next morning, and after I got off the train I took a street car and rode into the city and went to the flop-house there on State street where Pat Kelley and I had stayed as we passed through Chicago that summer on our way out to the northwest, and went to bed in one of the little cell-like rooms and slept until the middle of the afternoon. Then I got up and went to a store over on South Clark street where I bought me a new outfit from the hide out, a suit of clothes, underwear, shirt, socks, shoes and a hat, collar and tie, and went back to the flop-house, where I took a bath, and put on the new outfit, which if I remember right cost me around about twenty dollars, all told, for everything. Gee, I wish I could do that now, but no such luck, for in these days of old high cost, and boot-leg hooch I am telling you brother it can't be done.

Well after I got all dressed up I went to the Great Northern Theatre[42] and saw a show, the play was called A Texas Steer, and it sure was funny. I remember that there was a little midget with the show who came out and sang the song (just because she made those goo, goo, eyes) which was very popular at that time, and he made such a hit with the crowd, that they called him back three or four times.

Now after the show, I had something to eat, then I went down to what was called the old Dearborn Street Station[43] in those days, and bought me a ticket on the C.&E.I. and rode home on the cushions like a gentleman.

Well, I sure was glad to see my mother and the rest of my folks, and they were glad to see me. It felt good to be home again, and my old pal Pat Kelley was home, and back working at his old job in the Foundry. He told me that after I got separated from them the night we all left Fargo to go up to Grand Forks, that he only worked long enough in the harvest to make a stake to bum home on.

Well, I was only home a few days until I was back in the machine shop working as a machinist helper,[44] and I worked there this time up until about the first of June, when the machinists pulled a strike in the shop and the company run some non-union scabs down from Chicago to take their places. So one day, old man Peck, the superintendent, overheard another boy and I while we were over in one corner of the building eating our noon-day lunch and we were sympathizing with the striking union machinists and giving the non-union scabs heck, so that made old man Peck mad, and he tied a can on us right there, but I did not care, for it was nice warm weather by this time and my feet were itching for another ramble around the country anyway, and besides I had another stake saved up by this time and I was ready to go.

Chapter III

*W*ell, one day shortly after I got fired out of the machine shop, one of the striking machinists by the name of Eddie McKee (better known as Whitie McKee, on account of his real light hair) and I made up our minds that we would take a hobo trip around the country while the machinist union was trying to effect a settlement with the Sprag Manufacturing Company where we had worked at the time the strike was declared.

So we hopped a coal drag on the C.&E.I. and beat our way up to Chicago, where we shipped out from an employment office to a job as track laborers on the Chicago & Northwestern railroad over near Marshalltown, Iowa,[1] but when we got to Marshalltown, we jumped the job and beat it on out to Omaha, where we shipped out on a job on the Union Pacific as mule skinners near Laramie, Wyoming, but when we reached Cheyenne,[2] we jumped the job again.

Well, Whitie and I both agreed that this shipping-out racket to railroad jobs for a couple of dollars office fees and then riding the cushions for four or five hundred miles, was sure the cat's whiskers, but we was crowing too soon and although we did not know it, but when we got ready to leave Cheyenne for Denver, our troubles had just started for, after we left Cheyenne we sure did meet up with some hard boiled brakemen and railroad bulls.[3]

Well Whitie and I layed around Cheyenne for a couple of days and tried to get a job in the Union Pacific shops there, but there was not much doing there right then, so one night we grabbed a south-bound rattler and headed for Denver, but we got kicked off about two miles out of town and had to walk back, so when we got back near the train yards we went over to the jungles where some other hoboes had a campfire going, and stuck around there until morning, and as we were walking through the yards to town to get some breakfast, we met old Jeff Carr the yard bull, who was [an] all around Wyoming bad man, and he was mounted on his big white horse, driving a bunch of hoboes before him, and I remember that he was swinging one end of his rope and every time that he got close enough to a man, he would give him a whack with it, so he chased us quite a ways out on the prairie before he left us.

Well, to get back to my story, Whitie and I had to dig up a dollar a piece to a brakeman to get to ride to Denver in a box car, and after taking in the sights there at Denver for a couple of days, we caught a freight on the Santa Fe and by playing hide-and-seek with the train crew all night, we arrived at Pueblo, Colorado,[4] on Sunday morning and stayed there that day and night and the next day just about noon we grabbed an eastbound freight on the Santa Fe and headed back east, but we did not get very far on that train, for Whitie and I had made up our minds not to dig up any more and these brakemen on this division of the Santa Fe, sure were hardboiled, and after we had rode about two or three miles out of town, both brakemen came into the empty stock car that we were riding in and each one of them carried a brake club (which generally is a sawed-off pick handle)[5] and the big tall guy says: Where are you bums going, and what you riding on? Then Whitie showed them his machinist union card and they told him that he could ride, but as I said that I did not have anything, they told me to hit the grit, and as Whitie would not leave me, he said that he would get off too, and by this time the train was hitting it up at a pretty good clip, so I asked the big tough guy, that done all of the talking, if he would not let us stay on until the train slowed down a bit or made the first stop, then we would get off. And he said to me: Naw, get off before I knock you off, so Whitie and I swung down and let go, and man-o-man, when the ground jumped up and hit me, I sure thought that I was done for, and boy, we did not stop rolling until we hit the bottom of the high fill. And besides being almost knocked out, our clothes were mussed up and we had scratches and bruises all over us.

Well, we finally got up and brushed off our clothes the best we could, then we walked back near town and waited in the jungles on the bank of the Arkansas River with some hoboes until after dark, when we caught another freight train, but we did not take any more chances this time of getting unloaded, for we crawled under a box car and rode the rods,[6] where the train crew could not get at us while the train was running and we made it this time as far as Rocky Ford,[7] which is a little town just a few miles west of La Junta.[8]

Well, after we eat some breakfast, we went over to a little park and slept until about noon on the grass, then we got up and went over to the depot and bought tickets and rode from there on over to La Junta, where we arrived about 2 P.M. on a passenger train.

So we went into a little restaurant to get a bite to eat and the cook happened to be a young fellow that I knew back home. And after exchanging greetings and a lot of talk, he asked us where we were stopping, and we told him that we had just blowed into town and expected to stop in a box car that night if the bulls did not give us the bums' rush out of town, so he says, if you are here tonight, come around to the back door and I will slip you some meat and other stuff so that you can go over to the jungles and stew up a mulligan.

So after dark we went around to the back door as he had told us to and sure enough, he had a piece of meat, some potatoes and onions and a can of tomatoes, salt, coffee and a loaf of bread all fixed for us. So we took the layout over to the jungles on the river bank near the Santa Fe yards and cooked up a swell mulligan stew for our supper and then we sneaked over into the Santa Fe yards and crawled into an empty mail car that was parked on a track near the jungles and slept on the narrow couches that the postoffice department furnishes for the railway mail clerks to rest on while they are on long runs. Now I guess that the Santa Fe yard bulls did not think that any bums would have the guts to sleep in one of Uncle Sam's mail cars that had cut out there in La Junta, for we were not bothered and slept there until late the next morning.

And that day we went to the Santa Fe shops and we were lucky for we both got a job.

So that evening we went to the shop foreman and asked him if he could square us for a place to board and he gave us an O.K. slip to a lady that run a boarding house and we went up to her place and she had us to fill out a Santa Fe Company boarding house form and sign it, which she turned into the company, for this way she was protected and sure to get her board bill. Well that night after supper Whitie and I wrote letters back home to let our folks know where we were at.

Now after we had been working there about fifteen days, Whitie got a letter from the secretary of the machinists' union telling him that the strike had been declared off and everything was settled and for him to come back as his old job was waiting for him.

So we bunched our jobs and dragged our time [collected wages] and got ready to beat it home. Now we had made up our minds that from hereon we were going to use our guts and try and ride passenger trains as much as we could, for the freight crews in this part of the country were so danged hostile that they were causing us too much trouble and we were told that the negro train porters were just about as bad as the freight brakemen and at that time there was a negro porter that went by the nick name of Diamond Dick, that run between Dodge City, Kansas and La Junta on the Santa Fe, as passenger train porter, and they say that he was a bad coon from Memphis, for the same night that we left La Junta Whitie and I talked with a young fellow that said he had got tangled up with this Diamond Dick guy, and he showed us the backs of his hands, which were still swollen from being stepped on by Diamond Dick just the night before, for the fellow said that he was decking it on top of one of the Santa Fe's westbound fast trains (decking it on top, means riding on top of the passenger coaches) some place east of La Junta, when this big burly coon came right upon top after him and tried to throw him off while the train was running, but the fellow was holding onto some small iron pipes that ran along on the car roof, so the big smoke stomped on his hands in order to make him let go and the young fellow was pretty husky himself, so he let go of the pipes and grabbed the old black boy around the legs and said to Diamond Dick: If I roll off I will drag you with me, so the old hard boiled coon got scared and compromised with the fellow by telling him to get off at the next stop, which happened to be La Junta.

Well after hearing this fellow's story, Whitie and I were scared out of trying to ride the blind[9] or decking on top, so we decided to try to ride the pilot [cowcatcher] of the engine and instead of staying too close to the depot, where the bulls and train porters were watching everything, we walked up the track a short distance east of the depot and hid under a box car to await there for a fast passenger train that was then changing engines at the station.

Now it is a rule on all railroads that when a passenger train changes engines and starts on its way again, that the engineer must make what is called a running air-brake test, to see if the brakes are working properly.

So in this case, after the engineer got his train moving good, he made the usual air-brake running test, and lucky for us, he had set the brakes so hard that they had almost pulled the train down to a stop right close to where Whitie and I were hiding, and all we had to do was to duck out right quick and scramble up on the pilot, where we set down with our backs to the front of the engine.

And the whole thing could not have been done any slicker if we and the engineer had rehearsed it all over before hand, but dear reader don't make a mistake by thinking that it was any smooth acting on our part, for if that engine had not slowed down right where she did, I am sure that we would not have had the guts to try it, but as it was, old lady good luck had pulled the magic strings and set us right up there on top of that engine pilot, and there we were sailing down through the country at a fierce clip, and the dang grasshoppers and other bugs were pelting us in the face almost like we were passing through a hail storm.

But all we could do was to sit up there and hang on for dear life for the engine was rocking and swaying like a ship in a storm as she went tearing down that track through the night. Whitie says to me, gee, Brownie, what if we should hit a cow, and I said to him, for the love of Mike, don't talk about cows for these grasshoppers are bad enough, for oh boy, we were sure taking one exciting ride while it lasted. The beam of light from the electric headlight on the engine stuck out in front of us and lit up the right-of-way for about one hundred yards ahead of the engine, and we could see jackrabbits and other small animals go hurry scurrying off in the dark at the side of the track as the train approached them and one old jackrabbit thought that he could out-run us and went galloping down the middle of the track ahead of the engine until we overtook him and then he turned and jumped like a bolt of lightning to one side and was lost to sight in the dark as we flew past. And again at times we would see some wild range cattle too near the track for comfort, as there were no fences along the right-of-way and we were afraid that some loco steer might run onto the track instead of running away from it, for some of the crazy brutes would stand and stare at the headlight until the engine got almost to them.

Now the light beam from the headlight, shining on the track, made the rails look like two silver ribbons that were being unreeled out of the darkness ahead of us and swallowed up right under the pilot below us as we went sailing along through the dark night and gee, we were getting thrills and chills in turn, one after the other.

Now I don't know how long it took to make the run from La Junta, Colorado, to Coolidge, Kansas, a distance of one hundred and two miles,[10] for it was all down grade and they made it without a stop and I think that I am safe in saying that it was not one bit over one hour and thirty minutes for this part of the Santa Fe road was known as the racetrack at that time between La Junta and Dodge City.[11]

Well, anyway, when she pulled up and stopped at the water tank to take water at this little town of Coolidge, which is located just a few miles east of the state line, between Colorado and Kansas, Whitie and I jumped down from our perch on top of the pilot and ran out in the dark and layed down on the ground, but we were too late for the engineer spied us as he got on the ground to oil around, and he told the negro train porter who was there watching the blind, that he had better keep his eye on us, so we were at the river's end as far as getting any further on that train.

But we did not have long to wait, for there was an orange train pulled in after the passenger train pulled out,[12] and we were figuring on ducking under a car and riding the rods, but just before the train started, the head shack came along and he said to us, where are you boys going, and we told him that we wanted to get to Dodge City,[13] and he says you got any money, and we told him we would give him two bits apiece. So he said, give it to me and get on, for the four bits will buy me a pint when I get into Dodge.

So when the train started to pull out we loaded on and as the cars were all reefers loaded with oranges from California, we climbed up on top and rode into Dodge as the old boomer brakeman had called it and went over to a restaurant to get something to eat. But when we came back to the train yards our orange train had pulled out, but in a short time we caught a drag of empty box cars and rode it to a place called Greatbend, Kansas,[14] where we got ditched, for by this time it was daylight.

And that night we caught a passenger train out of Greatbend for Kansas City and we decked it on top until we reached Topeka, Kansas,[15] just before daylight and when the train pulled in and stopped we got off and were hiding behind some box cars when a man came and opened both side doors of the head baggage car of the train that we had rode into town on, and went away and left them open. And a fireman on a switch engine that was standing near by, hollered to us boys and said, come on, hurry up and get into that empty baggage car before she pulls out. So we ran over and climbed in and crawled over in behind some long boxes that were lying length wise across the car, but it was still too dark to see what they were, but after the train had gone quite a little distance, we crawled back over the middle of the car, close to the door and by this time it was light enough so that we could see to read the writing that was stenciled on top of the boxlids and we discovered that these boxes contained dead soldiers that were being shipped back from the Philippine Islands, and I remember of reading on top of one box lid, which went something like this: John Doe, Co. A, 47 U.S. V., killed in action at the battle of Luzon, and as my brother, Tom, was a bugler in Co. I, of the 47, U.S. V., which was in the Philippine Islands at that time,[16] I got very much interested and read all of the inscriptions on the box lids, thinking I might find his name on one of them, as we had not heard from him for a long time, but it turned out that he was not there among the noble dead.

Well to get back to my story, we rode in this car until the train pulled into the station at Argentine,[17] where the Santa Fe yards were at and as we were climbing out, we jumped right into the arms of the Santa Fe yard bulls, and I think that there must have been about a dozen of us all together, so the bulls marched us up to the town hall jail and before locking us up, they searched all of us and took everything that they could find in our pockets away from us, but Whitie and I had most of our money which was paper, planted on our person and the dicks did not find it and all that they got off of us was about three dollars between us, then they locked all of us up in a large bare cell and we layed down and slept on the floor until that afternoon, when they came and took all of the fellows that they had took much money off of up to court and the poor devils got fined ten dollars apiece. Then they came and took Whitie and two or three other fellows and I, that they had only got a small amount from and turned us loose and and told us to get out of town or they would give us thirty days on the rock pile, so Whitie and I took a street car and rode over into Kansas City and after getting something to eat we went out to the Chicago & Alton[18] yards and just about dark we grabbed a fast passenger train on the C.&A. for Roadhouse, Illinois,[19] and decked it on top until morning when we climbed down and were riding the blind right behind the engine and just before we got to Roadhouse the fireman came back over the tank and ask if one of us would come over on the tank and shovel down some coal for him, as this train was a fast hard run and he had used up all of the coal in the front part of the tank, so I climbed over onto the back of the tank and picked up an extra scoop shovel and shoveled and pushed the coal from the back and sides of the tank up in front where he could reach it, for it sure kept him busy baling coal into the firebox to keep the old girl hot.

(Now the firemen, so I am told, on most of the big engines of today, have mechanical stokers and apparatus to push the coal from the back of the tank up to the front end where they can easily reach it, which is operated by steam or compressed air, but they did not have anything like that when I was firing a coal burner on the road, for in my day, when the coal got so far back in the pit of the tank that we could not reach it, if the head brakeman did not take pity on us poor firemen and shovel the coal down for us we had to shovel it down ourselves.)

Well when we got to Roadhouse we grabbed a north bound coal drag on the C.&A. and rode it to Bloomington, Illinois,[20] where we caught a fast east bound L.E.&W.[21] freight and rode it home to Hoopeston and now here I was back home once more, after being gone on a wild goose chase for a little over a month, and had only worked about twelve or fifteen days of that time.

Well the strike was all settled and Whitie went back to his job in the machine shops, but old man Peck would not give me a job any more, so I stayed home and helped my stepfather in his tin shop until about the first of August [1899] and then I got restless again and made up my mind to beat it out to Wyoming and try to get me a job of railroading on the Union Pacific as I was now passed twenty years old, and could pass for twenty-one.

So I told my mother that I was going to follow in the footsteps of my father and become a railroad man, for it was in my blood and the railroad was calling, and after bidding my mother and all the rest of them goodbye, I beat it for Chicago and as I was all alone this time, I did not lose any time, but shipped right out on a Government job over the C.B.&Q. to Burlington, Iowa.[22]

Now this job was on the Mississippi river, doing rip-rap work,[23] whatever that was, and when I got to Burlington, I saw the river, but missed the job, and kept right on going, and if I remember right, I followed the C.B.&Q. across the state of Iowa to Council Bluffs,[24] where I took a street car and crossed over to Omaha and made the rounds of the employment offices and they were all crazy for men to ship out into Wyoming to all kinds of jobs along the Union Pacific, for I was told that old E. H. Harraman[25] was practically rebuilding this road from Cheyenne, Wyoming, to Ogden, Utah, and there were hundreds of men strung out all along the line, clear across the state of Wyoming and part of Utah at all kinds of different camps, making cuts and fills, building bridges, straightening out curves in the track, cutting down grades and boring tunnels.

Now a man could get almost any kind of a job that he wanted, but the most of them were big camp jobs and as I had my mind made up to go railroading, I wanted to ship to some job at, or near, a division point, where I could try to get a job in the train or engine service as a brakeman, fireman or maybe a job of switching in the yards.

Well there were so many jobs to pick from, that a fellow did not know what to do, so finally in my rounds from one employment office to another, I got into an office where they were shipping out laborers to a job in Rawlins, Wyoming,[26] and as the map showed Rawlins to be a division point, I paid the two dollars office fee and signed up for the job.

And that evening some more fellows and I were taken down to the Union Pacific depot where we got aboard of what was called the hobo car, which was coupled on the rear end of second No. 3,[27] and started on our way to Rawlins, and when we arrived at Cheyenne the next day, they coupled another hobo car that had come from Kansas City on behind ours.

Now I remember that our train was a double-header out of Cheyenne, with one big new engine, and a little old standard eight-wheeler,[28] and the little old engine had a diamond-shaped smoke-stack, the first that I had seen since I was a small boy and these little old eight-wheelers were the first original passenger engines used on the Union Pacific back in 1868.

Well, after we left Cheyenne and started up Sherman Hill,[29] the two engines puffed and snorted as they wound their way around up over this big mountain which is said to be eight thousand feet elevation above sea level.

And when we reached the top of Sherman Hill we were up in the Rocky Mountains, and it was not long after that until we pulled into Laramie, Wyoming,[30] which was the first division point west of Cheyenne.

And after leaving Laramie our train proceeded on to a little place called Medicine Bow,[31] where they stopped and took coal and water, after which it resumed its run to Rawlins, which was the end of my journey.

And now I want to say right here, that this little town of Rawlins was a humdinger, for she was a rough baby in those days. The main street which was called Front street, ran parallel with the U.P. tracks and was composed mostly of saloons, restaurants, and gambling joints, which never closed their doors, only just to keep out the cold, for they were open for business both day and night, for there was always a roving bunch of railroad camp workers coming and going.

For most of these men would work on a job just long enough to make a stake, and then they would blow into town for one heck of a big drunk, and they would stay in town as long as their money lasted, or until they went broke playing the many games of chance.

And many of these poor working stiffs that came to town, were rolled for their wad before they had a chance to spend it, for the crooked bartenders were always looking for a chance to short-change some poor drunk, and there was cheating tin horn gamblers who's games were not always on the square, and then there were plenty of ruffians and all around bad men who hung around these joints, that done the dirty work as henchmen for the crooked saloon and gamekeepers.

Now it was nothing to see drunks laying around in the back rooms, and the back lots of these joints, which were all fenced in with high board fences, and sometimes dead men were picked up in back of these places, who had died from a knock on the head, or a stab in the back, now of course there were many drunken fights, but I am sure that some of the men lost their lives through methods unknown to the public at large, and in most all such cases, it was just another stiff that had drunk himself to death, as this explanation seemed to suit everybody, they just let it go at that.

Now the job that I had shipped out to was that of tearing down the old stone roundhouse which had been built in the year of 1868, when the Union Pacific railroad was first put through, and they were tearing down this old roundhouse so that they could build a new brick one in its place big enough to accommodate the big new engines that the U.P. company were installing on that part of the road.

Now on this job we worked ten hours a day, and our pay was two dollars a day, and we had to pay four dollars a week for our meals, which was very punk, believe me, and of course we had to sleep in bunk cars, which was old box cars worked over with pine board bunks for us to sleep in, and our dining room was an old-time passenger coach, with a long table in the middle and with another old coach coupled onto one end which was used for a kitchen.[32]

Well after I had been there about six weeks, we finished tearing down the old roadhouse, and started to build the new one.

Now as I said before, I came out in this part of the country to try to get started to railroading, and after the new roundhouse was finished, I went to the roundhouse foreman and told him that I had served two years at the machinist trade, and that I would like to have a job as machinist helper if he could use me, and he says why sure, you show up in the morning and I will put you on, so next morning I was right on the job at seven o'clock, and the foreman put me to work helping a machinist in the roundhouse on what was called running repair work, that is, if an engine is ordered out on a run, and her engineer finds any little thing wrong that ought to be fixed before leaving the roundhouse, he goes and gets hold of the running repair man and brings him to the engine and shows him what needs to be fixed.[33]

Now each and every engineer when he comes in off a trip is required to make out a work report (in a book kept for that purpose in the roundhouse) of the repairs that he wants made on his engine, while she is laying in between trips, but as a rule the poor old engine does not get more than one-half of the work done on her that her hoghead [engineer] has reported in the work book.

And then again, if they done all of the work that some hogheads reported, they would have to jack up the whistle, and build a new engine under it.

Well, to get back to my story, I worked there in the roundhouse until I took down sick with the mountain fever, along in March of 1900, and an old miner who occupied the room next to mine in the old Rawlins Hotel, went out on the mountain side, and gathered some mountain sage that grows there in Wyoming, and made me some tea with it, and although it was worse than quinine to take, it sure done the business, by breaking up my fever, and in a few days I was up and around again. And around about the first of April, I went back to work in the roundhouse again, and one day after I had been back to work for about a month, or some time in the first part of May, the round-house foreman came to me, and says Brownie, they are putting on a work-train out at Tipton,[34] just west of Red Desert, and I am going to send you out there as an engine watchman, and your duties will be to coal up the engine, by shoveling the coal from a gondola (coal car), clean the fire and hoe out the ash-pan, and wipe off the engine and keep her as clean as you can, and the engineer will be your boss, and will keep your time and send it in with his fireman's and his own, you are to take all of your orders from him and do what he tells you, then he says to me, you had better go home now, and pack up your things and get ready to leave, and report back here to me in the morning.

Well, it all sounded too good to be true, for this was another step nearer my goal, for I had decided that I wanted to be a locomotive fireman, and I was really closer to my desire than I expected, so with an unbounded joy that I am unable to express, I beat it over to the hotel and paid up my bill, and throwed what few things I had into an old suitcase, and I was all ready to go, and as it was along about mid-afternoon, I went out on the front porch and sit down, and the air was very clear as I let my gaze wander around over the scenery of the country, and there was old Elk Mountain, fifty or sixty miles away, with its blue, hazy, wooded slopes, reaching up almost to its crown of white silvery snow, and the distance was so deceiving that to a person who did not know might think that one could walk over there in two or three hours. What a wonderful country I thought to myself, as I sat there and looked on mountain peaks, further south over in Colorado, and pretty soon, I caught sight of a small black moving object away out there among the sagebrush and greasewood bushes, and wondered what it could be, and after watching it for awhile, first losing sight of it, and then picking it up again, as it swung around the point of a hill, or a pile of rocks, on the trail, ever coming nearer and nearer, until I finally made it out as the overland stagecoach, drawn by six horses, on its daily run between Rawlins and the mining country, which lay a hundred miles or more south of there, and pretty soon here they come, clipping right along up Front street, the six horses in a long swinging trot, that did not slacken until the driver pulled them up and swung them around the corner and up to the stage coach station, and stopped just a little ways from where I was watching, and it sure was some pretty sight to see, the six fine, rangy horses, the big heavy stage coach, with the driver sitting upon the box, with his long whip, and big white stetson hat, and a six-shooter strapped around his waist, and the express guard, who sat beside him, with two big six-shooters strapped on him, and a Winchester rifle held across his lap, gee, it all gave me a thrill that I cannot explain.

Well, the next morning I reported to the round-house foreman, and he told me that he was sending the 1721,[35] and her crew, and that I was to ride out to Tipton on the engine with them, and that the 1721 was going to doublehead and help a westbound freight train as far as Tipton.

So when the crew was called, they came over to the round-house to get the 1721 ready to go out and the foreman took me to the engineer, and told him that I was going along with them, as their engine watchman, and for him to take care of me, as I was under his orders from now on, so I climbed up into the cab, and set on the fireman's seatbox, and pretty soon the head brakeman of the train that we were to double-head came and took us over into the train yard and coupled the 1721 on ahead of their engine which was another big 1700 class[36] (seventeen hundred class) and as the conductor was there with the running orders, we soon got started, and as the two fine, big, mountain engines went puffing and snorting up the heavy grade west out of Rawlins, I was so thrilled with my first ride in the cab of an engine, that I hardly knew what to do with myself, and as I watched the fireman standing on the deck, swinging the fire door open and shut, by grabbing hold of a chain which hung down from the roof of the cab to the latch on the fire door, as he shoveled scoopful after scoopful of coal into the roaring hot firebox, and the glare from the fire would reflect on his hot, red face, and the heat from the open door would start the smoke curling up off his overalls, and after closing the door he would step to the gangway between the tank [tender] and the engine-cab to one side, and lean out to get a breath of fresh air and also to let the draft that sucked through the gangway cool his heated body for a few moments, and then he would grab the chain again and swing open the heavy door and put in another fire, for the engine was working hard going up this mountain grade and it was up to the fireboy to keep her hot.

Well it was practically up grade all the way to a little place called Wamsutter,[37] which was on top of the Continental Divide, where we stopped to take coal and water, after which we proceeded on our way to Tipton, where they cut the 1721 off from the train which went on its way west to Green River,[38] the next division point.

Now the train crew that were going to be in charge of the work-train, were all ready there, for they had dead-headed out in their caboose on another train ahead of us, and the conductor already had a line up on everything when we arrived, and he told the engineer that the work-train's job was that of taking the flat-cars which were loaded with gravel, that were brought in there by the gravel-trains from a gravel pit west of there, out on the new line between Tipton and Red Desert, and unloading them, which was done by an extra-gang of Greeks,[39] or bohunks as the railroad men called them, and this gang of Greeks lived in a string of bunk-cars that had been spurred out there a few days before, and their foreman was a big red-faced Irishman by the name of Tim Murphy, better known as Big Tim.

Chapter IV

*W*ell they got started that afternoon, and unloaded one train of gravel, after which they came back into Tipton with the train of empty flats, and shoved them into a storage track, and then the crew tied up [stopped] for the night.

I remember there was a carload of coal, which stood on a short spur-track and they spotted the engine alongside of it so that I could coal up the engine tank during the night, for that was my biggest job that had to be done on this, my new job as an engine watchman.

Now before the engineer and fireman left me to go over to the section house where we were all going to board and room, they showed me how to to work the injectors, which puts fresh water into the engine-boiler, and the fireman showed me how to use the slash-bar with which you break up the clinkers with, in the firebox, and then how to hook the clinkers out with the clinker-hook, and then he told me how to bank the fire for the night after I got it cleaned, so that it would keep up steam in the boiler all night, so that the engine would be steamed up and ready for them the next morning.

Well, after they left me I started in on my new job, with a feeling that I had never experienced before on any other job, for working on and around an engine sure was fascinating to me, so the first thing that I did, was to put on one of the injectors and fill up the boiler almost full, then with the slash-bar I broke up the clinkers in the firebox and hooked them out with the clinker hook, and throwed them out on the ground, then after shaking the ashes down through the front section of grates, I took the ash hoe and pushed the live fire from the back half of the fire-box, up to the front half onto the clean grates, and then I shoveled in several scoops of fresh coal on top of it, then I proceeded to clean the back half in the same manner, after which I got down on the ground and crawled under the engine, and hoed out the ash-pan (for they did not have the hopper-dump-ash-pans in those days as they have now) then I crawled out and got up on the engine and scooped in some more coal on the fire near the fluesheet,[1] and banked the fire for the night, after which I climbed upon the fireman's seatbox, and took a good long rest, and a nice little snooze for myself.

Well, after having a rest and a snooze, I got over on the carload of coal, and started to work down in one corner to the floor, by picking up the lumps of coal with my hands, and tossing them over onto the tank, and after so long a time which seemed ages to me, I got the tank all coaled up, and I will confess that I did not get any kick out of this part of the job.

So after coaling up the engine, I took a good rest in the engine-cab, then I took a bunch of clean waste[2] and crawled through the small narrow door alongside the boiler, just ahead of the fireman's seatbox, onto the running board just above the drive-wheels, and proceeded to wipe off the boiler-jacket that covered the boiler, and then I polished the bell and cleaned the headlight.

Then I got down on the ground, and took the old dirty waste and wiped off the drive-wheels, and the side-rods, and the steam-cylinder jackets,[3] and by this time it was breaking day, and in a short time the camp began to come to life, and I could see the little camp fires burning, as the Greeks in little family groups began to cook their breakfast on the open fires out on the ground alongside their bunk cars, for they boarded themselves, eating and living in their own natural way.

So I got up on the engine, and took the ash-hoe, and pulled some of the fire back and scattered it all around over the fire-box, then I put on the blower which causes an artificial draft up through the fire which makes it burn, after which I shoveled in a lot more coal and she began to pick up steam which showed fifty pounds pressure on the gauge at that time, and when she had picked up to one hundred and seventy-five pounds I shut off the blower, and by the time the engineer and fireman got there she had her regular two hundred pounds working pressure.

Well, the engineer said everything looked fine and dandy, and the fireman complimented me for my good work, and told me that some day I ought to make a good tallowpot [fireman], and those few remarks from them made me feel rather stuck up over my first night's work.

Well, as I had been up for twenty-four hours without much sleep, I went over to the section-house where I had already made arrangements with the Swede section foreman and his wife to board and room, and after eating some breakfast, I went to bed and slept until some time in the afternoon, then I got up and took a stroll around the camp, which consisted of the section house, and another smaller house where the Japanese sectionmen lived, and a small telegraph office, where the old bachelor telegraph operator lived and worked.

Well, I stalled around there until the work-train pulled in off the new line to get another train of gravel, then I got on the engine and rode out to the new line with them, and the fireman said that he was going to learn me how to fire the engine, and I told him that was just what I wanted to do, so he showed me how to handle the scoop shovel so as to scatter the coal in the fire-box in order to keep a nice bright level fire, and he also showed me how to turn the scoop shovel over upside down in the open firedoor, and look for bright spots in the fire, for by this means you could see just what kind of a fire you had in the firebox, and if the exhaust was pulling holes in the fire which showed as bright spots, he told me to always keep the bright spots covered with fresh coal, for if I did not the exhaust would pull so much cold air in through the holes that the steam would drop very fast when the engine was working hard.

Well, I would get up every afternoon and make a trip on the engine with them, and the fireman would always let me fire the engine on these trips and I soon got so that I could keep her hot without any trouble, and it happened after we had been out there for four or five days, the engineer took the cramps in his stomach, from drinking the bad alkali water, and as he and his fireman were oldheads on the road, they were entitled to main line work, so the engineer got sore, and sent a message to old Billy Nilind, the master mechanic at Rawlins, and told him if this work-train out here on the desert was all that they had for him and his fireman, that they were through, and to send another engine crew to relieve them, for they were coming back to Rawlins where they lived, and had their families and homes, so old Billy Nilind wired back that he would try and have another engine crew out there in a day or two, and he kept his promise, for on the second day after that, here came the 1727,[4] double-heading on a west bound extra to relieve the 1721 and her crew, which in turn got orders to run extra from Tipton to Rawlins.

Now by this time I had gone through the siege of cramps, and was getting used to the water, so that it did not bother me any more, but the new fireman on the 1727 took the cramps after he had been there about three days and he was feeling pretty rotten, so I would go along with them and fire the engine for him, but as he did not get any better, he sent a message to Rawlins for them to send another fireman to relieve him, and they wired back that they did not have another extra fireman on the board, and that he would have to stick on the job, and that made him sore, so he grabbed an eastbound extra, and beat it back to Rawlins, leaving the job and his engineer flat.

Well, of course when the fireman left, that tied up the work-train, so the engineer got busy and sent a message to Rawlins, telling that his fireman had left him and was headed back for Rawlins, so he asked for instruction as what to do, for Brown, the engine-watchman, had been firing the engine for the last two days for the sick fireman, but he could not keep on firing the engine all day, and work all night as engine-watchman too.

So Rawlins wired back telling the engineer that they did not have any extra fireman, and for him to take Brown, the engine-watchman, for his fireman, and they would dead-head another boy out of the round house on second No. 3, that afternoon to Tipton as engine watchman, and the first time that the engine came into Rawlins for repairs and boiler-wash-out, to have Brown report to the master mechanic's office, and fill out an application and take the regular examination, both physical and time card [operating timetable] and book rules, and when the engineer showed me the message, I could hardly believe my own eyes, for it sounded too good to be true.

Well I was now the regular fireman on the work-train engine, 1727, for the time being anyway, and when the other boy arrived at Tipton to take over the job as engine watchman, I told him all that I knew, and showed him what to do, and believe me I was just about all in, for I had been working both day and night, trying to hold down both jobs.

So the engineer let me take his book of rules and time card, so that I could study up for my examination, which I had to take the first time that we went into Rawlins, and after I had been firing for about ten days, we got a message from Rawlins telling us that engine 1720[5] and her crew were coming east on an extra, and that they would change off with us, and that we would bring their train on into Rawlins, so when the engine crew on extra 1720 read a copy of the message that we had got, I thought that the engineer and his fireman were

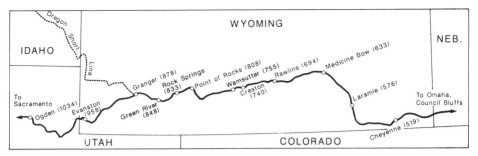

Union Pacific's "Overland Route" in 1900. The distance from Council
Bluffs, Iowa, is given in parentheses.

going to croak, for man, oh man, they sure were sore, and they
cursed the train dispatcher, the superintendent, and all of the Union
Pacific officials in general, for they sure did hate to be pulled off of
the main line work and put on a work-train, but my engineer and I
were just as glad as they were sore, for our engine was getting in
pretty bad shape, her boiler was dirty, the flues needed boring out,[6]
and she was foaming so bad that we had to carry the water so low
in the boiler, that it was not safe any more, for there was danger of
burning the crown-sheet,[7] or of blowing her up.

Well, after the head brakeman had cut the 1720 off from the train,
he coupled us on, and the conductor got an order from the train
dispatcher that extra 1720 had arrived at Tipton and was annulled,
and that engine 1727 would run extra from Tipton to Rawlins, so
we got a highball [approval to move] and started out, and when we
got into Rawlins that evening, I went over to the old Rawlins Hotel,
and after supper I went around to the saloons, and gambling joints
and give things the once over, and then I went back to the hotel and
took a bath, after which I piled into bed and slept until morning,
and got up feeling fine.

So after breakfast I reported at the master mechanic's office, where
they gave me three copies of an application to fill out, and I had to
state therein where I had been working for the last five years, and
what kind of work that I had been doing, besides answering many
questions, and filling out that application was one heck of a job for
me, as I had never run up against anything like that before, and after
I got all through, the chief clerk gave me just an oral examination
on the time card and book of rules, and I remember that he impressed
upon my mind that rule G[8] said that I could not, and must not use
intoxicating liquors, and then he made me recite the rule 99,[9] which

[53]

is the flagging rule, and it says that when a train stops where it is liable to be overtaken by another train, the flagman must go back at once a safe distance that will insure protection to his train, and must take with him the proper signals as prescribed in the book of rules, to stop a following train, which is a red flag and torpedoes by day, and a red and white lantern, fusees, and torpedoes[10] by night, and it further states that on descending grades or where there is curves, or if the weather is stormy, or foggy, the flagman must use his judgment, and go back far enough to insure full protection to his train, and when he has arrived at that point, he will at once place one torpedo on the right hand rail in the direction that the following train is approaching, and remain there until relieved by another flagman, or until he has been recalled by the whistle of his engine, after which he will place another torpedo on the same side two rail lengths from the first one, and if it is after night he will leave a red fusee burning in the middle of the track besides the two torpedoes, to protect his train while he is returning, for the flagman must bear in mind that this is the time of greatest danger, now that is not just the same as it is in the book, but it is something like it.

Well, after I answered a number of the questions, the chief clerk gave me an order to the doctor, and I went over and took the physical examination,[11] and the eyesight and hearing test, then I came back to the master mechanic's office, and the chief clerk gave me a timecard, book of rules, and a switch key, for which I had to sign for, then he gave me an order and told me to take it to the roundhouse foreman, and that he would take care of me, so when I gave the order to the foreman which was an order to mark me up on the fireman's extra board, he says to me, well now Brownie, you are a real sure enough fireman, and we are fixing up one of the old mountain hogs [locomotives] for you and a new engineer that we just hired, to take back out to Tipton for the work train engine, and I asked him where she was at, as I wanted to take a look at her, and he told me that she was the old 1288,[12] further around in one of the stalls, so I walked around to where she was at, an' boy, there was quite a difference between her and the new big 1700 class engines for they were big ten wheelers [4-6-0's], with wagon top boilers, with lots of room in the cabs, but the little old 1288 was of the mogul-type, and she had a ten foot firebox, long and narrow, and the fire-door was down almost even with the deck, or rather where the deck should have been, as this type of engine was known as a deckless hog.

Well she sure was one of the old babies on the Union Pacific, and some of the old timers said that she had been a whale in her day, but it looked to me like that her day was gone forever, and man, oh man, I'll never forget the first trip that I made on her on our way back to Tipton. They fixed her up and got her ready for us, and we double-headed with a westbound extra, but they did not put us in the lead, but instead they coupled us next to the train with a big 1700 in front of us, for my new engineer whose name was Blood (I thought it was rather a funny name) did not know the road well enough to handle the air, and for my part I felt like giving up before we started, for the fire door was back so close to the coal-gate in the front of the tank that I did not have room enough to get a good swing with the scoop shovel, to put the coal up in the front end of the firebox, and besides the fire-door was so low down that I had to almost stand on my head and sort of raise the scoop full of coal up high, then bring it down in a nose dive and volplane [glide] it in through the door, and then give the shovel handle a sort of jiu-jitsu twist that snapped the scoop out from under the coal, and most of it fell in a pile about midway the fire-box, and it seemed to me that my new engineer was trying to run over the big 1700, that was in front of us, the way he was working the old 1288, and boy, oh boy, how I worried and sweat and shoveled and shoveled was something fierce, but I could not keep her hot, but that did not worry Mr. Blood one little bit for he kept pounding her on the back just the same, and we were making a lot of noise if nothing else, but I think that the 1700 was pulling us along most of the time.

Now I will never be able to understand how I kept her alive until we reached Tipton, and I sure was tired and disgusted when we got there, believe me, and as it was late in the evening when we arrived, I was glad to turn her over to the night watchman, after which I crawled off to bed, but the next morning I felt better, and made up my mind to learn how to fire than danged old hog.

So after my engineer and I eat our breakfast, we went over to the old 1288 and the watchman had her all steamed up for us, and while Blood, the hog-head, was oiling around, I took the scoop shovel, and by taking about one half of a shovelful at a time, I practiced different curves, angles, and twists, so as to see which was the best way to land the coal up at the front end of that long fire-box, and pretty soon the train crew who cooked, eat, and slept in their caboose, came over and met the new engineer, and he told the conductor that he had never done any railroading in this western country before, and that he would appreciate any help and pointers that the train crew could give him, as he already knew that I was a new fireman, and was having troubles of my own.

So the head brakeman took us around and coupled on to a string of loaded flats [flatcars], which the Greeks with their shovels, were already climbing onto, and pretty soon we headed out on to the new line, and proceeded down to where they wanted to unload, and in the meantime I was still practicing with the scoop-shovel, and after about three days, I sort of got the hang of it, so that I could place a scoop of coal any place in the fire-box that I wanted it, for I had learned the simple twist of the wrist that done the trick, and after that I did not have much trouble with the old girl.

Well my engineer turned out to be a pretty good sort of a fellow, and about every two weeks they would relieve us, and we would bring the old 1288 into Rawlins for boiler washout and minor repairs, and I always looked forward to these trips in to Rawlins, for we always layed in there for a couple of days, and it gave me a chance to sort of kick up my heels and play around a bit.

Well I remember that we had been at Tipton for about three months, or around the fore part of August [1900] when we got through with our job there, and moved our camp to a place called Creston,[13] a few miles east of Wamsutter, where we stayed for about a month, and then they sent big Tim Murphy and his gang of Greeks some place else along the line, and we of the work-train crew were turned over to the bridge and building department, which had the job of setting up the snow fences along the new right of way, so instead of having to stay out in a camp any more we tied up in Rawlins every night, and each morning we would start out with a train load of snow fences, which were put together in sections, something like a camp folding chair, and about all the men had to do, was to unfold them and set them up, after which they would stake them down, so that the strong winds could not blow them over.

Well they kept us on this job until it was finished some time in the latter part of September when the work-train was pulled off, and I was marked up on the extra board for main line work between Rawlins and Green River, the next division west of Rawlins, and I had not been on the extra board long when one afternoon, some time in the middle of October the call boy[14] called me for second No. 3, engine 642,[15] one of the little old standard eight wheelers [4-4-0] which was one of the old time passenger engines, and as I had never fired a passenger run yet, I sort of felt weak in the knees, for I was afraid that I could not hit the ball, and as I had heard how those grouchy old passenger engineers hated to take out a new green fireman on their runs, I was almost scared stiff, and just the thought of meeting up with one of those old birds on an engine gave me the shivers, but there was no way out of it for me, I had to go, so I went over to the round-house, and looked up the old 642, and began to get things in shape, when the hog-head showed up, and he was an old Englishman, by the name of Tom White, and when he saw me, he says, ay hi say me lad, ow long ave you been firing han hengine, and I told him about six months, but most of it had been out on a worktrain, and that I had only made a few trips on the main line, on through freight, but this would be my first trip on passenger, and he says, well second No. 3 is not a eavy train, hand the old 642, is a good steamer, so those few words of encouragement from him made me feel lots better, and I sort of got over my scare.

Well we got the old girl ready, and pretty soon the passenger engine herder came and took us over to the station to await the arrival of second No. 3, and when No. 3, run in two sections, first No. 3, always carried the baggage-car, smoker, chair-car, and pullmans so that left the mail-car, Wells-Fargo Express,[16] and the two hobo cars which were loaded with laborers for second No. 3, which was running a few hours late that day, and by the time that we got started out of Rawlins, it was late in the afternoon, so old Tom took it easy and gave me a chance, until he saw that I had picked up confidence in myself, after which I had no trouble in keeping the old 642 hot, and about dusk that evening we pulled into Wamsutter where we took coal and water, and old Tom was right about the 642 being a good steamer, but the old girl had all she could do to wiggle up some of those grades with the four car train that we had, so we went rambling along, running them downhill, and pulling them uphill, until we reached Bitter Creek,[17] where we stopped and took water.

Now this little place of Bitter Creek could not be called a town, for it was only a sort of headquarters and supply station for sheep herders outfits, and it was a very common sight to see sheep herders there with their camp wagons getting supplies, and some times you would see cowpunchers and mine prospectors there with their pack horses supplying themselves with grub stakes, for it was miles and miles, both north and south, before you would strike another railroad, for these parts were unsettled except for a few big cattle ranches south of there, and some sheep outfits to the north (so I was told), and it was a pretty wild country yet in the year of 1900.

Well after we took water and started out, I saw a hobo get on right behind the tank on the blind, and as he was dressed something like a sheep herder, I did not think anything about it, so after we had gone some little distance, we heard somebody holler hands up, and when I looked around, there set my sheep herder hobo on top of the coal-gate, with a big six-shooter in each hand. One was pointed at old Tom White, my engineer, and the other one was pointing at me, and the first thing that struck me, that he was going to rob old Tom and I of our money and railroad watches, but instead, he climbed down off the coal-gate, and says to old Tom, slow down, and old Tom was so excited that he grabbed the brake-valve handle, and gave them the whole works, and almost stopped the train right there, but the bandit says no, don't stop here, pull on down around the curve, and you will see a camp fire alongside of the track, where my pals are waiting, and that is where I want you to stop.[18]

So old Tom White says to the bandit, I say what in the bloody 'ell is this, a 'oldup? And the bandit says no, my pals and I are just a little hard up and we are going to touch the express company up for a little loan, as they are rich and able to stand it, so after rounding the curve, we saw the campfire and old Tom pulled up to it and stopped and there were three more bandits there, and they were all armed to the teeth, they each had two six-shooters strapped on them, and their cartridge belts had a double row of cartridges all the way around and besides this, they each one carried a repeating rifle in his hands except one, who carried a sawed off repeating shotgun, so when we got stopped the bandit who was on the engine, says to old Tom and I, come on, get down on the ground, which we did, and he climbed down after us and it turned out that he was the leader of the gang for he began to give orders as one of the other men handed him a rifle, and we had not been on the ground but a couple of minutes when the conductor came running up to the engine and says to old Tom, what's the matter White? What are you stopping here for? And before old Tom could answer him, the leader of the gang says to the conductor, come on line up here, we will take care of you, and then the conductor says, what is going on here anyway? and the leader says it don't matter what is going on, you just do what we tell you, then the leader told two of his men to go on the other side of the train, and not to allow anybody to get off. Then he and his other man made the conductor and old Tom and I walk back to where the express car was coupled onto the first hobo car and then he told me to get under there and uncouple the air and whistle hose, and unhook the toggle chains[19] and pull the pin, which uncoupled the express car from the hobo cars and then the conductor says to the bandit leader, are you going to leave these two cars loaded with men stand here? and the bandit leader says, sure, why? Then the conductor says, will you let me go and send my flagman back to protect the rear of the train? for there was a freight train ready to follow us out of Bitter Creek, and I am afraid that they will come tearing around the curve and plow into us, but the leader of the robbers says to him, if your flagman is a railroad man, he don't have to be told to go back and flag, and the bandit robber was right, for we could see the flagman's red and white lanterns as he went back up the track to flag.

And about this time there was a man came out of the front door of the head coach, and started down the steps to get off on the ground, but the leader of the train robber bandits says to him, get back in that car! And the working stiff says, Who the heck are you? and just then the bandit stuck the muzzle end of his rifle up against the guy's belly, and says, I told you to get back, and I mean what I say. And when the fellow saw what he was up against, he sure did scramble back up the steps, and hurried into the car, and he must have spread the alarm, for some of the car windows were raised and three or four guys stuck their heads out to see what was going on, so the leader fired one of his six-shooters into the air three or four times and the guys sure ducked their heads back in and slammed down the windows. Then the leader called to his two men on the other side and told them to come on up and get on the engine. Then we all went back to the engine and got on, and as I was just about scared out of my wits I was afraid to make a move unless they told me to, as I asked the bandit leader if I could put in a fire, and he says, sure, go ahead, don't let your engine die. (And do you know, from the way that guy talked I have always thought that he was an ex-railroad man.)

Now up to this time the bandits had not bothered the mail clerks or the express messenger, so after pulling down the track for about two miles from where we left the two hobo cars, we stopped again and all got down on the ground and the leader says to the conductor, what time is it? So the conductor pulled out his watch to look and the bandit says to him, That's a pretty nice watch you got there and the conductor says, yes, and I suppose you are going to take it away from me, too, but the bandit laughed and says, no, we are not going to take anything away from you men, for you have to work for what you get, and as long as you do what we tell you, we will not bother you, for the Wells-Fargo is rich, and we are going to borrow some money off of them, and in the meantime he had sent one of his men around on the other side, then while the bandit with the sawed off shotgun, guarded old Tom and I, the leader and his other man stood out from the track a little ways, so that the light from the cars could not shine on them. Then the leader told the conductor to go and knock on the door of the mail car, and tell the mail clerks to come out. So the conductor went to the side door and knocked and hollered to the mail clerks to open up and come out, which the three of them did. Then they joined the engineer and I, then the conductor had to go to the express car and knock on the door, but he hollered for the express messenger not to shoot, for he was not one of the bandits, but the conductor of the train, then he told the express messenger he had better open up and come out, but the messenger would not do it, so the bandit told the conductor to tell him if he did not come out and be dang quick about, that they would blow him up car and all. And after the conductor told the messenger what the bandit said, he opened the door and came out and joined the rest of us, then the bandit leader asked him if he knew the combination of the big through safe, and the messenger told him no, that it was locked in Chicago and was not opened again until it reached Frisco. Then the bandit says, What about your small local safe, and the messenger says, there is no money in it, and I don't even know what is in the big safe. Then the bandit leader says, Well I do, and we are going to get it, too, if we have to blow it to pieces.

So they made us cut the engine off from the two cars and then the bandit with the sawed off shotgun, climbed up on top of the tank and then the bandit leader told all of us to get up on the engine and run her down about a half mile before we stopped, so when the engineer stopped the bandit who was guarding us with his sawed off shotgun, told us to get down on the ground and walk up in front of the engine and set down in the middle of the track where the electric headlight from the engine would shine on us and while he was guarding us there he told us that it would not be good for any of us to try to escape, for he had six shells in that shotgun and every shell was loaded with ten buckshot, and that he could get all of us before we got out of range. So old Tom White spoke up, and says 'Ay I say, you don't think that we are that bloody foolish, do you, and that wise crack from old Tom made the bandit laugh, and after that he began to talk and joke with us, and he told us how he and his pals had been in and around Bitter Creek for a week or more. He said that they had passed off as sheepmen, but they had not ex-posed all of their firearms, for so many shootin' irons might have given them away. He also told us that they had packed in by trail from over the Colorado line south of there, and that their leader had been getting code messages from the east, and that they knew just when this big shipment of gold was coming through and what train that it would be on and then he told us how near they came blowing up the rear car on second No. 3, two nights before that, when she stopped at Bitter Creek, and the conductor ask him why, and he says, because it was all dark and we thought it was loaded with officers of the law, who had got next to our little game, and were trying to set a trap for us, but we found out just in time that it was some railroad official's private car, and that they had all gone to bed, and that was all that saved them so we figured from what he told us, that they had been in touch with somebody on the inside, that worked for the express company. So after we had been sitting there talking for quite a little while, we heard an explosion and the train robber that was guarding us, says, there she goes, they have blown the safe open, and a short time after that, we heard three gun shots and the bandit says, all right, come on, that is the signal for us to come back, so he herded us all back on the engine but he was foxy enough not to let any of us get too close to him and while we were backing up to where we had left the two cars, he rode up on the tank again where he could watch all of us. So we backed up to the cars and coupled on, but the leader bandit told everybody to stay right on the engine except the conductor, who he allowed to go back to the rear end of the two cars. Then we backed up to where we had left the hobo cars and coupled onto them, and in the meantime our flagman had stopped the freight train, and the engineer and fireman and head brakeman of the freight train were there with our flagman, and most of the men of the two hobo cars were out on the ground, standing around in little groups talking and all of us trainmen went with the express messenger to inspect the express car and it had a big hole in the side and part of the roof was blown off right above where the big safe was sitting. Well, the safe was a total wreck and things were scattered around every which way, so after the inspection they decided that the cars was in a good enough condition to proceed, and after getting everybody back on the train we pulled out, and when we came to where we had left the bandits we saw them there with their saddle and pack horses, getting ready to beat it, and they hollered so long boys as we pulled by.

So we proceeded on west to the next open telegraph office, which was called Point-of-Rocks,[20] about twenty miles west of Bitter Creek and we stopped there while the conductor and the express messenger sent a detailed report by wire, after which we went on to Green River, the next division point, which was the end of our run, and I heard the next day that when the express company got all the cargo transferred to another car, as the damaged car was cut out there at Green River, that they found several twenty dollar gold pieces scattered around on the floor under the express packages, and it was reported that the train robbers got about sixty thousand dollars in gold. So the next day old Tom White and I double-headed with the 642, east, with No. 2,[21] the express and mail overland limited which was a pretty heavy train, and when we got back to Rawlins, I was marked up on the fireman's extra board again.

Now, I was told that there had been several express train robberies on the Union Pacific in the past, especially through Wyoming west of Cheyenne, and most of the time in those days the Wells-Fargo Express Company had armed guards in all of their express cars, and the guards were armed with two six-shooters and a sawed off shotgun, and one guard rode in each express car with the messenger, who was also armed with a six-shooter and he had a sawed off shotgun standing up in a rack where it was handy, and I was told that these armed guards were noted Wyoming gunmen that were quick on the draw and dead shots, and I was also told that there had been an express robbery just a year before the Bitter Creek holdup, at a place called Fort Steel,[22] just sixteen miles east of Rawlins, where the bandits killed the engineer by hitting him over the head with a six-shooter and right after that the express company put the armed guards back on again, and just before the Bitter Creek holdup they had taken them off again.

Well, just as soon as the Union Pacific and the express company got word at Cheyenne about the Bitter Creek holdup, they made up a special train at that place consisting of a baggage car, loaded with saddle pack horses, dining car stocked with provisions, and a Pullman sleeper and rushed a bunch of picked men, sheriffs, cowpunchers and noted all-around western gunmen out to Bitter Creek and took up the trail, but as the train robbers had about twenty-four hours start of the railroad posse, it was never able to catch up with them, for it was said that the train bandits were headed for robbers' roost, over in Colorado in the hole-in-the-wall country, which was said to be a place where cattle rustlers, horse thieves, stage and train robbers hung out to escape the clutches of the law.

Well, I fired extra between Rawlins and Green River until about the first part of December [1900], when they began to pull off work trains along the line and close down the camps for the winter and the board was cut, and the most of us younger men in the service were layed off.

Well, when they cut the board there at Rawlins and layed all of us extra men off, of course we had to leave there and go some place else looking for work, and this thing of traveling around looking for a job, is what makes a boomer out of a fellow, and that is the reason that the boomer never stays any place on any one job long enough to get promoted, but keeps jumping around over the country from place to place, and working as a brakeman, switchman or a fireman, on different railroads where business is good, and when business falls off where he is working, so that he can't make any money on the extra board, in most cases if he don't get layed off, he bunches the job on his own accord, and drags his time and beats it to some other part of the country and gets a new job on another railroad and sticks through the rush until things get too dull, then he is on his way again, looking for new adventures and a chance to have a heck of a good time, if there is a good time to be had. So this is the life of the boomer, who is a happy-go-lucky, not caring-a-hang sort of a cuss, here today, and there tomorrow, not giving a dang where he is, for he may be up in Montana, on the big G,[23] or down in Texas on the S.P.,[24] or he might be working back east on the New York Central lines or he may be firing a big oilburner on the Santa Fe, out of Needles, California, where the winters are fine.

Well, to get back to my story, after I got laid off at Rawlins, I got a pass and went to Green River and there I met a young fellow who had been the head brakeman on the work train that summer at Tipton, but he was now braking on the main line, so he asked me what I was doing in Green River, and I told him that I got cut off the firemen's board at Rawlins, and was looking for another job. Then he told me that Trainmaster Sheridon there at Green River was his uncle, and he would take me over and see if he could get his uncle to give me a job, and I says, gee, Billy, your talk sure sounds good to me.[25] Go on and lead me to this uncle of yours. So we went over to the trainmaster's office and Billy told his uncle that he had worked on the work train at Tipton with me that last summer, but since then I had got cut off of the firemen's board at Rawlins and was looking for a job of braking, but the old man told me that he had all the brakemen that he needed, then he says, the only thing that I can do for you right now, is to give you a job of switching here in the yards.

So I told him that I sure would be glad to get the job. Then he said all right, and told his clerk to give me an application to fill out, after which I went over to the doctor's office and took the physical examination, hearing and eyesight test. Then I came back and got marked up on the switchmen's extra board, and I was the only man on the board, for it was pretty cold there by this time, and most of the boomer switchmen had left for warmer climes, so the next day at noon I went to work with the crew that had the half and half shift. That is, we started to work at 12 o'clock at noon and worked until 12 o'clock midnight, for, yard crews in those days worked twelve-hour shifts.

Now, the boomer switchmen all claimed that this Green River yard was the worst job on the system, and when a boomer did light there, he only stayed long enough to make a stake and then he would be on his way again, but as old man Sheridon, the trainmaster, had been an old boomer conductor, and a yardmaster himself, he would always give the boomers a job if he needed a man, and some times he would hire them and give them a chance to make themselves a stake when he really did not need them.

Well, I got a regular job right off the reel, for one of the men on my crew quit and beat it out of there, and said he was going back to Oakland, California, where he would not have to eat snowballs and mustard, and I will tell the world that to me my new job was some tough game, for at the west end of the yards, we had to work around a curve, and if we had a hold of a long cut of cars, our engine was away out on the big river bridge that spanned the Green River from which the little division point town took its name, and it was hard to see and pass along hand and lamp signals, and as the yard was not level, the man working the field (farthest from the engine), would have to climb up and ride the cars in, as they were kicked into the different tracks and set up the hand brakes to keep them from running back out again.

Now, I remember one afternoon I was riding a big box car that the engine had kicked in, and while I was tugging at the hand brake, my car banged into some more cars that were standing on the same track, which caused the brake ratchet to jar loose, allowing the brake to unwind, and as I had a firm grip with both hands on the brake wheel, it picked me up and threw me over on the other car, and I was still so excited after I had climbed down, I thought that the engine was coming down another track further over, but instead, it was on the track next to me, and the end of the pilot beam swatted me in the back and set me sprawling headlong between the two tracks as the engine went on by me. Oh, boy, I thought that something had put the Indian sign on me that day for sure, and I remember one night not long after that, we were working up in the east end yards, and they kicked an old coal car in loaded with sand, and I grabbed her and climbed upon the west end (the direction that the car was traveling) to set up the hand brake, and as the old brakestaff was long and very much eaten with rust, when I swung all of my weight on the brake wheel in trying to slow the car up before it banged into the other cars, the old rusty brake-staff broke off just above the ratchet, and down off the end of the car I went, but the swing of my body that had caused the staff to break off, carried me off to the left side and I landed between the two tracks with the brake wheel still clutched firmly in both hands, just as the car load of sand crashed into the other cars, and the end board which was loose, slammed up against the other car that it had struck, which was caused by the shifting of the load of sand, and, boy, if that old rusty brake staff had not broken off just when it did, causing me to fall off the end of the car, I would have been mashed as flat as a pancake, and I thought to myself, Brownie, that old jinks will get you yet, but it is all in the game, and most railroad men believe that they will not get it until their time comes.

Now, my foreman, Eddie Fishback, who had charge of the engine, and my partner who's name was George Thorn, sure were two booze hounds, and they would send me over to the saloon some nights to buy them a pint of hooch, and to keep in good with them, I had to buy a pint once in a while myself.

Now, I remember while switching there in the Green River yards, I boarded and roomed at the old Elkhorn Hotel over south of the tracks from the main part of town, and it was run by an old German by the name of Egg, and if you ask me, he was some egg too, and he had two Swede girls working there, waiting on table, cooking and washing dishes, and these girls were sisters, and the oldest one was named Leana, and the younger one was named Anna, and as I used to quit work at midnight, I would go over and go to bed and sleep until about 9 A.M. in the morning, when I would get up and go down to the kitchen and talk to the two girls, and old Egg would get so mad, that he would almost blow up, and the girls told me that he was jealous of them. So finally one morning he could not stand it any longer, and he flew into a rage and fired me out of the kitchen and told me to stay out.

Well of course that made me pretty sore, for I had began to like Anna pretty well by this time, but after that I did not have much of a chance to talk with her, so one morning not long after that the two girls came hurrying upstairs with tears in their eyes and woke me up, and they said, 'ho, Brownie, you had better quit switching in the yards, for poor Mike Banks got killed last night, and they have got him now over at the freight house in a box car, and the girls felt pretty bad about it, for Mike had boarded and roomed at the Elkhorn just the same as I did, so I got up and went over and took a last look at poor old Mike, as he lay there in the boxcar on a grain door, and believe me, the sight of him made me feel creepy, for he was almost cut to pieces.

But I stuck to my job, and along about the middle of February, 1901, just after I had passed my twenty-second birthday, my crew was pulled off there in Green River, and I was transferred to another job at a place called Granger,[26] about thirty miles west of there, where a branch of the Oregon Short Line[27] made connections with the Union Pacific, and I worked with a switch crew who were switching jointly for the U.P. and O.S.L. railroads and our work up there was that of cutting the O.S.L. trains into and out of the U.P. trains, as all of the passenger trains on both roads made connections there, but this place of Granger was a heck of a place to live, for I have switched cars right there in Granger when it was forty below, and I don't mean maybe, and at times the cold raw wind felt like it was cutting your nose right off your face.

Now, after one of those Wyoming blizzards would pass, and the weather would moderate so that people could get around, I have been told that the sheep ranchers sometimes go out and find their sheepherders frozen to death, or they would be so badly frozen that it would be necessary to amputate their feet or hands in some cases.

Now, when they sent me up to switch in the yards at Granger, I was transferred under the jurisdiction of the trainmaster at Evanston, Wyoming, who had charge of the eighth and ninth districts of the Wyoming division,[28] which was that part of the Union Pacific from Green River to Ogden, Utah, so one day after I had been there about six weeks, or in the first part of April, the agent there at Granger who sort of acted as a yardmaster over us switchmen, showed us a message from the O.S.L. railroad superintendent at Pocotello, Idaho,[29] which stated that the Oregon Short Line company would discontinue to furnish a man to coal up the Union Pacific switch engine (which had to be done by shoveling the coal from a coal car, as there was not any coal chute there at Granger) and the switchmen on the crew would have to coal up their own engine, so when the agent sprung that little joke on us, we all pulled a one crew strike, and tied everything up for a short time, until the agent finally got us to agree to coal up the engine until he could take the matter up with Mr. C. M. Ward, the trainmaster at Evanston, and in a couple of days the agent told us that Trainmaster Ward was making a trip to Green River, and that he would stop off and talk to us boys, in regards to the matter, but as I wanted to get away from Granger I used this trouble for an excuse to quit, so by the time that the trainmaster got to Granger, my boomer blood that I had inherited from my father, predominated within me, and I had quit the job and Mr. C. M. Ward wired Evanston to deadhead another man to Granger to take my place, and he fixed it up with the boys on the crew to allow them an hour overtime each day for coaling up the engine.

So Mr. Ward got to talking to me, and he says, Well what are you going to do now, Brown? And I told him that just as soon as my check came, that I was going to head west and look for another job. Then he asked me how I would like to go braking out of Evanston, and I told him that would just suit me fine, and he turned to a freight conductor there, who was signing up for train orders, and told him to carry me to Evanston in his caboose and then he instructed the agent there to forward my check to his office at Evanston as soon as it came, so I hurried over to where us boys slept, and grabbed what few things I had and came back and got on the caboose just before they pulled out.

Well, it was about midnight when we arrived at Evanston, and the conductor told me that I could stay there and sleep in the caboose until morning, so I thanked him for the favor, for it saved me the trouble of getting out in the cold and going to a hotel where I would have had to pay for a room, and the next morning after I had eaten some breakfast, I went over the trainmaster's office, as Mr. Ward had instructed me to do, and he had already wired his chief clerk there at Evanston to take care of me when I showed up, and of course the clerk was expecting me, and when I told him who I was he gave me an application for me to fill out.

Well, the examination was not so hard for me now as I was getting used to it, so after I passed the doctor, I came back to the trainmaster's office, and the chief clerk asked me a few questions regarding the time card, and book rules, and especially about the flagging rule No. 99, then he gave me an order to the yardmaster, and I went over to the yard office and was marked up on the brakemen's extra board, and it turned out that the yardmaster, who's name was Rupe, had known my father, and he told me about braking partners with him on the old I.B.&W. years before, running between Indianapolis, Indiana, and Bloomington, Illinois, on a local freight, and I told him, yes, that I remembered when it was, for we were living in Crawfordsville, Indiana, at the time, and when my father's train stopped there to do its local work, I would go with my mother to take a big basket of lunch for my father, and sometimes he would let me ride in the caboose while they were doing their switching there in the train yards.

Well, the next morning I was called for an extra east, and I went out braking ahead [head brakeman], for a conductor by the name of Bill Berry, and he was a nut, if ever I saw one on a railroad. I was told that he came into Evanston a few years before, and got a job of braking and finally he got promoted up to be a conductor, and boy, he sure was some homeguard, too, for he was most always crabbing about his dang fool brakemen doing things that would cause him to lose his job, for he was one of those birds that are always worrying about the things that never happen.

Now when I got into Green River on my first trip, I went over to the old Elkhorn Hotel and saw the two Swede girls, Leana and Anna, and they sure were surprised to see me there, and I was glad to see them, too, and I thought that Anna looked sweeter than ever, and they asked me if I had come back to switch there in the Green River yards. So I told them, no, that I was now braking on through freight on the main line out of Evanston, and that I would be able to see them quite often from now on, and it happened I was in the kitchen doing this talking to the girls, and old man Egg came in, and if looks could have killed me, I sure would have been a gonner, for that old bird sure gave me a dirty look, but he did not mean anything in my young life, for every chance I got I went around to the kitchen and talked to the girls. And if I was in Green River in the evening, I and a young switch engine fireman, who liked Leana pretty well, would set in the dining room after supper and talk to them, for there was no place of entertainment to take them to in that little burg.

Well, a few months after I started braking I came into Green River one trip, and I found that the girls had quit and gone. So I asked Carl, the switch engine fireman what had happened to our girls, and he told me that old man Egg got so hostile with them, that they quit and went back to their home in Rock Springs, and that was the last that I ever heard of them.

Now, after bucking the slow board for about a month, I had the bad luck of catching old Bill Berry's car regular, for he was such an old crab, that nobody wanted to brake for him, and I remember that I was braking behind, and the head brakeman was a big over-grown young Irishman by the name of Mike Loam, and he was off a ranch up in Bear River Valley,[30] right close to where old Bill Berry, our conductor, came from, and Mike was the youngest of five of the Loam brothers working out of Evanston on the Union Pacific at that time.

There was big Bill Loam, a freight engineer, running an engine between Evanston and Ogden, and there was Joe Loam, firing a passenger run between Evanston and Ogden, then there was Johnnie Loam, a freight conductor, running a train between Evanston and Green River, and there there was Charlie Loam, braking on freight between Evanston and Ogden, and last but not least, there was kid Mike Loam, braking partner with me for old Bill Berry, between Evanston and Green River, and after I left Evanston in 1902, I was told by another boomer that had worked out of Evanston two or three years after I had left there, that Joe Loam, the passenger fireman had got set up (meaning that he had got promoted up to be an engineer) and then got killed soon after that, then after Joe, Johnnie, the conductor, got killed next, and then Charlie, the brakeman, got killed after Johnnie, and Big Bill Loam, who was the oldest of the bunch, quit running an engine and went back to their father's ranch, up in Bear River Valley, about twelve or fifteen miles out of Evanston. Away back in 1909, I happened to see kid Mike Loam, but only got to talk with him for a few minutes, as I was riding a west bound passenger train on a pass, and Mike just happened to come by the depot where I had got off to sort of stretch my legs a bit, but he did not remember me until I told him who I was, and reminded him of the time that he and I broke partners for old Bill Berry. So Mike told me that it was true about his three brothers getting killed, and of his brother, Bill, going back to the ranch, and that he was now running a train between Evanston and Green River and I asked him if old Bill Berry was still there and he says, yes, with all of his worrying, about losing his job, the old crab is still here, and is now running passenger train between Green River and Ogden.

Well, to get back to my story where I left off, after I broke for old Bill Berry for about six months, I went to the trainmaster's office one day, and asked the chief clerk if he would let me transfer onto another car, so he assigned me onto Big Tom Shell's car, and I broke for Big Tom all the rest of the time that I worked there as a brakeman, and my partner was an old boomer by the name of George Poe, who had just came there and hired out as a brakeman, and boy, I am telling you that he was a hobo money rustling fool, for he sure did like his booze, and the more bo money he could pick up, the more booze he could buy.

Now, I will never forget one night in Evanston, we had just pulled in from the east with a train of empty fruit reefers and they had called us to double right back to Green River with a long drag of freight, and empty box cars (of course that was back in 1902, before the sixteen-hour law[31] was in effect) and after we had went into the depot lunch room, and put a good feed under our belts, we were all set to try and get out of there ahead of No. 4,[32] an east bound passenger train, and as my partner, George Poe, was braking ahead, he had gone to the roundhouse and was bringing the engine around to couple on, for the train was already made up, and the yard crew had taken our caboose off of the train of reefers up in the east end yards that we had just brought in, and brought it down with their switch engine and coupled it on to the rear end of the drag just a few minutes before, and I was walking from the caboose over toward the head end looking the train over and coupling the airhose (for in those days the train crews had to couple their own air hose, and test the air brakes), when all at once a man came running up to me in the dark and I was holding my lantern up taking a look at him, when he says, I want to go to Ogden, and I could tell by his broken English that he was some kind of a foreigner, then he told me that he was a Greek interpreter, and was with a gang of fifty Greeks who had been working on an extra gang and that they all wanted to go to Ogden, and would give me fifty dollars to take them in an empty boxcar, and oh boy, when I heard that, I thought I would drop dead, for here we were going east, and they wanted to go west, and with the thought of losing the fifty bucks, I had almost lost my voice, but when I did come out of it, I managed some how to tell that we were not going to Ogden, but were going east to Green River, and just about this time my partner, old George Poe, walked up to us, for after he coupled the engine on, he came walking back coupling up the airhose until he met us while we were talking, and when I told Poe what the fellow wanted, I thought that poor old George was going to flop right down there and croak on the spot, for he was a hound for his bo money, but this Greek guy kept saying, I want to go to Ogden, and he evidently must have been turned around, for after I told him that we were headed east, he says I have got a gang of fifty men over there behind the depot, and we will pay you a dollar a piece to let us ride to Ogden, and I almost felt like taking a swing at him, for I thought he was kind of rubbing it in, for here was a chance that would never come along again in a life time, where a gang of men would come along and offer and beg us to take fifty bucks in cash to let them ride over a division in an empty boxcar. Boy, it was too much, and I was so sore because we were going east, that I wanted to bite myself. Gee, it sure was a tough break for us that night, and when poor old George finally came out of his trance, for it had knocked the wind out of him too, he says to me with almost tears in his eyes, Listen, Brownie, this guy keeps saying that he wants to go to Ogden, so let him bring his gang down here and we will load them all into an empty boxcar, collect the fifty bucks, then lock the door and they will not know the difference, and I says, listen old-timer, I hate to lose that money as bad as you do, but I am not thinking of kicking off just yet, for when those Greek babies woke up and found themselves in Green River, instead of Ogden, the Union Pacific Company would be wiring our folks for instructions as to where they wanted our remains sent to. No sir, nothing doing on that score, so we walked on up to the head end, and he cut in the air behind the engine, and while the hoghead was pumping them up, old George says to me, If we only had time to take them up in the east end yards, we could load them into one of the empty reefers that we just brought in, and get the money, for they will be sending a crew west with that drag of emptys before long, and the Greeks will get to Ogden, and we will get the fifty bucks, and I says, sure, that will be jake if we can only do it, but just then Big Tom Shell came down from the dispatcher's office with our train orders, as the night yardmaster had already given him his waybills, and a switch list[33] with a lineup of the train, he was all ready to go, so he came to the engine and asked the hoghead if the air had pumped up all right and the hogger told him yes, that the gauge showed that the train line was holding pretty good. So, after we all read the train orders and compared time, Big Tom says to the engineer, Well let's get out of here for we want to try to make Altamont[34] for No. 4. Do you think we can make it? And the hogger says, yes, I think we can. So Big Tom says, all right, let's go.

Well, that bursted the last bubble of hope for old George and I ever getting our hands on that bunch of Greeks' fifty bucks and while I was standing there by the main line switch, which was just across from the lunch room, waiting for our train to pull out on the main line, a boomer brakeman by the name of Jack Taylor came out of the lunch room, with his lantern in his hand, and says to me, Highball the switch, Brownie, I will take care of it (he meant by highball the switch, for me to go ahead and get on, that he would close the switch for me). So I swung my lantern over my head and gave the men on the head end a highball, which is the all right, go ahead signal, to leave town, and the hoghead gave two long blasts of the engine whistle which was an answer to my highball, so while I was waiting for the caboose to come along, I says to Jack, Are you called to go out? and he says, yes, we are getting an extra, west, a drag of empty reefers, and I says, yes, we just brought that string of emptys in and doubling right back out again. And Jack says, Ride 'em old head, ride 'em, for the more mileage you make, the bigger the old pay, check you know, and I says, say Jack, do you want to pick up fifty bucks of bo money? And he says, do I, boy, lead me to it. So I told him to go over and talk with that gang of Greeks in back of the depot, for they wanted to go to Ogden, and there would be fifty bucks in it for him, and he says to me, Kid, if I land them, I will slip you ten bucks the very next time I see you, and I says O.K., as I swung onto the rear steps of our caboose and watched him close the main line switch.

Well, as I had the story told to me afterwards by Jack's partner, the hind [rear] brakeman of the crew that night, it seems like, that after Jack closed the switch for me, he went over behind the depot and got in touch with the gang of Greeks, took them up and loaded them into an empty reefer and locked the door, but he did not live up to the code of honor between brakemen on a crew, for instead of splitting fifty-fifty with his partner, the hindman, he stuck the whole works in his pocket and kept it, and the hind man didn't know anything about the Greeks until they arrived in the yards at Ogden the next morning, and instead of Jack going back and unlocking the door and letting the Greeks out, he cut off his engine and took her to the round house, and then went on over to the railroad boarding house near by, where some of the brakemen and engine crews eat and flopped on their trips to Ogden.

Now it happened that the yardmaster was walking through the yards shortly after Jack's train pulled in, and he heard somebody pounding and hollering in one of the cars, so he went over and let the gang of Greeks out, and they sure was raving mad, and the interpreter told the yardmaster that they had paid the head brakeman that came in on that train fifty dollars to bring them down from Evanston, but they expected him to let them out when they got into Ogden. So the yardmaster smelled a long tailed rat, and figured here was where he was going to pull down some easy dough. So he went over to the boarding house and singled Jack out to be the guy that he was looking for, and he says to him, Are you the head shack that just came in on that extra from the east? and Jack says, sure why? And the yardmaster says to him, Well I just unloaded your car load of live stock for you, and if you want to keep on working for the Union Pacific, you are going to kick through, and split that fifty bucks with me, and Jack told him nothing doing, that he could go to heck and jump in the lake, for he did not know when he would ever have fifty smacks in his jeans again at one time, and that he was ready to bunch the job anyway, as he did not crave riding out on top down them Wasatch Mountains and twisting up handbrakes with a pickhandle nohow.

So the yardmaster wired Mr. C. M. Ward, the trainmaster at Evanston, and spilled the beans of the whole affair, and Mr. Ward wired back that brakeman, John Taylor, was discharged, let out and canned on the spot, and that they were dead-heading an extra brakeman down to take his place on the crew, so Jack was canned by wire, and as I never saw him after that I did not get my ten spot that he promised me.

Now, I remember another time while I was braking there out of Evanston, we were called for an extra east sometime after midnight, I think it was around about 3 A.M. in the morning, for I remember we just had time to make Bear River, a passing track about five miles east of there, for No. 4, so we tore out of Evanston and beat it over to Bear River and headed in, and after I closed the main line switch, I told Big Tom Shell that I was going to take the pipe wrench and go and look over the train line, for the caboose gauge showed that there was a bad leak somewhere. So I started over toward the head end, but I had not got very far when I saw old Poe's lantern bobbing up and down as if he might be running, so in a few seconds he came running up to me all out of breath, and he says to me, Listen, Brownie, don't you go up near the head end until I go back and get Big Tom's gun, and I says, why, what's the matter? Then he told me that while he was looking for hoboes, he stuck his head and lantern in one of the boxcar doors and he saw a big nigger in there with a gat [pistol] about two feet long, and the nigger had all of the rest of the boes lined up along on one side of the car and was robbing them of what jack that they had, and he says to this big black boy, Say, coon, what do you think you are doing there? And the old black boy told him that it was none of his blankety blank business, and if he did not get away from there, he would fill him full of lead, and poor old Poe did not wait to hear anymore, but tore out for the caboose as fast as he could to get Big Tom's six-shooter. So I went on ahead a few car lengths further and found the leak, which was in a branch pipe and I fixed it by cutting out the car, that is I closed the cut out valve between the train line and the triple valve, under the car,[35] and just then I saw No. 4's headlight as she shot around a curve and whistled for Bear River, and in a few seconds she went roaring by like a cyclone. And as Poe was not at the head end to head us out, the fireman got down and opened the switch so that we could head out, and as the caboose came along I swung on and Poe was telling big Tom about the bad coon, so when we got out on the main line, I dropped off and lined up the switch and gave the engineer a highball, and he whistled off and we proceeded on up the mountain grade to the Aspen tunnel at Altamont, and as there was a red board,[36] we had to stop, so big Tom took his six-shooter and he and Poe walked over to the head end to look for the bad coon and to sign up for the train orders that we were to get there. And of course I had to stay back and flag, for we were standing on the main line, so when Big Tom caught the caboose as we pulled out of there, I asked him if he had found the bad nigger? And he said no, that the other hoboes told them that after he had chased Poe away, while we were headed for No. 4, down at Bear River, that the coon had taken all of the money away from them and jumped out of the car and beat it off into the dark, and that was the last that they saw of him, and it sure did peeve old Poe because the old black boy took all of the bo money, but he was a good sport and let the poor hoboes ride anyway.

Well, I remember another item that we were going east on an extra, and old George Poe had laid off for a round trip, and we had an extra man for my partner that trip, but he was not a boomer, for this was his first job and he had been braking just long enough to get tough and hard boiled, and when it came to making the hoboes dig up or hit the grit, he was a bad actor, just like some of the shacks that I had met up with when I was hoboing my way around over the country before I went railroading. So, on this trip we had crawled and wound our way up around the mountain as far as Altamont,

and we had headed in there to meet some west bound train, so I
started walking over from the caboose toward the head end to look
the train over to see if everything was running all right, and when
I came up to where the head man was standing on the ground tossing
rocks up into an all steel ore car, I ask him what was the big idea?
and he told me that there were two bums in that car that would not
dig up, and that he was going to rock them off the train, and I told
him to wait a minute and I would climb into the car and talk to
them. So I climbed up over the end of the car which was almost as
high as a boxcar, and then down in the hopper bottom where the
two fellows were standing, and I saw right away that they were
foreigners of some kind, for they were dark and swarthy and wore
big heavy mustaches, so I tried to talk to them, but they did not
seem to understand English, and while I was trying to make them
understand, this bozo, the head brakeman, came walking across on
some strips of iron that was riveted along on the inside of the car
for the brakemen to walk across on when the car was empty, and
when he got to where we were standing, his feet were just on a level
with our heads, and he hauled off and took a kick at the guy nearest
to him, and if the poor fellow had not ducked in time, the brakeman's
foot would have caught him right in the face, so the fellow reached
down and grabbed one of the rocks that the brakeman had tossed
into the car and the other one pulled a big knife out of his clothes
some where and started after me, and I dang near broke my neck
getting up out of there, and when I did get out, I gave that head
brakeman one of the best cussings out that he ever got, and I told
him if he ever pulled another stunt like that when I was in a car with
some hoboes that I would kick him in the face, and also told him
just for that, to leave those fellows alone and let them ride, and I got
deep satisfaction in seeing him stretched out on a caboose bunk at
Green River about a month or six weeks after that, with a bullet hole
through each leg, and the story as told to me, went something like
this: He, this hard-boiled brakeman, was going east this trip, and
when his train started to pull out of Granger, he saw two hoboes
that were dressed in soldiers' uniforms climb into an empty boxcar,
and he went in after them, and when he asked them what they were
riding on, they told him that they were broke, as they had been mus-
tered out of the army out in Frisco, and were trying to get back to
their homes in the east, but he told them that their troubles did not
cut any ice with him, and if they did not have any money, they would
have to hit the grit. So the two fellows unloaded and ducked under

another car onto the rods, but this dirty skunk jumped out of the boxcar and gathered up some rocks and ran along by the side of the train and pelted the two fellows until they had to come out from under the car, and the brakeman grabbed onto a car ladder and was climbing up, when one of the ex-soldiers pulled an army colts six-shooter and let him have it through both calfs of his legs, as the shack drawed his body up on top of the roof of the car and most of the boys on our division that knew him like I did said that he only got what was coming to him.

Well, I'll never forget the time that I was initiated into the Brother-hood of Railroad Trainmen (known as the B.of R.T.),[37] there at Evanston, Pulpit Rock Lodge, No. 324, for they sure did have fun with me (yes brother trainmen, I swallowed hook, sinker and line) and I was just about scared stiff, and oh, boy, if I could have gotten away, I would have went right through one of the windows, sash, glass and all, but I sure felt mighty proud after it was all over, and I bought me a big stinger pin, and wore it on my coat lapel (stinger is the nickname for B.of R.T. members), and when I would meet a boomer brakeman traveling through, if I did not see a stinger pin or a watch charm on him, I would flag him to see if he belonged to the trainmen, and if he did, I would shake hands with him, and call him brother and in most cases he would come back at me something like this: Well I sure am glad to meet you Brother Brown, you say that you belong to No. 324? Well I belong to so and so down in San Antone, but listen brother I haven't eat since I left Cheyenne. How is your piebook?[38] Is it still working? Then I would pull the old piebook out and tear off a bunch of coupons and give to the worthy hungry brother, and send him on his way over to the beanery to scoff as we used to call it when we fed our faces, and on my rambles as a boomer around over the country, I have fed them and they have fed me, for that is part of the game among brotherhood railroad men, for if I am working and got a piebook, I feed him, and if he is working and I come along he feeds me, and if I am working and he is traveling, I carry him, or square him for a ride over the division, and if he is working and I come along he does the same thing for me, for that is the code of honor, that rules among brotherhood rail-road men.

Now, I remember while I was braking out of Evanston there was a little brown cur dog that made his home at the switch shanty, and we all called him Boomer, and he was a sure enough railroad dog, too, believe me, and he would not have anything to do with any body except the railroad boys and if the notion took him, he would hop onto a caboose when a train was pulling out of Evanston, and it did not make any difference to him which way the train was going just so he went, for he would go to Ogden or Green River with one crew and come back with another. So Boomer was making a trip east with us one time, when I was braking for old Bill Berry, and we stopped at Granger to pick up a car load of sheep, and when the sheepman came into the caboose as we were pulling out, old Boomer was going to chew him up right there on the spot, but I made him get up on top of the cushions on the bunks and lay down, but every move the sheepman made, Boomer would start to growl and bark and old Bill Berry was sitting at his desk at one end of the caboose, going over his waybills and he hollered back to me, and said if I did not make that danged dog keep quiet that he would kick him off, and I patted Boomer on the head, and says to him, Did you hear what old Bill said? He says if you don't stop being so hard-boiled, and lay down and keep quiet, he is going to kick you off the train, and old Boomer licked my hand and wagged his tail and whined, almost as if he understood what I said to him.

Now speaking of Boomer, reminds me of one time when Kid Mike Loam and I were braking for old Bill Berry, we were going east one trip on an extra, and we got an order at Altamont to take siding and meet a west bound extra at a little place called Carter,[39] about thirty miles west of Granger. So after we had headed in at Carter I was walking over toward the head end, looking the train over, and Kid Mike walked back from the head end and met me and as the west bound extra had not showed up yet we were standing there looking at an old sheepherder who was sitting on his roll of bedding, not far from the track, and he had a little pack burrow and two sheep dogs with him and he says: Hey, brakie, how much will you charge me to ride to Granger with my whole outfit? And Mike looked at me, and we laughed, and the old man looked at us, and says, No foolin', I am not kiddin' you, I mean it. So Mike says to him, we will take you and your whole family for one big round dollar, and the old sheepherder says O.K., it's a bargain, as he handed Mike the dollar, and then he and Mike grabbed the burrow and lifted it up into a boxcar. Then we threw in his bedding and other junk, but the dogs would not let Mike or I touch them, so the old man lifted them into the boxcar and climbed in after them. Then we closed the door but did not fasten it, but left it so the old man could open it and get out at Granger, and just then the westbound extra whistled into

Carter, so Mike hurried to the head end, and when they pulled by Mike opened the switch and we headed out, and went on over to Granger. Now old Bill Berry had been back in the caboose all of this time and did not know anything about the old sheepherder and his outfit. So when we pulled into Granger and stopped to take water, I told old Bill that the order board was out, so he went beating it over to sign up for the orders and by the time he got over to where the old sheepherder was, the old man had the door open and was unloading his outfit, so old Bill says to him, say where in the blankety blank heck did you get on at, and the old man told him how he had paid the brakies a dollar to ride from Carter to Granger, and Mike told me after we got into Green River, that when we stopped in Granger, that he started back to help the old man unload, but when he saw old Bill coming over ahead, that he jumped through between the cars and hid on the other side of the train, and he said that it was all he could do to keep from bursting out laughing when old Bill blowed up, and old Bill was still all burnt up when he caught the caboose as we pulled out of Granger, and he says to me, you dodrotted brakemen are going to get my job yet, it is bad enough for you to always be carrying them bums, but when you go to hauling sheepherders and all of their livestock, that's too much, that is going the limit. But I did not say anything for it was all that I could do to keep from laughing right out in his face, for he had the sorriest look on his pan that I ever saw, and then he says when you danged fool kids get me canned, I have got an old span of mules up at the ranch in Bear River Valley, and I guess I will have to go up there, and try to make a living with them, and I would almost bet that I saw tears in his eyes. Gee he was one home guard that was always worrying about losing his job.

Well after I had been braking there for about a year, or around the first part of May, 1902, I took a notion that would like to go back firing again, for I sure do love an engine, and I went into Mr. C. M. Ward's office there at Evanston one day (I will state here that Mr. Ward besides being trainmaster acted as division superintendent), and asked him if he would let me transfer into the engine service as a fireman, and he says to me, you used to fire out of Rawlins didn't you Brown, and I told him yes that I had (he knew, for I had to put that in when I made out the application for the job of braking). Then he says, yes, I think it can be arranged all right, and a few days later, I was called into his office, and he says to me, well Brown, I have arranged everything with the master mechanic for you to go firing, and have transferred you over under his jurisdiction, and you are already marked up on the firemen's extra board, so you go to my chief clerk, and turn in your lantern, and brakeman's badge, as you will not need them while working as a fireman, so I thanked him, and after getting fixed with the chief clerk, I beat it over to the round-house and told the call-boy of the engine crews where he could find me, and I also left my name in the call book for the night call boy.

I remember the first trip I made firing out of Evanston. I was called for train No. 19, a fast freight, engine 1504 (fifteen-O-four),[40] and these fifteen hundred class engines that the U.P. was using up and down the Wasatch Mountains between Evanston and Ogden were almost the same type as the 1700's that I had fired out of Rawlins, except they were larger, and were twelve wheelers, where the 1700's were ten wheelers, and the boilers of the 1500's where they came back into the cab, were square, and looked like the end of a young boxcar, and these engines were so big and heavy and so nicely balanced on their springs and equalizers that they almost rode like a Pullman car.

Well after I was called and signed the book, I went over to the depot lunch room, to get something to eat, and it was near midnight, and I only took my meals at the boarding house when I was there at meal time, so when I came into the lunchroom, all togged out in a new suit of overalls, with a big blue handerkerchief tied around my neck, cap, and a new pair of firemen's gautlet gloves, the cute little Irish waitress behind the lunch counter, by the name of Mollie O'Day, says to me, gee, Brownie, where are you going all made up like a tallowpot? and I told her that I was a tallow-pot now, and was called for No. 19, and she says what are you going to eat? and I says Oh give me some boomer's delight, ham and eggs, fried potatoes, and coffee, and when she brought my order in to me, she says what did you do Brownie, quit braking to go firing? and I told her yes that I had transferred into the engine service, then she laughed and says you know the old story Brownie, all it takes to be a fireman is a weak mind and a strong back, and I laughed back at her, and says yes that's me, kid, and she says who are you firing for? and I says why I don't know, for this is my first trip, and I don't know these west end hogheads and tallow pots very well, because I have always worked on the east end ever since I had been here, and besides I have not been over to the round-house yet, but the call boy told me that I got the 1504, and then she says, oh that's old Dad Murdock's engine, I guess Jack Conley, his regular fireman must be laying off, and I says yes I guess so, and when I got through eating and started to go, she says well good luck Brownie, I hope you can keep her hot for old Dad, for if you don't he might turn you in when you get back, and I laughed and says, well if all it takes is a weak mind and a strong back, I won't have any trouble keeping her hot.

Well, when I got over to the roundhouse old Dad Murdock was already there, and he says to me, did you ever fire one of these 1500's before? and I says no, but I used to fire the 1700's out of Rawlins, on the seventh district, and I don't see much difference except these engines are a little larger, and then old Dad said that he thought that I would make it all right, as I was a pretty husky looking kid, so pretty soon the brakeman came after us, and we were soon on our way. I remember we had a time order on No. 8,[41] an eastbound passenger train, and we just had about enough time to make Wasatch,[42] a little open telegraph station at the top of the Wasatch Mountains, so we beat it over there and headed in with some time to spare, and as soon as got into clear, I went out and covered the headlight,[43] and pretty soon we could hear old No. 8's engine puffing and snorting as she came dragging her heavy train of pullman's up the mountain grade, and before long we saw her headlight come swinging around a curve and she soon went rolling by, then I went out to the front of the engine and uncovered the headlight, and we were soon on our way again.

Now it was sixty miles down the mountains from this little place of Wasatch at the top of the hill, to Ogden[44] where you strike the great Salt Lake Valley, so after we got going, old Dad says to me, now kid it is all down hill from here, and we will fill her up about half full of water, and you can let your steam drop back to about a hundred and eighty pounds, and bank your fire pretty good up in front, along the sides, and in the back corners, so I done just as old Dad told me, then I climbed up and set down on my box seat and leaned out of my cab window while the big mountain engine rocked and rolled as she went shooting around the sharp curves, and gee what a thrill and a kick I was getting, but at the same time, something in my mind kept telling me, never mind kid, those that ride must pay, and you will pay on the return trip, and old Dad Murdock was setting over on his side of the cab with his head leaning out of the window and his eyes glued on the track ahead and working the brake valve handle setting up and then releasing the air brakes, keeping his train under control as he dropped it down the mountain, and the two brakemen were out on top of the train, with the pops turned up, and at the steepest points in the grade, they would set up the binders[45] with their brake clubs, and at the flat places let them off again. Gee, that was the life, and there is times while writing these memories, I get so thrilled that I wish I could go back and live my life all over again.

Well, we pulled into Ogden the next morning just after daylight, and after putting the engine away, old Dad and I went over to the boarding house, and eat some breakfast, then I piled into the hay and slept until late in the afternoon, and was just getting up when the call boy come to call us for a fruit express extra, so after we eat some supper, we went over to the roundhouse and got the 1504 ready, and we were soon on our way, back to Evanston with an orange train, but oh boy, it was quite different going back to what it was coming down, for we had a sixty mile pull up those Wasatch mountains to the top of the hill at Wasatch, but as I was young and husky, it did not bother me much except the heat from the big square boilerhead, and the fire box when I would swing the big door open to put in a fire, for we were not going very fast, while winding up around through the canyons and mountain passes, and there was not any breeze stirring to cool me off between fires, and the only time that I would get to rest was when we would head in to meet a passenger train, and I think that was only a couple of times on the whole trip, but when we reached the top of the hill, I climbed upon the seat box and took it easy for the last seventeen miles into Evanston, for it was slightly down grade, and old Dad let them coast into town, where we arrived some time after midnight, so after old Dad and I washed up in a bucket of warm water on the deck of the engine, we rolled up our overclothes and locked them in our seat boxes, and then we went over to the lunch room to get a bite to eat before going home to bed, and when we came into the lunch room, Mollie O'Day says why hello Dad, I see you brought Brownie back alive, and old Dad says yes, but I think he got pretty well het up, for it sure was hot coming up the mountain tonight, and I says yes Mollie I have got both a weak mind and a weak back tonight, after spading coal up that sixty mile pull, and Dad is right, for I sure did feel the heat tonight while coming up the hill, and I am too tired to eat anything but a piece of pie and drink a glass of milk, then I am going home and hit the hay, believe me, no foolin'.

Well I fired the 1504 for old Dad Murdock for about two weeks, when his regular fireman reported for duty, and I was marked up on the extra board again, and I layed in about a day and a half before I got out again, so one morning I was called for an extra east, and I caught the 1664,[46] and her regular engineer was a big Swede by the name of Nelson, but was known on the division as old Wooden Shoe Nelson, but believe me he was some hoghead, and we knew each other, for I had made many a trip with him when I was braking there on the east end, and when I came over to the engine after being called, he was sure surprised to hear that I had quit braking to go firing, and he says to me, did you ever do any firing before Brownie? and I says sure, and he says where at? and then I told him about firing out of Rawlins, and what a time I had trying to learn to fire old 1288, when I was on work-train, and he says what, you fired the old 1288? and I says yes, and then he says why that's the old mountain hog that I learned to fire on several years ago, out of Cheyenne, and while we were waiting for the brakeman to come after us, he told me what a heck of a time he had trying to fire her on his first trip, and then I told him what a heck of a time I had with her on my first trip, the time that we double-headed with an extra west from Rawlins to Tipton with a new engineer by the name of Blood, and then we both had a big laugh, and after that we got real chummy.

Well, I held his engine for thirty days, and I never fired for a better man in all of my railroad career, and I remember one trip into Green River, we had got in there in the evening and after a good night's sleep, I got up the next morning feeling pretty good, and there was some kind of a German celebration, and a whole mob of Germans had come over from Rock Springs that day, and they were having a parade, led by a little German band around through the streets, and then they marched out to a little baseball park, where they were going to have speaking, and a ball game afterwards, and of course I followed the parade to the ball park just the same as almost everybody else did, and they had the beer-wagon from the Sweetwater brewery (a small German brewery there in Green River) to bring out a load of keg beer, and everything was free, and man oh man, talk about your celebrations, why by the time the speaking was over, everybody including the little German band and the two ball teams were so soused and slopped up on beer and feeling so good that the band did not know whether it was playing a hot time in the old town, or ain't we got fun, and I was feeling just as good as the rest of them, so about three P.M. in the afternoon the call boy finally found me out at the ball park, and he says what the heck Brownie, I been looking all over town for you, then he says here sign this book for an extra west, and kid you had better get a move on you, for you are delaying the train, but that did not cut any ice with me, for I was so full of Sweetwater beer that I did not care right then if the U.P. ever run any more trains or not, but I finally got over to the round house, and old Wooden Shoe Nelson was there and had the engine ready, and he and the head brakeman were waiting for me, so I crawled up into the cab and set down on the seat box, while the brakeman was taking us down into the yards to couple us onto the train, but old Wooden Shoe did not say a word to me, and while they were pumping up and testing the air, I managed somehow to get into my over-clothes, and as the conductor was already there with the train orders, we soon got started.

Now leaving Green River going west, there was a ten mile pull up what was known as Peru hill, and although I could hardly stand up on the deck, and it was all I could do to see the pointer on the steam gauge, I kept the old mill hot, but I'll never be able to tell how I done it, but anyway by the time we reached the top of the hill I was wringing wet with sweat, and feeling fine, so we rambled right along over to Granger, where we stopped to take water and sign for orders, as the red board was out, and by that time I had sweat most of the beer out, and my head had cleared, and I began to be myself again, and after I had taken water, and we were waiting for the captain [conductor] to come with orders, old Wooden Shoe Nelson opened the fire box door, and took a look at my fire, then he raised up and swung the door shut, and I thought here is where I get a heck of a bawling out, for I thought he must have seen a heck of a looking fire in there, but instead of bawling me out, he says, boy you sure have got a pretty fire in there, and then I was more scared than ever, for I thought the fire must be in one heck of a shape, so when he got down on the ground to read the orders with the conductor, I slid down off my seat box and took a look at the fire myself, and to my great surprise, I did have as pretty and level a fire as any tallow pot would care to look at.

I remember one trip I was going west out of Green River on a heavy drag of loads, and I was firing one of these 1600 class engines,[47] for a young engineer by the name of Charlie Shoemaker, who had just been set up from a passenger fireman on the west end between Evanston and Ogden, where he had done most all of his firing, and when we got up to the Aspen tunnel, and were pulling through, we got stalled in the tunnel on account of oil being on the rails. Now this Aspen tunnel was bored through the backbone of one of the Wasatch group of mountain ranges, and was on what was known as the Spring Valley and Aspen Tunnel cut off,[48] which did not only shorten the distance in mileage, but gave the company engineers a chance to make the east and west approach to the tunnel a maximum grade of about two percent,[49] and the tonnage rating for these 1600 class engines up these grades was thirteen hundred tons [of train].

Now it happened when the Union Pacific Company was building this Spring Valley cut off, and boring the Aspen tunnel, they struck the first oil in that part of Wyoming, if not in the whole state of Wyoming, and the first was struck in the tunnel just about a quarter of a mile in from the east end, and the next was found when the Company was drilling for water down at the little coal mining town of Spring Valley, about six or eight miles east of the tunnel, so when the tunnel was finished, they tried to cement off this small vein of oil but it always gave the train crews much trouble, for the oil would seep through and drip down on the track and oil the rails, and as it was up grade going west through the tunnel, if the engineer did not have his air-sanders working good, so that he could keep the rails sanded, he was liable to get stalled when drive-wheels of the engine struck this oil on the rails, for they would lose their grip and start spinning around and around, which of course would cause the train to stall.

Well, to get back to my story, when we pulled into the tunnel and struck the oil on the rails, the drivers lost their grip and spun round and round, before the young hoghead got the throttle closed, and the exhaust from the smokestack had filled that part of the tunnel where we were at, so full of coal smoke and gas from the fire-box of the engine, that besides being unable to see, we were becoming unable to breathe, for the want of air, but as I had been caught in this tunnel the same way before, I grabbed the water bucket that we carried on the engine, and drawed it full of fresh water from a faucet in the side of the tank, and then I grabbed a big bunch of clean waste and soused it into the bucket of water and got it soaking wet, and gave it to the engineer and told him to hold it over his face and breath through it, and of course I did the same thing myself, until the draft through the tunnel cleared the smoke and gas out, and in the meantime the head brakeman who had been riding on the engine, had jumped down on the ground and was laying down on his belly with his face just above the surface of a small ditch of spring water that run along the side wall of the tunnel, which enabled him to breathe. Well when the smoke and gas cleared out so that we could see, and breath the good cool fresh air again, Charlie Shoemaker, the young hoghead, says to me, Brownie what do they do in a case like this, and I told him that we always waited for the conductor to come over (for when a train stalled, the hind man went back to flag, and the conductor always set up a few binders on the rear end to hold them before going over to the head end), so we waited for Big Tom Shell to come over, as he happened to be our conductor this trip, so he told the head brakeman to go back about fifteen car lengths and make a cut and we would double out [take out the train in two sections], then he went to one of the telephones there in the tunnel, and called up the operator at Altamont just outside of the west end of the tunnel, and told him to hold everything, that we were stuck in the tunnel and was going to double out to the passing track there at Altamont, and the operator told him to come ahead that he would protect us, so I lit the red lantern and gave it and a red fusee to the brakeman and he went back and made the cut, and after hanging the red lantern on the head car of the part of the train that we were leaving there, he gave us a highball with his fusee, and we pulled out to Altamont and set the cars out in the passing track, and big Tom and the brakeman tied them down with some binders, then big Tom stayed there at the telegraph office to make a report to the train dispatcher of what had happened to us, while we and the brakeman went back and got the rest of the train, and as the tunnel was about a mile long, it was pretty dark in there, so we eased back down through the tunnel until we saw the red lantern on the head car and coupled on, then while the air was pumping up, the head man went back and let off the binders that big Tom had set up, and we called in the flagman, and the only way we had of knowing when he was in, he opened the angle-cock[50] on the rear end of the caboose, and set the brakes, and when he closed it again, the brakes released, and that was the signal for us to go ahead, so we came out to Altamont and headed in, for we could not get out of there for No. 2, the fast mail, and when she arrived and departed, we pulled out and went on into Evanston, the end of our run.

Well to go on with my story, I fired there out of Evanston until the latter part of August, 1902, when the boiler maker and machinist unions pulled a strike all over the Union Pacific system, and almost tied up the whole works, especially there in Wyoming, for the water was very bad, and if the engine boilers were not taken care of, they would soon be leaking so badly that an engine would die right out on the main line, which they were doing at the time I left there, so when conditions got so bad that many freight trains were lying in the passing tracks along the route on account of dead engines, they cut the firemen's extra board there at Evanston, and layed off a bunch of us younger men, and the company gave me a pass to Omaha, as I had made up my mind to go back to Hoopeston, Ill., and see my mother, after being away from home for three years.

Well when I got to Omaha, I went over to the Chicago and North Western[51] railroad yards, in Council Bluffs, and found out from the yardmen that there was a regular fast freight due out at seven P.M. for Chicago, and I made up my mind to tie into the conductor on this highball [fast] run to see if he would carry me over his division, as I was now a railroad man and in good standing in the order of the Brotherhood of Railroad Trainmen (B. of R. T.) so about six thirty P.M., I went over to the yards again, and the train was already made up, with the engine and caboose coupled on, and the air brakes were being tested, so I tied into the conductor for a ride, and he sent me to his hind man, and he said if the hind man would vouch for me, that I could ride, so I went back to the caboose where the hind man was, and told him what the conductor had said, then I showed him my Brotherhood traveling card, and receipts, and told him that I was a trainman off the U.P. in Wyoming, and was headed for Chicago, then he put me through the works and saw that I was right up-to-date, and when the conductor came to the caboose, the rear brakeman told him that I was jake (meaning that I was up-to-date, and in good standing in the B. of R. T.) and as the skipper was a Big-O himself, he said O.K. (Big-O is slang for Order of Railway Conductors, known as the O. R. C.)[52] So at seven P.M. they pulled out of there right on the cathop [on time], and believe me they sure did wheel them too, and about nine P.M. the hind man says to me, listen brother, don't you want to take a flop in the hay, and get some shuteye, for we run right through on this run two divisions to Marshalltown [Iowa], and I told him that I would be glad to. Now this caboose had upper berths something like a pullman (of course not so fine), for the North Western handled lots of stock trains, and these berths were for the accommodation of the traveling stockmen, so he pulled down one of them and fixed the bed, and I piled in and had a good sleep, and when we arrived in Marshalltown the next morning, the conductor squared me out on the same train with the next crew, and I rode with them to Clinton, Iowa,[53] on the west bank of the Mississippi River, and the next crew that got the train at Clinton took me right into Chicago, so I rode the same fast freight across two states, from Council Bluffs, Iowa, to Chicago, Ill., with three different train crews, and they were all good Brotherhood men too, and I could not keep from thinking how different it was to be a railroad man and belong to one of the big brotherhoods, and get to ride in a caboose, than to be a poor hobo, and have to ride in a boxcar.

Well, after looking around Chicago for a day, and taking in a good show, I caught a fast redball freight out of the Twelfth Street freight house yards there in Chicago, and rode in the caboose to Hoopeston and home, and my mother and the rest were all glad to see me, and I was glad to see them too.

Chapter V

*W*ell, after visiting at home for about ten days, I went over to a little town about twenty miles west of Hoopeston, by the name of Rankin, Ill.,[1] and got a job firing on the Lake Erie & Western, and the master mechanic sent me over to Lafayette, Ind.,[2] about fifty miles east of Rankin to take the examination, and when I got there I went up to the superintendent's office, and gave the clerk the sealed letter that I had brought from the master mechanic at Rankin, and the chief clerk ask me if I had a railroad watch, so I showed him my twenty-one jewel Bunn-special[3] that I carried at that time, then he gave me a card [employee's or operating timetable], and told me to go over to the watch inspector, and have my watch examined. Well my watch and I passed all O.K. (I will mention here that they did not have any doctor's examination there on the L.E.&W. at that time.) Then I went back to Rankin, and was marked up on the firemen's extra board, and I have to laugh when I think of the first trip that I made. The engines were little ten wheelers [4-6-0's], but the little runts could drag an awful long string of cars through that level country.

So I was called the next morning for No. 54, a second class regular freight run, and engine No. 335.[4] Well I went over to the roundhouse, to get the 335 ready for the run, and the engineer was already there, and of course he asked me the same old questions, did you ever fire an engine before? and I told him that I had, and he says where at? and I told him out in the Rocky Mountains on the Union Pacific in Wyoming, and then he says to me, well this No. 54 we are getting out on is a hot-shot run, and they expect us to make the time, and

I told him that was O.K. with me, but I says what do you do with the scoop shovel and coal pick, gauge lamps, and all of the other things when you come in off a trip? and then he says why you know we don't have regular engines here, for the engines are all in the chain gang [locomotive pool], first in first out, and I says what's that got to do with the tools? where do they keep them? and then he says why we have to rob one engine to supply another, and I says do you mean that I have got to go over there and rob that engine that just pulled in over the cinder pit? and he says yes, go ahead and get everything that you can find, so I did, but I did not find a heck of a lot, and I had to grab some of the things that we needed off another engine, and it reminded me of the time that I used to work on the farm, for when we busted anything, we would tie it up with binder twine, or patch it up with haywire and go ahead until we busted something else, and believe me, that little old one horse road sure was haywire at that time.[5]

Well we finally got started out, and the train sure was a long one, or at least it looked that way to me, for they did not pull them that long out in the Rocky mountains, where I had just came from, so when we got over to Hoopeston, we stopped about a mile west of town, and cut off the engine and run down to the water tank, and took a tank of water, then we went back and coupled onto the train, and called in the flagman while we were pumping up the air, then the hoghead called for the interlocking signals,[6] which governed the crossing there in Hoopeston, and in a few seconds the semaphore arm on the distance signal dropped down to clear, which gave us a clear right of way over the C.&E.I. crossing, so we whistled off, and got a highball from the hind end.

Now the town of Hoopeston lay down in sort of a sag, and we had to take a run down through there in order to make the grade on the east side of town, and as it was just before daylight, you should have seen the fireworks coming out of that smokestack. And I was down on the deck shoveling in the black diamonds when we passed the depot and hit the C.&E.I. crossing, and it sounded like we were making four hundred miles an hour, and when we hit the east grade the hogger dropped the old Johnson bar[7] down almost in the corner, and widened on her some more, and oh boy, it was just like watching the Fourth of July fireworks to see the skyrockets shooting out of that old smokestack, and he kept patting her on the back until he put them over the hump, and pretty soon we were rambling right along again, and that little old hog was talking to them all the way, so we beat it over to a place called Templeton[8] and headed in for No. 3,[9] a westbound passenger train, and while we were lying there I took the ash hoe and crawled under the engine, and hoed out the ashpan which was chuck full, as it was very shallow and had to be hoed out every chance I got.

Well after No. 3 arrived and departed we pulled out of there, and went on over to Lafayette, where we stopped on top of the hill just west of the Wabash River bridge, and called with four long sounds of the whistle for the towerman in the block house to line up the interlocking system and give us the right of way, for besides crossing the Wabash River there, we also crossed the Monon Route, and the Wabash Railroad.[10]

So pretty soon we got the distance signal which told us that everything was all lined up for us, and the hoghead whistled off and got a highball from the hind end, and away we went down the hill and across the Wabash River bridge, around the curve past the depot, then first over the Monon tracks, and across the Wabash Road, and up another hill to the coal chutes at a place called East Lafayette, where we stopped and took coal and water, after which we proceeded on over to Frankfort, Ind.,[11] after taking another tank of water we rambled on toward Tipton, Ind.,[12] the next division point which would be the end of our run and when we got within about four miles of Tipton the engineer says to me, well fireboy it is all down hill from here to Tipton, and the firemen always take a bunch of waste and go out on the running board and wipe off the jacket while we are coasting down into town, and I looked across at him, and says what fireman, and he says why all of the firemen of course, and I says no, not this fireman, for this is one fireman that don't wipe off the jacket while he is coasting into town, for he is going to set up on the seatbox and watch the scenery go by, and then the hoghead says, oh you are one of them boomer tallowpots what don't care for his job eh, and I says to him, I would not care for a heck of a lot, if I cared for this job, and besides the L.E.&W. Co. is only paying me two dollars and twenty cents a hundred [miles] for firing this coffee mill, and not to wipe off the jacket, and I told him where I came from they paid a fireman two dollars and seventy-five cents a hundred miles, to fire an engine, and they had wipers in the roundhouse that got paid for wiping them off, but he did not say anymore until we got in, and after we put the engine away and got all washed up, then he says to me, Brown how would you like to have a good cold bottle of beer before eating supper, and I says that would just hit the spot, lead me to it, your talk sounds good to me, then he says I have got a friend over here in the bottling works, that is always good for a couple of bottles, so we went over to the bottling works and hysted a good cold bottle of beer apiece, then we went over to the boarding house nearby, for supper, and he asked me how I was hooked up and I told him that I had money, but thanked him just the same, and he turned out to be a heck of a nice fellow.

Well, after I fired there about six weeks, I got disgusted with the idea of having to rob Peter to pay Paul, ever time you wanted to get an engine ready to go out on a run, so I bunched the job, and told them to send my check to the agent at Hoopeston, as that was where I would be, so I went back to Hoopeston and stuck around until my check come, and while I was there I got a letter from the master mechanic at Evanston, Wyo., calling me back to my old job on the U.P., but I did not go for I wanted to ramble around and see different parts of the country, so one day I bid my mother and all the rest of the folks goodbye, and headed for St. Louis, where I got a job of firing between there and a little place called Newburg, Mo.,[13] on the Frisco railroad.[14]

Now this little town of Newburg was a division point on the Frisco system about half way between St. Louis and Springfield, Mo.,[15] and it lay down in a deep valley of the Ozark mountains, and going east out of there we had an eight mile pull up what was known as Rolla hill, to the little town of Rolla[16] which was right at the top of the hill, and going west out of there we had a fifteen mile pull up what was called Dixon hill to the town called Dixon.[17]

Now they used the same system on the Frisco road that they did on the L.E.&W. where I had just came from, that is the engines were in the chain gang, or in the pool as they called it on the Frisco (engines in the pool work first in first out, and do not have regular assigned crews) and as the road was doing a rush business, they were short of power, and the engines were kept on the go all of the time, therefore they did not get the right amount of repair work done on them that should have been done, and the result was, that the engines were badly run down and in a heck of a shape, and who ever had charge of buying the fuel coal which the Frisco burned in their engines should have been sentenced to fire one of those old battleships all the rest of his life, with that dirty cheap slack coal that they gave us to fire the engines with, for in all of my railroad career, I never saw such a conglomeration of muck, which clinkered the fire so bad that it was almost impossible to keep an engine hot with it and every time we had an occasion to head into a passing track, I always had to be hooking clinkers out of the fire box, and cleaning my fire.

Well a short time before I went to work there, the Frisco had taken over the old Kansas City, Fort Scott & Memphis railroad,[18] and while I was there they brought some of the new ten wheelers[19] over from that road to use on the Frisco main line, and I was firing for an old hoghead by the name of Moore, who was better known on the road as old Cyclone Moore, for he was another Casey Jones type of an engineer for he would go tearing down hills, shooting around curves through those little Missouri towns just like a cyclone, so the natives down there in the Ozarks nicknamed him old Cyclone Moore, and all of the boys on the road called him Cyclone.

Well after I had been firing there for a short time, old Cyclone and I were called there in Newburg one morning for a stock extra east, and when we got over to the roundhouse, we saw that they had us lined up for one of those new ten wheelers off the other road, and I remember that she was the 520,[20] so old Cyclone says to me, Brownie, I hear that we are getting twenty cars of stock out of here, and they tell me that these new ten wheelers can run like a scared deer, and kid if you will keep her hot, we will give them longhorns back in there in the caboose (meaning the Texas cattlemen, enroute with the cattle) the dangest ride from here to St. Louis that they ever had in their lives, so the head brakeman came and took us over in the yards and coupled us onto the stock train, and we had just got the air pumped up and the brakes tested, when the skipper [conductor] came over with the train orders, and the train dispatcher had put us on a schedule order, running extra from Newburg to St. Louis with rights over all except first class [passenger] trains.

Well that schedule order sure did tickle old Cyclone, as it gave him a chance to go some, and believe me the dispatcher had made it plenty fast, for he knew old Cyclone would wheel them if given a chance. (Now a schedule order is a special fast running order, written out on a No. 31 train order form,[21] giving the leaving time of the extra train at all timecard stations along the route, and the crews of opposing trains all get a copy of this order, which they used to check against the schedule extra, so that they will know when to head in and get out of the way.)

Well after we got out on the main line, old Cyclone saw that we had a rotten tank of coal, as it had been raining and the coal was wet, and there was a big bunch of wet mucky slack right up in front, so old Cyclone jumped down on the deck and took the scoop shovel and said that he would fire the engine while I got up on top of the tank and shoveled all of the good coal that I could find from the back and sides of the tank up to the front end, and he shoveled all of the wet muck out on the ground, because if he had put it in the firebox, it would have only made clinkers instead of steam, then I got down on the deck and took the scoop, and pretty soon we pulled through Rolla at the top of the hill, and from there on the country was rolling, and old Cyclone would get them going so fast down one hill, that he would run them up over the next one, and as the track was very crooked, winding around through those hills, I sure had one heck of a time trying to stand up on the deck of the engine, for she was rolling and swaying around something awful, and trying to hit the fire door with a scoop of coal kept me pretty busy, for boy, old Cyclone was sure giving us all a ride for our lives, and who ever told old Cyclone that those new ten-wheelers could run, sure knew what he was talking about, no foolin', and those twenty cars of stock was just enough to make her fan her tail.

Well our first stop was a place called Iron Mountain,[22] where we stopped to take coal and water, and after leaving there we wheeled them over to a place called Pacific,[23] where we headed in for some westbound passenger train, and from there we beat it just as fast as the old 520 could turn a wheel, for old Cyclone was going to town with that train load of cattle, and when we pulled down and stopped at Twenty-first street there in the St. Louis Terminal yards, I sure was tired, but the old Cyclone had put the stock train and the Texas longhorns into St. Louis right on schedule.

Well after we took the engine back to the roundhouse, I went over to my boarding house on Shoto [Chouteau] Avenue and hit the hay for about four or five hours, when I was called again for a red-ball fast freight No. 33, but I got over to the roundhouse, I met old Cyclone, and he told me that we had lost our ten-wheeler the 520, for they had doubled her right back with another crew, and we caught an old battleship, that sure was some scrap heap, and I was so disgusted making the trip back to Newburg, shoveling slack and hooking out clinkers, cleaning the fire, and crawling underneath the engine to hoe out the ashpan, that I swore to myself, that if I ever got back to St. Louis, I sure would bunch the job and drag my time.

Well the next trip out of Newburg, instead of going east, I was called for an extra west to Springfield, Missouri, so I lost my old hoghead, Cyclone Moore, and went out with a strange hogger that I did not know, and I remember we had an old seven hundred class single compounded engine,[24] with a light train of emptys, of about fifteen cars, and the captain asked the hogger if he thought that he could make Dixon at the top of the fifteen-mile hill for No. 4 (now No. 4, was an east-bound fast passenger train known in those days as the meteor),[25] so the hoghead told the skipper that he thought that we could make it if the fireboy could keep her hot, and I told them to hop to it, that I would do the very best I could, so we pulled out of there, we sure did go tearing up that hill with our short string of emptys, but about half way up the hill, what few lumps of coal that were on the tank, of course had to get shook down and lodge at the bottom of the coal gate, and block everything for me, so that I could not get any coal on my scoop shovel to put in a fire with, and I grabbed the coal pick and went after them to break them up, but the danged things were almost as hard as flintrock, and I had one heck of a time trying to break them up, and between pounding those lumps of coal and trying to get enough loose coal to put in a fire with, I was just about the busiest guy in seven states, and of course, as I was not having trouble enough, when I struck one of the lumps of coal with the coal pick, a small piece of sharp edged coal had to fly into one of my eyes, and it almost put that lamp on the blink for the time being, and the head brakeman who was riding upon my seat box, happened to look around, and he saw what I was up against, so he jumped down off the seat box and climbed up over the coal gate, down into the coal pit, and dug some of the biggest lumps out with his hands, and throwed them back on the tank, then he took the coal pick and began to pound the rest of the lumps until he got them all broke up, so that I was able to get my scoop full of coal each time, and by shoveling coal like a steam shovel, until we reached the top of the hill at Dixon, I was able to hold the steam at about a hundred and fifty pounds, so we headed in there at Dixon for No. 4, but did not have any time to spare, for we could see her smoke over the top of a little hump, and here she came shooting around the curve, and went tearing by like a cyclone, and oh boy, we sure had a close shave that time (you know I often think if the passengers riding on a fast train, sometimes knew what close calls they have, they sure would be half scared to death), but you know the old saying is, a miss is as good as a mile, and what you don't know don't hurt you, and believe me there is a lot of truth in those old sayings, at that, for there has been times in all of our lives, if we knew, things might have turned out a whole lot different.

Now they kept me on the west end for some time between Newburg and Springfield, but one day along in the middle of December [1902] they called me for an extra east, and when I got into St. Louis, I bunched the job, and went up to the main office, and got my check, after which I went over to East St. Louis[26] to the big four train yards,[27] and tied into the skipper of a fast run, for a ride with him over to Mattoon, Ill.,[28] for my Brother Tom was now braking out of there on the east end of this same pike, between Mattoon and Indianapolis, Indiana, and as the skipper belonged to the big O's, he told me to go talk to his hind man, and if he said I was O.K. for me to pile into the dog house [caboose], so after the rear brakeman put me through the works to see if I was up-to-date in the B.of R.T., he told his captain that I was there with the goods, so I rode over to Mattoon with them, where we arrived the next morning, and I went over to the Railroad Y.M.C.A.,[29] and asked them if there was a Big Four brakeman stopping there by the name of T. H. Brown, and they told me yes, that he stopped there, but at present he was out on the road, so I stuck around there that day and night, and the next day he came in off the road, and I met him, and we had quite a visit, for we had not seen each other for a long time, and we told each other of our railroad experiences, and he asked me where I was headed for, and I told him that I would go to work there out of Mattoon, if I could land a job, and he told me that I could get a job easy enough, but he says you don't want a job here, for it sure is the bunk, then he told me that had been figuring on bunching it himself, so I told him to go ahead and drag his time, and we would hit the road together, and look for a job some place else, so he bunched the job and got his check, and we rode over to a place called Charleston, Ill.,[30] where the Big Four crossed the Toledo, St. Louis & Western (better known at that time as the Clover Leaf Route),[31] and we went up to the trainmaster's office there in Charleston, and the trainmaster was a big red-faced Irishman by the name of Danny O'Brien, who had been promoted up from a passenger conductor, and he was sure a fine old fellow believe me. So when we asked him if he was hiring any brakemen, he told us yes, that he needed some brakemen to work out of Frankfort, Ind., on the east end, and as he was getting ready right then to go to Frankfort on No. 6, he would take us right along with him. (No. 6 was a fast passenger train, known in those days as the commercial traveler.)[32] So when No. 6 pulled in, we got on with him, and when the conductor came through to take up the tickets, Danny O'Brien told him that we were two brakemen that he had just hired, and that we were deadheading to Frankfort with him, and as it was about midnight when we arrived there, Danny told us to come up to the superintendent's office the next morning, and make out applications, and take the book of rules and time card examination (there was no doctor's examination). So the next morning we got all fixed up, and were marked up on the brakemen's extra board.

Now I remember that I was called and made my first trip on Christmas day [1902], on an extra east from Frankfort to a place called Delphos, Ohio,[33] the first division point east of Frankfort, and the conductor that I made the first trip with was a young fellow that had just got set up from brakeman to be a conductor, and he belonged to the trainmen (B.of R.T.) the same as I did. Well we had a good trip, and got into Delphos some time after midnight, and we went to bed in the caboose, and slept there until about 9 A.M. the next forenoon, when we got up and went over to a boarding house near the yards, and got some breakfast, after which we went back to the caboose, and as I was braking behind, I got busy and cleaned and filled the handlamps and the two big markers, and swept out the caboose (handlamps mean the conductor's and brakemen's lanterns, and the markers are those two big lanterns that you see on each side of the rear end of any train that shows a red light to the rear, and green lights to the front and sides), and after I got through, we set around and talked until the call boy come and called us for No. 43, a hot shot westbound fast freight, so after getting the train at Delphos, we highballed right through to Frankfort, and had a nice trip.

Well I broke extra out of Frankfort for a little while, then they sent me to Delphos to switch at night in the yards, and as it was along in January, 1903, the winter weather was something fierce, and I was never stuck on switching at nights, especially in the winter time, so after I had been there for a couple of months, or around about the middle of March, I had a small stake saved up, and I was ready to go, so I sent Mr. K. A. Ghoring, the superintendent at Frankfort, a message and told him to send a man to relieve me, for I had hired out there as a brakeman, and not as a switchman, so they wired back for me to stick a little while longer, and they would send a man to take my place, and let me come back to Frankfort and brake out of there.

Now I remember one night while I was switching there in the Delphos yards, there was a crew called for an extra north out of there for Toledo, and as I had done all of my braking and switching up to this time, out in the Rocky Mountains, I had not yet got out of the habit of cooning up on top of the cars and setting up the hand brakes, while switching and making up trains, and I had set up so many binders on this train that we had just made up for this crew, that when they got ready to go, the little ten wheel Rhode Island engine[34] could not start the train, and the rear brakeman come over the top from the hind end, letting off the hand brakes, and I heard him holler down to his conductor and say, I sure would like to know who this blankity blank mountain boomer snake [switchman] is, that leaves all of these binders set here in a level yard, I shore would tell that saphead aplenty, believe me. I was working over just two or three tracks from him, and I sure had a good laugh, and got a kick out of what he said, but the old home guard was right, for it was not necessary to leave so many binders set, for the yard was practically level.

Well along about the first of April they sent a man from Frankfort to relieve me, and I deadheaded back to Frankfort and was marked up on the brakemen's slow board, but I only had to buck the extra board for a short time until I caught a regular car, braking ahead for a little conductor by the name of Fred Knapp, and my partner the rear brakeman, was a big, good-natured Irishman by the name of Jack Hanly, and they both lived in Delphos, but when away from home, they cooked, eat and slept in the caboose, and I had a room in Frankfort, but I eat with them on the road, and paid them two bits a meal.

Now when I first went braking there for the Clover Leaf, they only paid one dollar and ninety a hundred (miles) but about the time I was assigned to my regular car, the brotherhoods had been up and met the general manager, and had got a slight raise, and some better working conditions, and we brakemen were raised to two cents a mile, and overtime at the rate of ten miles an hour, or in other words we got twenty cents an hour for overtime after we had been out over thirteen hours and thirty minutes, for as our division was one hundred and thirty five miles long, and at the rate of ten miles an hour, we got paid for thirteen hours and thirty minutes, for making the trip, and the quicker we made it the better it was for us, for if we made it in one hour, or used the whole thirteen hours and thirty minutes, we got our two dollars and seventy cents just the same, and that is the reason that railroad men are always in a hurry to get over the road.

Now I remember I paid two dollars a week for my room and two bits a meal at the boarding house where I lived at there in Frankfort, and like most all boarding houses in those days, it had a saloon in connection with it, and the barroom was right joining the big dining room, and in the dining room there were two big long tables, where the food was put on in family style, and you could help yourself and eat all you wanted, and us boys while in off the road would loaf around in the barroom and play cards, checkers, and dominoes for little brass checks, which were good at the bar.

Now the man and his wife that run this place had a pair of twin daughters that waited on the tables in the dining room, and boy, I am telling you they sure were pretty, and they looked so much alike that it took me quite a while before I could tell them apart, but as they were pretty nice girls, they did not mix up much with us railroad boys, except of course they talked and joked with us in the dining room, but that was all, for their family were country people, and had moved in off a farm about six months before I went there to board, and it seemed like the farmers in the country had always heard about them wild rough brakies and firemen on the railroads, and they were not taking any chances.

Now this little Clover Leaf railroad at that time handled quite a lot of dressed beef out of East St. Louis from Morris and Company's big packing houses,[35] and they run many meat trains, most of them running as No. 42, in several sections, and the train dispatcher always tried to give these meat trains a clear track, for they had to get this dressed beef over the road as fast as possible, and I have seen one of those little ten wheelers take twenty-five cars of meat over that one hundred and thirty-five mile division in six hours, including all stops, for coal and water, train orders and railroad crossings where there were no interlocking systems, but the engines all had regular assigned crews, and were kept up in first class order, and the company furnished the firemen with good coal, and the engines were good steamers.

Now I remember that I was called there in Frankfort one morning, for first No. 42, but as she had not showed up yet, the hoghead, tallowpot and myself were all setting up in the cab of our engine talking, while we were waiting for No. 42, to pull in and pretty soon we heard her whistling in, and in a few minutes we could see her headlight as she came heading down the ice house track, where they were to leave the train spotted, so that the ice house crew could re-ice the meat cars, and when they stopped, their head brakeman cut the engine off, and headed her down the round house lead, and she pulled down and stopped right along beside our engine, and her hogger had just got down to look her around, when all at once her front flue-sheet[36] let go with a bang and a roar of escaping steam, for she had blowed up, and about one-half of the front end of the smoke box went up in the air and come down on top of our cab roof with an awful crash, and man oh man, I thought that some old jinks had tacked the Indian sign on me that time for sure, and boy, I did not wait for nothing, but I jumped through the cab window and lit on my feet running, for man I thought I was a goner, no foolin', but as luck would have it, there was nobody hurt, but several of us that were right near the explosion were almost scared stiff.

Now I remember another time when I was going east on a meat train, that we had stopped at a place called Marion, Ind.,[37] for water, and down about one-half mile east of the depot we crossed a river on one of the old-time low bridges, that would not clear a brakeman standing on top of a box car, so when we pulled out of there, I caught on about six or eight cars behind the engine and climbed up on top, and was riding with my back to the engine, and the engineer was taking a run down the hill to the river bridge, so that he would be able to make the grade which started up from the river bank on the east side, and I was standing up there, busy waving and flirting with a girl, who was waving me a high ball from the front porch of her house, not so far from the tracks, and I had forgot about the low bridge, when all at once I saw the girl throw up her arms, and cover her face with her hands, and I had just began to wonder what had happened to her, when biff bang, the tell-tale ropes that were hanging down over the track,[38] about two hundred feet from the end of the bridge, smacked me in the back of the head, and believe me nobody had to tell me what that meant, so I flopped down on the running board of the car just in time, and the next second I shot under the bridge, and boy, I am telling you it was a close shave, no foolin', and I did not flirt with any more girls while standing on top of a train going down through Marion after that, believe me.

Now while I was braking out of Frankfort, I used to chum around a whole lot with a little Irish fireman by the name of Frank Mahoy, who fired the 111[39] (hundred and eleven) for a prince of an engineer by the name of Fred Willcockson, and Fred thought of the world of his fireman, and would take Frank out on the engine at times when he was so stewed that he could hardly stand up on the deck, without holding to the fire door chain.

Now the Clover Leaf Road used to run Sunday excursions through the summer time, from Frankfort, Ind., to Toledo, Ohio, and return for one dollar a person, and these excursions always left Frankfort at about two o'clock on Sunday mornings, so one Saturday night I was walking up Main street with a girl friend of mine, and we met Frank Mahoy and his girl, and as Frank was pretty well stewed, his girl was trying to get him to go with her out to her home so that she could keep him from drinking any more, and she asked my girl and I to go along with them, for Frank said he would not go unless Brownie (meaning me) went with them, so we said O.K., that we would go, and when we got out to his girl's house, her old man had a lot of bottled beer on ice, and was feeling pretty good himself, and when he saw Frank and I come in, that was all the excuse he wanted to start throwing a party, so he began to open up cold bottles of beer, and I saw what was coming, so I went to the phone and called up the yard office, and told the night call boy where he could call me in case he wanted me.

Well after we had been there for about two hours, I was feeling pretty good, and Frank and the old man were just about snowed under, and the old lady, and the two girls were not feeling so bad themselves, and about that time the phone rang, and Frank's girl answered it, and she turned around and says, Brownie it is for you, so I went to the phone, and it was the call boy, and he wanted me for an extra east at one o'clock A.M., so I took my girl home, then I went to my room and changed my clothes, after which I went over to the beanery and took on a mess of ham and eggs and coffee.

Now my partner Jack Hanly was laying off a round trip, and I was braking behind this trip, so after leaving Frankfort, we rambled over to Kokomo[40] where we made our first stop and took water, and then we proceeded on over to Marion where we stopped again and filled up with water, and got some train orders, after which we were on our way again, and my conductor Fred Knapp and I were setting up in the cupola of the caboose, and after we had gone about three miles east of Marion, we heard a torpedo explode when our engine struck it, then we heard our hogger answer a flag,[41] and I stuck my head out of the cupola window, as I was on the inside of the curve, and I could see the flagman's red fusee as he swung it across the track to flag us down, and further up the line I could see the two big red tail lights on the rear end of the other train's caboose, so our hogger picked up the flagman then pulled up behind the other train and stopped, and whistled out a flag, so then I had to take my flagging outfit and go back to protect my train, and after I had been out there for about an hour, I heard the big chime-whistle of the old 111, as she whistled into Marion, for I knew the old 111's whistle, and I says to myself, gee, Fred Willcockson is pulling the excursion this morning with his old 111, for I knew it was just about time for the excursion to be coming along, and I thought to myself, this is one trip that Frank Mahoy is not firing the old 111, for his pal Fred Willcockson, for it had only been about three hours since I left Frank all drunked up at his girl's house, so while I was out there in the night thinking to myself, I heard the excursion pull out of the station at Marion and cross the River bridge, and I could tell by the way that the engine was working, that Fred had widened on her [opened the throttle] when he hit the grade on the east side of the river, and in a few minutes I saw the electric headlight swing around the curve as I flashed a red fusee and swung them down, and Fred answered my flag with two short sounds of his whistle, as he cut off and drifted up to where I was waiting to get on, and when the engine got up to me I swung on and climbed up into the cab, and to my great surprise there stood Frank Mahoy on the deck hanging onto the fire door chain, and he was still so pickled that he did not recognize me until Fred says to me, what is the matter up ahead Brownie, and I told him that I did not know, as there was a train ahead of us, so he pulled up behind our caboose and stopped, then he whistled out a flag to protect his train, and Frank crawled up on his seatbox and was soon sound asleep, and I asked Fred if Frank had any trouble keeping her hot, and he says no Brownie, I don't know how he does it, but it seems that the drunker he is, the better he can fire an engine.

Well in a short time we all got started again, and when we got over to a little town called Van Buren, [42] we two freight trains headed in and let the excursion go by, and we followed her out of there, so that day when we got into Delphos, I went over to Mother Bishop's boarding house for dinner, and as her oldest daughter, Anna, was pretty sweet on Frank Mahoy, I told her that the old 111 was pulling the excursion this Sunday, and I figured that they would be coming through Delphos about eight P.M. that evening on their return trip, and Anna made me promise to take her down to the depot that night when the excursion pulled in from Toledo, so that she could see and talk to Frank, and Anna and I were at the depot that evening when the old 111 come pulling in and we went up to the head end, and Frank and Fred both got down and talked to us, and Frank was as sober as a judge, and nobody would ever think that he had been loaded for bear that morning.

Well I worked there on the Clover Leaf until the first of November, 1903, when I bunched the job and dragged my time and beat it back to St. Louis, where I stuck around for about a week, then I went out to the Frisco yards where I had fired an engine the year before, and squared myself a ride in the caboose with a train crew who carried me to Newberg, then I rode with another crew from Newberg to Springfield, and when I got there I went to the trainmaster's office, of the old Kansas City Fort Scott & Memphis railroad, and got a job of braking between Springfield and Thayer, Mo.,[43] down through the Ozark Mountains, on what the natives down there call the Leaky Roof division,[44] and I want to say right here that it was the best job of braking that I ever had. I don't just remember what they paid there, but I think it was two dollars and twenty five cents a hundred, at that time, and all of the engines were of the ten wheeler type, and fifteen loads was a train down through those hills for that class of engine, and boy, what I mean they sure did wheel them, no foolin', for they would run them down one hill and up over the next one, but there was one grade when we were going south, known as Whetstone hill, that we always had to double with a fifteen car train. We would go down the north side of Whetstone just like a bat out of heck, and run them up the other side just as far as we could, then stop and make a cut about the middle of the train, and then double to the top of the hill with the first half and back the cars into a spur track built there for that purpose, and then go back and get the rest of the train and bring it up.

Now there were two hills going south where the brakeman had to ride out on top and turn up the pops (retaining valves) and the first hill was known as Stirling hill, from a little place called Stirling[45] down six miles into Willow Springs,[46] and the second was known as Koshkonong hill, from the little burg of Koshkonong[47] down ten miles into Thayer, the first division point south of Springfield.

Now I remember going south one time on an extra, and the engineer was an old boomer hoghead off the D.&R.G.[48] from Salt Lake City, Utah, and his name was Charlie Bordner. (I will tell of meeting him again when I was braking out of Salt Lake on the D.&R.G. later on in another chapter.) I asked old Charlie just before starting down Koshkonong hill how many retainers he wanted me to turn up, and he says what's the matter, do you think I need any retainers turned up going down these little hills, heck no, you don't need to turn up retainers for me, and boy, the way that old Rocky Mountain boomer could drop a train down a hill was enough to make an old timer love his mother-in-law, he sure knew his airbrakes, no foolin'.

Now I remember another time that I was called for an extra there in Springfield, and our train only consisted of the engine, six cars, and the caboose, and we were supposed to fill out to fifteen loads at Willow Springs, but when we got out to a little place called

Rodgersville,[49] about fifteen miles from Springfield, the air-pump on the engine went on the blink, and the conductor sent the train dispatcher a message telling him what had happened, and ask for instructions as what to do, so the dispatcher wired back and ask the engineer if he thought he could handle the six car train without any air, if he would let us go right on through to Thayer, without filling out at Willow Springs, and after talking it over with us two brakemen and the conductor, the engineer told the operator to tell the dispatcher yes, that with the help of the two brakemen on the hand brakes, that he could make it all O.K., and the dispatcher wired back and told us to go to it, so we pulled out of there, and by the time we got to Cedar Gap,[50] which is said to be the highest point in the Ozarks, it was dark and so foggy that we could not see three car-lengths ahead. So while the fireman was taking water, I walked back to the hind end, and discovered that we had lost our crummy [caboose], and I hurried back to the engine and told the hogger that we had lost our doghouse [caboose], and that I would take a red fusee and go back to the rear end, and if he could see the fusee when I gave him a back up signal, for him to answer with three short toots of the whistle, and then start backing up slow, which he did, and after backing up for about a mile, we met the skipper walking in with a lighted red fusee, so we picked him up and went on back about a half of a mile, where we found the caboose and coupled onto it, and then the hogger called in the flagman, and as soon as he came in, we pulled back into Cedar Gap, where we got some train orders, and then proceeded on our way, and after we had gone some few miles, the fog cleared up, but it went to raining and sleeting, and by the time we got to Stirling and started down the hill to Willow Springs there was so much ice on the rails that the engine could not hold them, for when the hoghead would hoss her over into the back motion,[51] the crushed ice on the rails would cause the drive-wheels to lose their grip on the rails and spin around backwards, and as she could not hold anything that way, the six cars and the caboose shoved her right along, so the hogger grabbed the whistle-cord, and began calling for brakes, and I took my lantern and scrambled back over the tank. And I had one heck of a time getting from the back end of the tank over onto the first box car, for everything was covered with ice, and when I finally did get upon top of the box car I could not stand up and walk, for by this time we were going so fast and the car was rocking from side to side so bad that I had to get down on my hands and knees and crawl to the other end of the car where the hand brake was at. After setting it up as tight as I could, I managed somehow to get over onto the next car, but the ratchet dog on that brake would not hold, so I did not try to go any further, but just sit there on the running board, with my lantern between my legs, and held on for dear life, for I'll tell the cockeyed world that we were going some, and I don't know how we shot around those curves and struck to the rails, for I was expecting them to jump the track any second and go crashing down the hillside among the rocks, for boy, I am telling you that we were sure riding a runaway train that dark, stormy night, down that mountain grade into Willow Springs, no foolin'. And as it was customary there at Willow Springs for the freight crews to leave their trains on the main line after taking coal and water, (that is if there were no first class trains due at that time) while they went over to the Dutchman's to eat, it so happened at this time that there was a northbound extra that had just pulled in and after taking their coal and water, the crew was just ready to go over and eat, but when they heard us coming down the hill calling for brakes every few seconds they knew right away that there was a runaway train coming, and they got busy right now, and started backing their train up to get out of our way, and they did not stop until they backed away up on top of a hill south of there. And believe me it was a good thing that they did too, for we came down through there like a cyclone, but when we run onto the rails where the other train had cracked the ice off of, and which they had also sanded, our engineer kept throwing her over into the back motion, and the drivewheels began to grip the sanded rails, which slowed her down a bit, but we did not get stopped until we went about halfway up the other hill. Then we backed down into the yards there at Willow Springs, and got in the clear, then the other train pulled down into the yards again and stopped, and we all went over to the Dutchman's to get something to eat. We were all so excited, that we were all trying to talk at once, and our engineer bawled my conductor and the hind brakeman out, for not getting out on top and try to help hold them with the hand brakes, and they told him that they had the caboose brake set up as tight as they could get it, but the brakes would not hold on account of the ice on the rails, and my conductor told me I was a fool for getting out on top, for at the speed that we were going the hand brakes were useless, and I told him that I had found that out. The funny part of it was, there was a young fellow riding on the engine as a student, learning to be a fireman, and this was his first and last trip, for he said that he got all of the railroading that he wanted in that one fast ride down the mountain that night. He rode back to Springfield with us in our caboose, for after the captain made a report to the train dispatcher at Springfield of what had happened, he wired us to set out the six cars, and return to Springfield light (with just the engine and caboose), so after turning our engine there on a wye,[52] we took coal and water and got running orders and returned to Springfield.

Now I remember another time while I was braking there, that we were coming north out of Thayer on a banana special-extra, with ten cars of bananas, and we were running extra on a schedule order, and the schedule was a fast one too, but we had a young green fireman, and he was having a hard time trying to keep the engine hot, and Billy James the hogger was a little worried because he was not making the time, but was falling down on the schedule, and when we pulled into a place called Mountain Grove,[53] about half way over the division, the operator had his order board out, so we stopped and took a tank of water, while the skipper went into the telegraph office to sign the orders, and instead of getting orders, the operator handed him a message from the dispatcher, addressed to Engineer James of banana special, wanting to know why he could not make the time, so Billy sent him an answer explaining that he had a new fireman, and although the boy was doing the very best that he could, he was unable to keep the engine hot. Now up to this time I had been riding back in the caboose, for we were all eating bananas that the messenger brought out of the cars when he would make an inspection, so I told my conductor and Billy James that I was an old tallow-pot, and if it was all right with them, that I would fire the engine the rest of the way into Springfield, and the captain said it was jake with him if I would do it, and Billy James says to me, Brownie if you will keep her hot, I will go to town on time, and when we get there, I will buy you the biggest drink of whiskey that you ever had, so I says fair nuff, hop to it, then I peeled off my coat and vest, and put on the fireman's gloves, and then we started for Springfield, and from Mountain Grove up to Cedar Gap it was pretty tough sledding, but I was keeping the old mill hot, and Billy kept patting her on the back. We pulled into Cedar Gap and while the fireman was taking water and Billy was dropping a little oil on her, I put on the blower and the injector both,[54] and at the same time I slammed a good fire into her, and by the time that we were ready to go, I had her hot and plenty of water in the boiler, and the operator came out and handed Billy a message from the dispatcher, telling him to come on, that he had a clear track. Now from Cedar Gap to Springfield the distance is about fifty miles, and the country is rolling and hilly, so when we pulled out of there, Billy say to me, well Brownie here we go and the next stop is Springfield, and I says go to it old kid, I am with you, and man oh man, the way that guy took those bananas to town was a caution, and I'll tell the world that I sure was one busy fireboy keeping the old mill hot, but we made up our lost time and pulled into Springfield right on the cat hop.

So after putting the engine away and washing up, Billy and his fireman and I all went over to Mike Kelley's saloon on the corner of the main stem and some other little street, and Kelley's bartender had a big bowl of Tom and Jerry[55] all made up, so we had a Tom and Jerry on Billy, then the fireman bought a round, and just then the conductor and hind man came in, and the skipper said that the next round would be on him, so we throwed them into us, and then I was going to buy, but they would not let me, for the hind man said that the next round was on him, and then to top it all off, Kelley's bartender said that the next round would be on the house. By that time the young fireman and I were just about cuckoo clock, so I took my lantern and wabbled down the street a short distance to the hotel where I roomed and boarded, and when I went into the dining room for supper, there was a cute little widow there I had stepped out with a few times, waiting on table. When she saw me, she says, why Brownie, what in the world is the matter with you, and I says nothing much, why; and she laughed and says why boy, you look like you had been sent for, but could not make the grade. So after eating my supper I went up to my room and piled into the hay, and slept until about the middle of the forenoon the next day, and when I got up I was feeling pretty good, except my arms and back were a little bit sore, for that was the first firing that I had done in little over a year.

Well I broke there on the K.C.F.S.&M. until the first of March, 1904, when business began to fall off, then I bunched the job and dragged my time, and got a pass back to St. Louis, where I went to work firing a switch engine for the St. Louis Terminal Railroad Association[56] (or the Bridge as it was known in those day by all of the boomers) and I had to ride all over the yards there in St. Louis, and East St. Louis, and through the tunnel that runs right through under the main part of St. Louis, which starts in near Poplar street, and runs under Eighth street up as far the Post Office, and there it swings around and goes east under Washington right up to the end of Eades Bridge,[57] and then the tracks goes on across Eades Bridge to the relay station[58] at East St. Louis, and this riding that I speak of was done on different switch engines, so that I could learn the system, before they would let me go to work, for all movement of trains and switch engines were under control of the thousands of semaphore fixed signals,[59] only except in special train yards used for storage, and for making up trains.

Well after I learned all of this system, the job was not worth it, for they did not pay enough money for all of the trouble that a fellow was put to, but I stayed there for about three months, or up to the first of June, for the World's Fair[60] was going on there in St. Louis, and I wanted to see as much as I could.

Now I remember the first engine that I was assigned to, after I got the job, was that of pulling passenger trains from Union Station,[61] and the relay station over in East St. Louis, but I remember that the last month that I worked there, I was assigned on the night switch engine over in East St. Louis working in what was called in those days the eastbound, and believe me it was some job. I guess about all of the old time boomer switchmen have switched cars in the eastbound in East St. Louis, or have heard all about it anyway.

I don't know what they do there now, but back in the days of 1904, I will tell the world, there was one place where they switched cars, believe me. I was told that they killed pin-pullers there quite often, although I did not see any killed while I was there. The pin-puller is the man on a switch crew that makes the cuts (uncouples the cars) while the engine is kicking the car into different tracks, and if the pin lifter is broken or disconnected, the pin-pullers have to jump in between the cars and get the pin with his hand, and that is where the danger comes in, for if he loses his hand hold or stumbles over the rails, the chances are he is a goner.

Now I remember that I was firing for a hoghead by the name of Jim Lett, and we carried a two gallon tin bucket on the switch engine, and after going to work at six P.M. we would pull up to the north end of the yard, then we would take up the collection for a can of beer. For there were five of us on the crew, and we would all throw in a nickle apiece, and then one of the switchmen would take the bucket and the two bits, and go over to a saloon near by and get it full of good cold beer, and after we licked that canful up, we would go up to Morris & Company's Packing house and dig out a few stray cars of meat, and bring them back down to the yards, and then we would all chip in another nickle apiece, and get another can of beer, and after lapping up that canful, boy I am telling you we were ready to switch cars, for by this time we were all feeling pretty good.

C.St.P.M.&O.

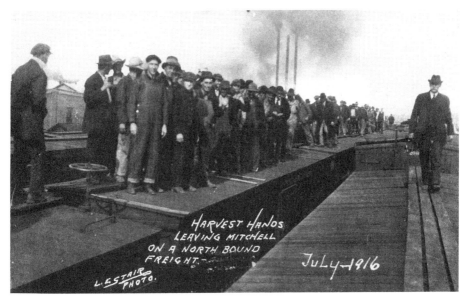

Harvest hands hitch rides on a Chicago, Milwaukee & St. Paul freight train in Mitchell, South Dakota, in July 1916. These "boes" are headed for the Dakota wheat fields. (Courtesy of the Center for Western Studies)

Hoboes clog a Chicago & North Western freight train bound for Oakes, North Dakota, on August 13, 1914. With so many riders, crew members probably were unable to extract any "bo" money. (Don L. Hofsommer Collection)

Early in the twentieth century, the E. H. Harriman administration underwrote a major rebuilding of the Union Pacific mainline through Wyoming. In this scene a crew widens a cut. (J. E. Stimson photograph; Union Pacific Museum Collection)

Union Pacific's #6, the eastbound Fast Mail, roars across Wyoming, ca. 1900. (J. E. Stimson photograph; Union Pacific Museum Collection)

The caption on this postcard reads "This Is the Way Trainmen Hooked the Cars Together in the Old Link and Pin Days. (Editor's collection)

Section men ballast the Union Pacific's mainline track near Bitter Creek, Wyoming, a station between Wamsutter and Point of Rocks, ca. 1901. (J. E. Stimson photograph; Union Pacific Museum Collection)

A powerful Bucyrus steamshovel loads a ballast car with rock as it widens a cut. (J. E. Stimson photograph; Union Pacific Museum Collection)

The new line of the Union Pacific across portions of Wyoming is seen to the right. An "extra" freight train, with white flags flying, waits on a passing siding. (J. E. Stimson photograph; Union Pacific Museum Collection)

Union Pacific's eastbound Atlantic Express, #4, nears Fort Steele, Wyoming, ca. 1900. The first three cars carry express. (J. E. Stimson photograph; Union Pacific Museum Collection)

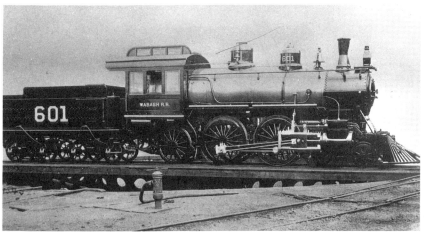

The Wabash Railroad, famed for its fast passenger trains, commonly used sleek Atlantic-type (4-4-2) locomotives to pull its "varnish." Pictured is #601, a Class E-1 locomotive, built by Baldwin in March 1898; the Wabash scrapped #601 in June 1931. (Gerald M. Best Collection, California State Railroad Museum)

Braking in Hard Weather

A. B. Frost drew several sketches of "The Every-day Life of Railroad Men" for the November 1888 issue of *Scribner's Magazine.* (Editor's collection)

Flagging in Winter

Trainmen and Tramps

Crewmen and minor Santa Fe officials gather in front of locomotive #940, a 2-10-2 built by Baldwin in 1903. (California State Railroad Museum)

Crew members of a Santa Fe freight train stand by their locomotive, #1642, a powerful, state-of-the-art 2-10-2 ("1600 Class"), built by Baldwin in 1906. The photograph was taken in California, ca. 1910. (California State Railroad Museum)

The Santa Fe's (neé Gulf, Colorado & Santa Fe) board-and-batten-style station in Somerville, Texas, ca. 1920. (Santa Fe Collection, Kansas State Historical Society)

A switch engine and local railroaders pose in front of the Santa Fe's Harvey House and depot in Needles, California, in 1907. (Santa Fe Collection, Kansas State Historical Society)

The Santa Fe's popular recreation hall for employees in Needles, California, is pictured on this ca. 1910 postal card. (Editor's collection)

Chapter VI

Well after I quit the Terminal Association there in St. Louis, I took a notion that I would go out into Kansas and get a job on some railroad through the wheat rush, so I rode the Frisco system back to Springfield, where I spent about a week with some friends of mine, then I went up to the Frisco office and got a pass from Springfield out to Wichita, Kansas,[1] and I remember that the train on which I was riding stopped at a place between Neodesha, Kansas[2] and Wichita to take coal and water, and while this passenger train was standing there, I got off to look around a bit, and there was a freight train laying there in a passing track, and I saw a brakeman come out from between two cars, right near where I was standing, and who do you suppose it was. I will give you one guess; it was nobody else but my old friend George Poe, who I had broke partners with on the Union Pacific out of Evanston, Wyo., for Big Tom Shell two years before in 1902, and I says to him, hello there George, you old hobo hound, what are you doing? still frisking your trains for bo money? but he did not recognize me right off the reel, then finally he began to laugh, and says, why hello there Brownie old kid, how is the boy, and I says just fine as we shook hands, and he asked me where I was headed for, and I told him that I was on my way to Wichita to make the wheat rush, so we visited and talked about old times when we were out on the Union Pacific, until my train started to pull out, and then we wished each other good luck as I got back on my train, and I never saw him again after that.

Well I landed in Wichita around about the middle of June, and as the wheat harvest had not started yet, none of the railroads were hauling any grain at that time, but I went to the Missouri Pacific[3] Office there in Wichita, and got a job of braking and my name was marked up on what was called the emergency board, for they were taking on men, although they could not use them until the wheat began to move, so they marked all of the new men upon this emergency board so that they would have them when the wheat rush started.

Well I layed around there waiting to go to work, until I was just about broke, so a boomer conductor, a fireman and myself, all tied into the captain of a little local passenger train that run out through a large wheat belt west of Wichita, on a branch line of the Santa Fe System, for a ride out in the country, for we had made up our minds to go out and work in the harvest fields so as to make a little stake for ourselves, while we were waiting for things to start rolling, so this skipper carried us out to a little place called Cheney,[4] about thirty miles west of Wichita, and we all got jobs as harvest hands, working in the wheat fields setting up bundles of wheat into big round shocks, and we got two dollars a day and board and room, and boy, if you ask me, it sure was some hot job, and the wheat where I was working was the bearded variety, and boy, what I mean, that wheat had whiskers that would do credit to a Jewish rabbi, no foolin', and the beards struck right through my clothes and into my bare skin, and between those beards sticking and scratching me, and the heat, it was just about all that I could stand.

Well I remember that I worked there for three days, and then it set into raining, and boy, it did not only rain, but it just poured, and the heck of it was it kept it up for about a week, and by that time the poor farmers' wheat crops in that section of the country were completely ruined, for the wheat that had not been cut yet was all knocked down flat on the ground, and the wheat that was in the shock had began to rot.

Well the young farmer that I had worked for paid me my six dollars (and honest, under the circumstances, I really hated to take the money, for he had to go and borrow it to pay me off, but I was broke and I needed it) so I went back into Wichita, and everything was beginning to be flooded, for the Arkansas River that runs down through the west side of the City of Wichita kept raising until it spread out all over in the low places of the city, and I saw the water in some of the lowest places running through the second story windows of the houses, and some places in the heart of the city the water was running up over the counters in the stores.[5]

Now the city of Wichita was practically cut off from the outside world as it were, for about ten days, for most of the bridges had gone out, and the rest were not safe to cross over and no trains could get in, and the trains that had got caught there could not get out, and practically all of the business there in town had been shut down. As it was right around the first part of July the weather was hot, and almost everybody turned the flood tie up into sport, by going boat riding and having wading parties, for men, women and children would put on old clothes and go wading afternoons and nights, and boy, I am telling you that everybody had lots of fun, and when a wading party of girls would meet a bunch of boys, they would get all mixed up and have lots of fun splashing and ducking each other in the water.

Now there were two Frisco freight crews tied up there in the Frisco yards, and I slept in one of the cabooses with one of the crews, and eat with them over at their boarding house where their credit was good, and then we all used my six dollars cash money to buy beer with, for besides sleeping and eating, all we had to do was to can beer and go wading and have a good time, yes I know that the State of Kansas was supposed to be dry at that time, for it was there in Wichita that the great and noted Carrie Nation[6] took her battle-ax and busted up her first saloon, but the dry business in Kansas at that time was good business for the boot-leggers just the same as it is now, for if you had the jack to pay for it, you could get anything you wanted, and it was . . . no blinding poison.

I remember that one of the Frisco brakemen and I had a date to go wading with a pair of little queens one night, but the danged Frisco road had to go and spoil everything for us, by getting one of the railroad bridges fixed back so that trains could get over, and the train dispatcher at Neodesha, Kans., the first division point east of Wichita, sent orders for the two crews that were tied up there in Wichita, to return to Neodesha running light with just their engines and cabooses, and as there was nothing for me there in Wichita, I wanted to get out of there and head back for St. Louis, and the only chance that I had of getting out, was by going with one of these crews, so I went with them, and the Frisco brakeman and I lost out on our date to go wading that night with the two little queens.

Well, when we got to Neodesha, I was told by some of the worthy brothers that was working out of there, that the train master had hired three brakemen the day before, and if I went up to the office and hit up the chief clerk I might get a job, but while I was talking to them on the depot platform, another brotherhood man walked up to us, and he had a little girl with him which he told us was his oldest child, and that he was broke and had left his sick wife and two smaller children with some friends back in Missouri, and he was traveling around over the country, looking for a job of some kind, so some of the boys that was working there dug down into their pockets and gave him some money, and I told the brother that I was broke and traveling myself or I would help him too, and then I says to him, listen brother, I was just going up to hit the trainmaster's chief clerk for a job of braking, but if there is a job here for a brakeman, you need it worse that I do, so you go up first, and I will wait until you come down, and he thanked me, then he beat it upstairs to the trainmaster's office, and sure enough the chief clerk hired him, and he come down stairs with a big smile on his face, and told the rest of us that he had made the grade, and landed a job. Then I went up and tried my luck, but the chief clerk told me that he had just hired a man, and did not need any more at present, so I tied into him for a pass to St. Louis, and he fixed me up and I left there that night on an eastbound passenger train. (I will mention here at this time, that the brotherhoods had it in their contract with the Frisco System in those days, that when a railroad man came along that is a brotherhood man, looking for a job, that if the company could not put him to work, they had to give him a pass to some other division along their line.)[7]

Well, I went on back to St. Louis, and from there I went over to Decatur, Ill.,[8] and landed a job of braking on the Wabash Railroad,[9] and I remember that I worked two ways out of there, between there and East St. Louis, and east out of there to Danville, Ill.,[10] and it was a pretty good job of braking too.

Now the Wabash sure did wheel their fast freights over the road, for the World's Fair was going on in St. Louis at that time, and they had to get their freight trains over the road and keep them out of the way of the passenger trains, for there were fifteen regular first class time-card passenger trains each direction every twenty-four hours, between Decatur and St. Louis, and some of these trains run in two and three sections, for the Wabash was doing a big World's Fair excursion business at that time.

Now I remember that I was going south out of Decatur one trip on a freight train, and we headed in at a little town called Bluemound,[11] and in the space of one hour's time, three passenger trains passed us going south, and three more met us going north, in other words while we were laying there in the passing track, just one hour, six passenger trains came and went, three north and three south, and this was on a stretch of single track too, for the Wabash at that time only had stretches of double track here and there along the route, but I saw more pretty train dispatching done there while I was working for the Wabash, than any other road I ever worked for, and in most cases where two trains either freight or passenger, had a meeting point with each other, both trains arrived there at about the same time, and there was no waiting and no delays.

Well I only worked extra on freight for a short time after I went there, until I was assigned into extra passenger service, and I worked as a brakeman, and flagman on passenger until the World's Fair closed, late that fall, when the company pulled off some of the regular passenger runs.

Now I remember while I was on passenger in the month of September 1904, I was coming west out of Danville, Ill., one trip on first No. 9,[12] the fast mail, and when we reached a little town by the name of Bement, Ill.,[13] where the Chicago division of the Wabash branched off from the main line, we crashed head on in a collision with No. 4,[14] an eastbound fast passenger train known as the Buffalo limited, and the way it happened was something like this.

Now between Decatur and Bement there was a stretch of about twenty miles of double track, and the dispatcher at Decatur put out a No. 31, meet order to No. 4, and first No. 9, and the order stated that the two trains would meet on double track between Bement and Decatur, and as first No. 9 was already running late with the mail that had to make connections with mail trains running west out of St. Louis, the dispatcher was giving first No. 9 all the help he could by not stopping her. Now No. 9 on the employees official time-card, was given time-card rights over all trains, and that meant that all other trains on the road must keep out of the way, and clear No. 9's time at all stations along the route, unless otherwise instructed by the train dispatcher, and in this case No. 4 had not yet met first No. 9, when she (No. 4) reached the east end of the double track there at Bement, and it was her duty to stay in the clear until first No. 9 arrived and departed, but the engineer that was pulling No. 4 made a statement afterwards that he overlooked his hand by forgetting his orders, so he came sailing down there and called for the switch with four toots of his engine whistle, and of course the poor old crippled up switch tender, not knowing anything about the meet order, lined up the switch and gave him a highball to come ahead, and got about half of his train out on the main line, when the fireman woke up to the fact to what his engineer was doing, and he holler over to him and says hey, we have got a meet here with first No. 9, and you had better get back into clear, for here she comes, but the fireman's warning had come too late, for as Bement was not a time-card stop for No. 9, big Jack Edwards who was pulling first No. 9 this trip with his big ten wheeler, the old 640[15] (six forty) was sure stepping right along trying to make up lost time, and Jack stated afterwards that by the time that he discovered that No. 4 was partly out on the main line, instead of being in the clear, all he could do was to plug her, and give them the works,[16] as he hollered to his fireman to unload, which they both did just before the two big engines come together, and he and his fireman both got pretty badly bruised and shaken up, and they were lucky that there were no bones broken, and it was pretty lucky for all of us, for although many people were injured, nobody was killed, and all I can say, is that it was sure one miraculous escape for all of us.

Now I remember at the time they hit, I was walking through one of the cars toward the head end, and when the crash came, I went sailing over the backs of the seats and piled up with a lot of the passengers in the front end of the car, and the crashing, grinding sound of iron and wood, and the terrific roaring noise made by the escaping steam from the two demolished engines, mingling with the screams and cries of the frightened and injured passengers, sure was something awful.

Now after I got myself untangled from the struggling mass of people on the car floor, I run back to the other end of the car and tried to open the doors so that we could get out, but as the car was sort of twisted out of shape, the doors were jammed in such a manner that we could not get them open, so we got the people out through the broken windows, and when I got out I could see them carrying injured people out of all of the cars on both trains.

Well, when the two engines come together, the impact was so great that they had reared right up, and they reminded me of two angry stallions fighting, and the combination baggage and smoking car which was coupled to the engine on No. 4 had telescoped the tank of the engine, and the front part of its roof was resting on top of No. 4's engine cab, and the baggage master on No. 4 was pretty badly crushed and broken up, from the trunks and other baggage piling upon him, but the big all-steel mail cars on our train were not damaged much, except being jammed together at the ends, and the glass broken out of the windows, and the mail clerks come out of it pretty good, except some cuts and bruises.

Now of course the Wabash Company rushed a relief train out from Decatur with doctors and nurses, which was followed by the wreck train to clear the wreck, and when second No. 9 came along, they transferred the mail over on her, and she also picked up the rear cars of our train that were not damaged very much, and took them and the passengers that were able to go, and went on her way to St. Louis.

Well, as I stated above, I worked there on passenger [trains] until the World's Fair closed, then they put me back on freight, braking extra out of Decatur, and I was living there at the time in the railroad Y.C.M.A., for I was a member and carried a membership card, which cost me five dollars a year, and this card entitled me to the many privileges given to the members, such as free baths, and reduction on room rent, meals, and many other things. There was a bowling alley, and pool room down in the basement, and lounging rooms on the first floor where the boys could play games, such as cards, checkers, and dominoes, and there was nearly always some boomer around there that could play the piano that sit in one of the rooms, and there was also a wonderful library of good books which was a gift from Helen Gould,[17] as the Wabash was part of the Gould System, and I remember of seeing Miss Helen as we called her at that time, and her brother, George Gould[18] come through Decatur one time on a tour of inspection of the road, hospitals, and the Y.M.C.A.'s.

Now the Wabash railroad had a system there at Decatur, that when there was a wreck occurred out on the line some place, they would blow four long blasts of the big shop whistle, which was the signal to notify the wrecking crew, and other Wabash men, so the Company kept a list in the telegraph office which was in the depot just across from the Y.M.C.A., and when any trainmen heard the wreck whistle blow, if they were any ways near the office, they would rush over and sign the list, and the first conductor, and the first two brakemen that signed the list were the men that made up the crew that got to take the wrecker out on its run, and all other trainmen who signed the list received a nice complimentary letter from the superintendent with merit marks added to their credit.

Well as the Y.M.C.A. where I lived was just across the tracks from the depot, I always had pretty good luck catching the wreck train if I was in off of the road, and making a trip out on the wrecker was sort of a prize catch for an extra brakeman, for it paid straight time from the time you left Decatur, until you got back, at the rate of ten miles an hour.

Now I remember one time I caught the wreck train, and we went out to a little town by the name of Sudoris[19] (or I think that was the name of it, any way it was about forty miles east of Decatur), to clean up a freight wreck, caused by the train breaking in two and running together again, which piled them up and killed three hoboes, and almost killed a fourth one.

And when we arrived with the wreck train, the crew of the train that was wrecked told the wrecking boss that they could hear someone groaning and moaning every once in a while, in the pile of wreckage, so instead of the wrecking crew starting right in to pull the pile of cars to pieces with the big hook, as the wrecking crane is called, they took some hand saws, and axes, and went to work cutting a hole into the pile of wreckage, and some time after daylight they had worked their way into where the poor fellow was at, and they took him out first, and although he was pretty badly smashed and broken up, he sure was glad to get out alive.

Now this young fellow was a cigar-maker, and after he got out of the hospital he got himself a job there in Decatur, and he was so grateful to the Wabash boys for saving his life that he used to come down to the railroad Y.M.C.A. and bring cigars and pass them out to everybody. One time I got to talking to him and when I told him that I was one of the train crew that brought the wreck train out there that night, he sure was glad to meet me, and he and I became very good friends after that. He told me one time when we were talking about the wreck, how he and his partner, another cigar-maker had left their homes in New York City and started out to see some of the western part of the country, and how their trip was brought to tragic end by that awful wreck, and he says to me, Brownie it is pretty tough to be pinned down by a lot of wreckage expecting to die every minute, and then to have your best friend die right along beside you while talking to him, and I asked him if he knew the other two young fellows that were killed, and he said no that all that he knew about them was that they had told him and his partner that they belonged there in Illinois and that they were coal-miners, looking for work, and that he believed that they were killed outright, when the crash came, for they did not make a sound after that.

Well I broke freight all that winter, and up to about the middle of March 1905, when the train master's chief clerk there at Decatur called me into the office one day, and says to me, Brownie, how would you like a regular passenger run between Chicago and St. Louis, and I told him I did not know until I tried it, and if he would promise me that he would let me come back on freight in case I did not like it, that I would make a try at it just for luck, and he said, O.K., fair enough, so I became a regular passenger brakeman, and I was assigned to brake for an old conductor by the name of Frank Woods, and he was a sort of funny old codger, and most brakemen did not like to brake for him.

Now there were five crews of us working out of Chicago on the Wabash day and night passenger runs between there and St. Louis, and we worked in the chain gang, that is first in first out, and our daylight runs were No. 11 (number eleven) and No. 14, and the night runs were No. 21, and No. 12, and the daylight runs No. 11 and No. 14, were known in those days as the Banner Blue Limited,[20] fast crack trains put on during the World's Fair in St. Louis, and they sure were beautiful trains to look at. The cars were all painted a royal blue, with gold gilt letterings and trimmings, and the interior of the dining and observation cars were the last word in trimming and fixtures.

And if I remember right, the running time for No. 11 and No. 14 was around about six hours for the two hundred and seventy six miles, between Chicago and St. Louis, including all stops, and a change of engines at Decatur, and I remember that our time card schedule many places along the route was sixty miles an hour.[21]

Now we would make a daylight trip, going south on No. 11 one day, and come back the next day on No. 14, arriving at Chicago at 5:30 P.M., then we would lay over in Chicago for thirty hours or up to 11:30 P.M. the next night, when we would leave Chicago on No. 21, . . . and return from St. Louis the next night on No. 12, arriving back at Chicago at 6:30 A.M.

Now all of these trains were pulled by the big 600 class engines, known as the Atlantic type, which had big seven foot drivewheels, and when it come to running, they were regular grayhounds.[22] I remember the first trip that I made with old Frank Woods. We were going south on No. 11, and when we reached Granite City,[23] from which place the Wabash passenger trains run over the St. Louis Terminal Tracks to the Union Station at St. Louis, old Woods says to me, now listen Brown, you want to look out while we are on these Terminal Tracks, for they are fierce about flagging, and you must ride outside on the rear platform and be ready to hop down on the ground with your flag in case we have to stop. Now I am telling you this for I don't suppose you know any thing about this Terminal system, and I laughed and says to him, no; I ought not to know anything about it, for I only fired a switch engine here three months, after riding all over the system on an engine to learn it, before they would let me go to work, then old Woods gave me a dirty look and says to me, well how in the blankity blank heck did you expect me to know that you had worked for the Terminal before, that is the trouble with you boomers, you work everywhere for a short time, but you don't stay any place very long at a time, and I says to him, no, but we boomers know how to hit the ball what little time we do stay, so old Frank Woods never bothered me after that, and I broke there for him until I quit the Wabash some time in the month of February, 1906.

Well a short time after I quit the Wabash, I went to work braking on freight for the Chicago, Milwaukee & St. Paul, running between Chicago and Janesville, Wisconsin,[24] and I caught a regular car the very first trip, as the main line boys did not like the Janesville branch as long as business was good on the main line, but after I had been there about two months, business began to fall off, so some old head come over from off the main line, and bumped me off my regular car (being bumped means that an older man [in seniority] takes your place on the crew) and I was sent to Milwaukee and marked up on the extra board to work out of there on the main line,[25] and while I was working there my brother Tom blowed in, but as business was so rotten he did not go to work, so I bunched the job and dragged my time, then he and I took a Lake steamer and went back to Chicago and where we met a couple other boomers who told us that the Santa Fe was sending them down into Texas to work, as they had a stock rush on, so Tom says to me, what do you say we take a trip down into Texas, and I says it's jake with me, for firing or braking on stock runs is just my dish, so we went up to the general offices of the Santa Fe there in Chicago[26] and told them what we wanted to do, and after showing them our service letters off of other roads where we had worked, they fixed us up with passes to Temple, Texas,[27] and we left Chicago that night on a Santa Fe passenger train and after riding about two days and nights, we landed in Temple, and when we got there we went up into the trainmaster's office and told the chief clerk that we were boomer brakemen and had been sent out from Chicago to help out in the stock rush, and just then the train-master came into the office, and the chief clerk says to him, look who is here, two boomer brakemen they sent out to us from Chicago, and I whispered to my brother Tom, and says look out, they are so tickled to see us that they might rush over and try to give us a French kiss on both cheeks, for they sure were hollering for experienced brakemen right at that time, for they had a big stock rush coming on, and they did not have enough men to move their trains, but one of the reasons they could not get men was because their examinations, both physical and book of rules were too stiff for some of the fellows, for down there you had to go before two doctors in those days, one for physical, and the other for eyesight and hearing test, and I am telling you that a fellow could not go down there in those days and kid them old Southern doctors into passing him. Nooo Saah; neveah could be done, and if a man was lucky enough to pass the doctahs, then he had to fill out a book of five hundred questions by writing out the answers to them, pertaining to the book of rules, and time card, in regards to train orders, movement of trains, and the proper understanding of semaphore signals, interlocking plants, and electric block systems, but as my brother Tom and I both had worked in and out of Chicago and St. Louis where we had learned all of this stuff, it was much easier for us than for some of the boys that had never got up against these things before.

Now I remember at that time there were about five or six of us boys over in the railroad Y.M.C.A. filling out our books, and it sure was comical to hear all of us ask each other questions. One guy would say, or rather would ask of another fellow, say what is the color of a transverse stripe on a home signal semaphore arm of an interlocking system? and then another fellow would ask, what does it mean by saying that a semaphore arm is depressed to an angle of forty-five degrees and another fellow would ask, say for the love of mike, what is a pot signal? and that is the way it went, gee, it was too funny for anything.

Well when my brother and I got our books filled out, we took them over to the trainmaster's office, and the chief clerk gave us an order to go and draw our lanterns and to be marked up on the extra board, and he also gave us our switch keys and brakemen's badges, then we got hold of the call boy and told him where he could find us as we were stopping at the Y.M.C.A. (better known as the Y) so we both got out that night, my brother on a stock extra, and I was called to deadhead on a passenger train to Cleburne[28] the next division point north of Temple, to take another brakeman's place on No. 33, a fast freight run the next day, and I held that car for about ten days until the regular man reported back for duty, then I caught another car braking behind for an old skipper that wore long whiskers, and he told me that he come from Tennessee. He says yassuh ah done been out heah in Texas a right smaht while, ah come out heah right aftah the wah, and ah been heah evah since.

Well I broke for this old skipper all through the stock rush, and I remember that they used to run us west out of Temple on the San Angelo branch most of the time, for that was where the most of the cattle were loaded, out at the end of the line, there at San Angelo, for the Santa Fe was the only road that run into there at that time.[29]

Now I was told by some of the old timers there that this little town of San Angelo had been a wild and wooly place back in the early days, for it was located right on the eastern edge of the great Panhandle cattle country, and I saw a good many wild rough ridin', rootin' tootin' cow-punchers there yet in 1906, for boy, when they were paid off after one of those big shipping roundups, they sure did crave their liquor, and when they got all likkered up, it seemed that about the only thing that they could remember was how to shoot off their big sixshooters and holler whoopee, ride 'em cowboy, ride 'em.

Now there in Temple the saloon keepers had the space all fenced in back of their saloon with a high board fence, and we railroad men would set around in these inclosures after payday, and form into little groups and rush the can, and talk and tell stories, and of course at such times there were always drunken brawls and fist fights, so one morning a friend of mine, an Irish lad by the name of Johnnie Johnston (who also had been sent from Chicago) met me in one of the saloons and he says come on Brownie, let's chip in and buy a can of beer, and I says O.K. I'll go you one, so while we were talking, there was another brakeman by the name of Martin who was pretty well likkered up, and he wanted to butt into our party, and help lap up our can of beer, but Johnnie told him nothing doing, so we took our can of beer and went out in back and set down on one of the benches, and while we were setting there talking and drinking, Martin walked out to where we were and started to pick an argument, so Johnnie told him to go on away for we did not want to be bothered, and Martin took it as an insult, so he pulled a .38 sixshooter out of his pocket and says listen bo, I come from Kentucky where they fight with guns, and he took a shot at Johnnie, but as Johnnie was jumping up at the time Martin shot, he missed him, and by that time Johnnie was on his feet, and he says why you son of a biscuit eater, I came from Chicago where they fight with their fist, and biff bang, Johnnie caught Martin with a left hook to the jaw, and then with a right swing to the old chin button, and down he went for the count, and as quick as a flash, Johnnie grabbed the gun out of Martin's hand and stuck it inside his shirt, as we beat it out of the back gate, just before the cops came rushing through the saloon (now this all happened lots faster than I am telling it) and by ducking through the alleys, Johnnie and I got back to the Y (Y.M.C.A.) and went up to my room and locked the door, and after planting the gun in my bed clothes, we went back downstairs again, and some of the boys that came in later, told us that the cops tried to make Martin tell who fired the shot and what had become of the gun, but all Martin would say was that he did not know, and as luck would have it, the call boy called Johnnie that night to deadhead to Summerville,[30] a little burg about seventy-five miles south of there to switch in the yards, so Johnnie put the gun in his suitcase and took it with him.

Well I worked out of Temple up until about the middle of July, when the stock rush was over, and the company began to pull off crews and I lost my old conductor from Tennessee with the long brown whiskers, and I was marked up on the extra board again, and one morning the call boy called me and told me to report to the trainmaster's office, which I did, and the chief clerk says Brownie we are going to cut the board and lay off a bunch of boys, but we need a man to go down to Summerville to switch nights in the main line yards and as you are the oldest extra man that is to be cut off the board I thought maybe you might want to go down there to a regular job of switching, and I ask him if Johnnie Johnston was still down there? and he says why yes, do you know Johnston? And I says yes, he is a friend of mine, so the clerk says yes Johnston has got charge of the night engine down there and if you go down there you will be one of his helpers, then I says all right I'll go, so he fixed me up with a pass, and I went back over to the Y, and throwed what few things I had into my little old O.R.C.[31] traveling bag and caught No. 3,[32] and deadheaded down to Summerville. When we arrived there about 4 P.M. in the afternoon I got off the train and asked one of the natives there if he knew the yardmaster? and what kind of looking fellow was he? so he says to me, well suh when yo'all see a big fat fahmary looking fellah with a big longhaon mustache, and wearing a big straw hat, that's him, so I laughed to myself and started to walk over to the yard office, but on the way I met old Tom Brooks, the yard master, and I knew him right away by the description that the native had given me, and I stopped and says to him, are you Mr. Tom Brooks the yardmaster? and he sort of swelled up and says yassuh, that's me, and then I says to him, well they sent me down from Temple to help you out in the yards a couple of nights, then he blowed all up and says, a couple o'nights heck, I wants a man heah for evah, and then he says to me, are yoall a switchman? and I says no I am a brakeman, and he bursted out with a string of oaths, and says, when them blankity blank dad blame fools, I tole them to send me some switchmens down heah, them crazy fools sends yoall bomeah brakmens down heah and yoall stays about foah nights, then yoall are done gone yondah, so I laughed and told him that I might stay longer than four nights if the job was any good, and he says all right, repote fo work at six o'clock this evenen, then I ask him if he knew where I could get a room? and he says why yas, mah sistah keeps roomeahs. So he gave me the address and directions how to get to his sister's place, and when I got up there I told her that her brother the yardmaster had sent me to her to rent a room, as I was going to work nights in the yards, and she says yas I have just got one room left and yoall kin have it, which will cost yoall two dollahs a week, and I told her all right that I would take it, then she called one of the negro servants who showed me upstairs to the room, and that evening I went down to the Harvey House[33] for supper, and I met my friend Johnnie Johnston and we were glad to see each other again, and he told me that I was to work with him as one of his helpers, and I told him that suited me just fine.

Now this little burg of Summerville was where the Beaumont branch left the main line and run off down to the Beaumont Texas Oil Fields, and the lumber country which was called the sticks by the natives,[34] and about all they hauled on this branch was oil and lumber, and much of the oil that come in off of the Branch was used as fuel oil for the Santa Fe engines, for all down through Oklahoma and Texas their engines were oil burners, and it was down there that I saw my first oil burning engine, and I promised myself right there if I ever fired another engine, it would have to be an oil burner. (I will tell later on in another chapter of firing the big oil burners out of Needles, Calif., across the great Mojave Desert.) For setting up there on the seatbox regulating the fire with a firing valve sure did beat standing down on the deck shoveling coal into an old battleship, as fast as the hoghead could throw it out of her.

Now they worked five engines there on the day shift at Summerville, and four of them worked in the private yards of the big creosoting plant there, where they creosoted most of the lumber that was brought up out of the sticks, and the fifth engine worked in the main line yards, breaking up and making up both branch and main line trains. The daylight crews were all home guards, natives that had been raised right around there in that part of the country, and the hoghead and tallowpot on the night switch engine were also natives, but we three switchmen on the night engine were boomers, for it seemed like the native yardmen did not like to switch cars at night (and I did not blame them either for I never fancied it myself) so I guess that is why they always had to use boomers on the night engine, for Johnnie and a little boomer from El Paso, Texas, and I were the only boomers there, and we three boomers sort of kept poor old Tom Brooks the yardmaster in hot water, for he was afraid that we might throw our lanterns up against the side of a box car any night and walk off the job, and leave him with the yards all blocked, for that used to be sort of a failing of the boomer switchmen in those days when they would get their snoots full of squirrel whiskey[35] and take a sudden notion to move on to some other part of the country.

Now I remember while I was switching there in Summerville, that there was a cute little blue-eyed blonde blowed into town one day, and she was a boomer Harvey House hash-slinger,[36] and they put her in the lunch room at nights to dish out the hash to hungry rough necks, that is we night yardmen and the train crews that were always passing through, and she went by the name of Billie, and boy, believe me, Billie was some gogetter. Why the business at the night lunch counter picked up one hundred per cent after Billie got on the job, for the grouchy old waiter that was on nights before she came, failed to click with the boys for some cause or other.

Now Billie was there with the salve, and she was an artist when it come to spreading it too, for the way she had of handing out the bushwah to each and every one of us poor bums was enough to make a guy fight his own daddy. Gee, but she sure was pretty, with big blue eyes and wavy, blonde hair (and it was not drug store blonde either), and that peaches and cream complexion that you like to touch, and a figure that would make the Venus de Milo look like some starved to death flapper who was trying to reduce. Her great success with all of us poor saps, lay in the manner by which she smothered each poor boob with a lotta corral dust, that made him think that he was just about ten jumps ahead of the rest of the mob in her favor, why she even had the young native hicks that never came into the lunch room before lined up at the old feed trough every night eating pie and coffee, or ice cream and cake, for boy, when it come to drumming up trade at the lunch counter she was a knockout, no foolin' but after she had been there for about six weeks they shifted her to some place else along the line, for she was a boomer, and like railroad men, she kept jumping around from one Harvey House to another all over the Harvey system which covered the Santa Fe and the Frisco system.

Now I remember one beautiful moonlight night while I was switching there in the yards at Summerville, we were weighing cars of lumber over the big track scales along about 9 P.M. in the evening, when one of the boys that switched there in the yards in the daytime, came over and told us to look out for Sharp (who was another daylight switchman), for he was over at one of the saloons all likkered up, and that he had a sixshooter, and was popping off his mouth that he was out gunning for Johnnie Johnston, so Johnston thanked the other switchman, and told him that we would keep a look out for Mr. Sharp, then Johnnie slipped over to his room in a boarding house nearby, to get his gun (that is, the one that he took away from Brakeman Martin that time there in Temple back of the saloon, when Martin took a shot at him,) but when he got up into his room he found that somebody had dumped everything out of his suitcase, and the gun was gone, and as Sharp lived there in the same boarding house, we figured that it was Johnnie's own gun that Sharp was out gunning with.

Now the whole trouble between these two young fellows was over a pretty little biscuit-shooter who dished out the garbage to the roughnecks over at the boarding house, where they both roomed, and this fellow by the name of Sharp was a native Texas boy, who was sweet on this little hasher, and he had been stepping out with her before Johnnie blowed into town, but after Johnnie appeared on the scene, she gave Mr. Sharp the air, and now she was stepping out sometimes with Johnnie, so it seems like Sharp had picked this beautiful night to steal Johnnie's gun, and after getting all pepped up with a fighting jag, tells everybody in the saloon that he is going over in the train yards gunning for Johnston.

Well it was not very long after the other fellow had told us until here comes Mr. Sharp, and we could see that he had the gun stuck inside of his shirt, for he did not wear any coat, so he walked up to about ten feet of where we were working, and then he says listen I want to talk to you Johnston, so Johnston set down his lantern and walked out to where Sharp was standing, and stood there with his arms folded, and asked Sharp what he wanted, then Sharp started in to calling Johnnie all of the dirty names that he could think of, and cussing him out something fierce so Johnnie finally says to Sharp, listen I know that you have got my gun there inside your shirt, but if you will lay it down I'll tear your can off, but Sharp kept on cussing Johnnie, and I knew that he would not stand for this much longer before he took a swing at Sharp, and that was just what Sharp was playing for, so that he would have an excuse to take a shot at Johnnie, so I swung my lantern and gave the engineer a stop signal, then I walked out to where the two boys were standing, and I says Sharp what in the heck is the matter with you. He started to tell me that it was none of my dang business, but before he could finish, I had caught him off his guard, and I swung my big heavy Santa Fe skeleton lantern, bringing it down on top of is head with an awful bang, breaking the glass globe in many pieces. But the blow did not knock him down, so he jerked the gun out from under his shirt, but before he could use it, I grabbed the gun barrel in my right hand, and his right wrist with my left hand, and wrenched the gun out of his hand, but he handed me a nice left hook on the jaw for my pains, and at the same time Johnnie landed on his jaw with a right swing that sent him down on his back. But boy, he was one tough baby, and he bounced right up again almost like a rubber ball, but as Johnnie had done some fighting in the ring while he lived in Chicago, he was pretty clever, and as Sharp rushed at him, he caught Sharp with a left hook to the jaw, then he clipped him with a terrific right swing on the chin, and down Sharp went again, and before he could get up, Johnnie used some more Chicago tactics, by putting the boots to him, for he kicked him and jumped on him until Sharp was out for the count. In the meantime I was standing there holding the gun in my hand, and before I realized what had happened Johnnie had grabbed the gun out of my hand and was kneeling down on one knee taking aim at Sharp's head, and was saying you blankity blank son of a biscuit eater, you tried to kill me, now I am going to kill you, and for a moment that seemed like ages the ghastly sight froze me in my tracks, and I seemed unable to move, but finally I came out of it, and jumped and kicked the gun out of Johnnie's hand before he pulled the the trigger, and the other switchman, the little boomer from El Paso, grabbed the gun up and ejected the bullets out of the cylinder before Johnnie could get it again.

Now this all happened a danged site quicker than I am telling it, and by this time old Tom Brooks who happened to be over in the yard office, came running over with some more of the boys, and Johnnie says to him, listen Brooks you take that gun and keep it, for this makes the second man that has come gunning for me with it, and the next one might get me. So old Brooks took the gun and put it in his pocket, then he and some other boys got Sharp upon his feet, and helped him over to his room, and put him to bed, and he was unable to go to work for a couple of days. In the meantime old Brooks had been talking to him, and showed him where he was in the wrong, so one evening a short time after that, he came over to where Johnnie and I were sitting on a bench just outside of the switch shanty, and he says, hello there Johnnie, I want to apologize for what I tried to do to you the other night, and to prove to you that I am shooting on the square, here is my hand, so Johnnie shook hands with him, and told Sharp that he was sorry too for what had happened and that he was willing to let by-gones be bygones, if Sharp looked at it that way. Then Sharp turned to me with a big grin on his face, and says, gee Brownie you shore did give me an awful wallop over the head with your lamp that night, and I says to him well that was no love tap you give me when you socked me in the jaw either, and we both laughed, and he says well I realize now that it was the only thing for you to do, for the chances are that the wallop saved our lives, for I might have shot Johnston and then I would have got the rope. So then I says, I am sorry that I had to hang my lamp on your head, but I figured that was about the only washout signal that would stop you, so in that case I lived up to the book of rules, and played safety first, then we all had a good laugh, and everything was jake, and we were all good friends after that.

Now this little burg of Summerville was mostly made up of negroes, and the Santa Fe system used negroes for brakemen running out of there on the Beaumont branch, and as these negro brakemen got in lots of overtime, they pulled down pretty good money each payday, and the way they and their wives put on the dog, and strutted their stuff around town there among the other coons was some show to look at.

And as a rule you could take a bundle of laundry to almost any of the negro cabins and get them to do your washing, ironing, and mending for about two bits a bundle, so one day I took my bundle of laundry over to a cabin and knocked on a door, and pretty soon it was opened by a well dressed colored lady, and I says to her, why I just brought my laundry over to see if I could get you to do some washing and ironing for me, and she swelled all up and says to me, why youall will hafto scuse me mistah, for I doan takes in no washin', and then I says in a tone of surprise, you don't? Why I thought most all of the colored women took in washing around here, and then she says, why ah cain't hahdly git nobody to do mah washin', and I says do you mean to tell me that you don't do your own washing? And then she puffed up like a toad as she says, Noo, ah never does mah washin', why mah husband is a railroad man, he is a brakes-man on the Santa Fee, then I says please excuse me for I did not know that, and then she smiled and says, Oh dats all right, evah body makes mistakes.

Well one payday the little boomer from El Paso that worked with us got all stewed up like a boiled owl and bunched the job, so old Tom Brooks wired to Temple for another switchman, and they sent another boomer down there to work with us, and he was an old fellow by the name of Doyal, a tall rangy longhorn (native of Texas) who told Johnnie and I that he had worked as a cowpuncher out in the Panhandle cow country when he was a young fellow, and then he said after that he had joined up with the noted Texas Rangers[37] and served with them for some time, then he went railroading, and had been booming around over the country ever since, so Johnnie and I nicknamed him old Fuzz, for he never shaved, but still he did not have long heavy whiskers, but instead his face was covered with a layer of curly, fuzzy hair.

Well I switched cars there in Summerville up until the last part of Oct., 1906, when my feet got to itching to go rambling again, so I told Johnnie that I had made up my mind to bunch the job and be on my way, for I was getting too much money ahead, to stay any longer, as I had saved up a stake of about one hundred and fifty dollars, and now I was too rich to keep on working, so old Tom Brooks got me a pass to Galveston, Texas,[38] and I went down there and layed around for a while and enjoyed myself bathing at the beach and having a good time in general, and after playing around Galveston for a while, I took a notion into my head that I would like to take an ocean trip, so I bought me a ticket for New York City, which cost me forty dollars first class, and went aboard the steamship Denver of the Mallory line[39] and started on my way to the big town.

Now everything went fine and dandy, until the second day out of Galveston, when we were away out there in the Gulf of Mexico, we run into a bad storm, and boy, I began to think my time had come, at first I was scared almost stiff, for I was afraid that the old tub was going to sink, but after a short time I got so deathly seasick that I just layed in my bunk and heaved up my insides, and just about that time I did not give a dang if the old scow did sink, for boy, I had never felt such a sicky sickness before in my whole life, and just the thought of something to eat made me feed the fishes all the more.

Well the next day after the storm had passed I was up on the promenade deck, and I was feeling pretty tough too, for my stomach was so weak and felt so funny, that I did not care much about anything, and while I was standing by the rail looking down into the blue, blue water, another passenger came up to me and ask me how I felt, and I says oh I feel pretty rotten, and then he says to me do you know what would be good to settle your stomach and make you feel better, and I says no, what is it, then he says, why a nice big piece of good fat bacon, and man oh man, I thought my stomach would turn inside out. Oh boy, but I sure was sick, and this fellow beat it away from me and joined his friends, and they got a big kick and a good laugh out of it, but I'll tell the cockeyed world it was no laughing matter to me, for the kick in my stomach right then had just about kicked me out. Gee, what a funny feeling seasickness is.

Well, by the time we reached Key West[40] I was feeling lots better, and I remembered while they were getting the ship up to the docks, we passengers lined the rails and throwed small coins down into the water just to see the young native boys dive for them, and boy, those kids were regular human fish, and it sure was some sight to see them dive and swim around in that water, so after they got the ship docked, I went ashore to get a drink of beer, and I asked a U.S. sailor standing there on the dock which way it was to the nearest saloon, and he showed me where to go right around a corner, and man, I sure got all slopped up on beer before I went back to the ship, which was getting ready to pull out, after which we left Key West and proceeded on our way to the big burg [New York], but I remember that I got pretty seasick again, and if I remember right, I think they said we were just off a place called Cape Hatteras [North Carolina]. Well anyway it was pretty stormy and the water was rough, so one evening we were all down to dinner, and I remember that the first officer of the ship who was a big red faced Irishman, sat at the head of my table and as my stomach was still pretty weak yet, it almost queered me from eating just to listen to that guy give the waiter his order, for just the thoughts of meat turned my stomach, so just about the time that I began to mince around a little bit, the front end of the ship went away up higher over a big wave, and then went away down again, and man oh man, you should have saw the stampede. I will swear that all of one half of the people in that dining room made one grand rush for the stairway, all trying to get up on the deck at once, and boy, I think I was leading the herd, and in a few seconds the rail was all lined up, and we were all feeding the fishes, and about all I lived on after that until we got into New York was fruit, tea, and beef broth, and I felt and looked like I had been on a hunger strike for some time.

Well we finally pulled into the big town, and I sure was glad too, for I will have to confess that I was a bum sailor, and seven days and nights on that old tub was enough for me, and I remember getting off of the danged thing I seemed to roll and pitch, and stagger around on my feet for a couple of days before I got right again.

Now I remember while we were coming up through what is called the upper New York Bay, we met a great steamship going out to sea, and if I remember right she was the Majestic of the White Star Line, [41] and boy, she sure was a big one or anyway that was the way she looked to me and I remember of seeing many other sights at that time, the great Statue of Liberty and the Brooklyn Bridge was two of them, for I remember that our ship docked some place in the east river almost under the Brooklyn Bridge, or rather just south of the west end of the bridge on the New York side.

Chapter VII

Well after landing I went up to the old Grand Central Y.M.C.A. which if I remember right was located at the corner of Fourth Ave and Forty-third street, right near the old Grand Central Station. Well anyway when I went into the Y.M.C.A. I showed the clerk at the desk my Y.M.C.A. membership card and registered for that night, and the next day I walked around in the neighborhood of Times Square at Forty-second street and Broadway, and took in a couple of good shows and many other sights. That night when I went back to the Y.M.C.A. to get a room for the night they had an English London Cockney there as a sort of night clerk and bed maker and all around flunky, and when I told him I wanted to get a room, he says to me why you stayed here last night, and I says sure, but what difference does that make? Why we have a rule here that a party can only stay every other night, and as you stayed here last night, you are not entitled to a room here tonight. And I says what is the big idea, then he says we have to save some room for the Pullman car conductors, that runs in here on passenger, and then I asked him if these Pullman conductors had these rooms rented by the month, and he said no, but we save them rooms anyway, and I says to him, say listen English, I don't care anything about these Pullman skippers, for I carry a railroad Y.M.C.A. membership card, and I know what I am entitled to, for I know in the Y.M.C.A.'s it's first come first served, unless a guy has got his room rented by the month, and my membership card is good at any and all railroad Y.M.C.A.'s at all times. And he says well I can't help that for the rooms are all reserved, and I says where do you get that stuff, and just how much jack are you getting out of these Pullman Johnnies for holding out these rooms for them. And he tried to tell me that he was not getting any side money, but I says listen Johnnie Bull, can the bushwah, for you can't slip anything like that over on me, as I have had it tried on me before, for I have lived and slept in more railroad Y.M.C.A.'s than you ever heard of, and I know my rights, and no English flunky is going to tell me where to head in at. So after I called his hand good and plenty, he gave me a room, for he saw that I was wise to his little game, and I never had any more trouble with him after that, for I got a room any time I wanted it.

Well after I had been there in New York City for about a week and took in some of the sights, I went up to the New York Central trainmaster's office at the Seventy-second St. yards,[1] there near the Riverside Park, and got a job of braking between there and Albany on the Hudson division of the New York Central Lines, which was a four track system that run right along the east banks of the Hudson River all the way.[2]

Now I was running on fast freight which was known at that time as A.R. One,[3] going north out of the City, and A.N. Six[4] coming back from Albany, and we only made one stop on that whole one hundred and forty-five mile division, and that was at Poughkeepsie[5] to take coal, for we scooped our water on the fly from long narrow troughs in the center of the tracks, and all the fireman had to do on these runs when he wanted to fill up the tank with water, was just to open up a small air valve which dropped a scoop down into the trough to pick up the water caused by the speed of the engine, and the scoop was connected to a pipe which conveyed the water up and dumped it in at the back end of the tank.

Now these fast runs that I was braking on were all through freight, and we never had to stop to set out or pick up cars on this Hudson division, for they had peddler runs that did not do anything else but pick up and set out, and the fast through freight runs used the passenger track on this four track system which were the two outside tracks, and the two inside tracks were for freight trains. Now I remember when we used to leave New York City at the Seventy-second St. yards on A.R. One, all we got was a clearance card, and after that all we had to do was to follow the clear paddles, as we called the semaphore signal arms, when they were set to give us a clear track, and we would go sailing along on the passenger running track until a fast passenger train got too close behind us, then they would cross us over onto the freight running track without stopping us and we would run right along on this track until the passenger train overtook us and passed us then they would cross us back again to the passenger track and let us follow the passenger train.

Now this crossing us over from one track to the other without stopping, was all done by the aid of the operators in the block towers[6] along the route, for the train dispatcher did not handle his trains by train orders, but done all of his train dispatching through his operators in the block and signal towers, who set all of the switches and lined the derails and crossovers of the interlocking systems, and also set the proper semaphore signals that governed the routes that the trains had to follow, and this was all done from the tower houses along the whole route, as the whole system was interlocking and electrically controlled.

Now we would come sailing along and maybe when we came to a signal tower, there would be a yellow light or a yellow semaphore arm displayed at the position of caution, which ever it happened to be day or night, and we knew by seeing these caution signals displayed, that we were going to be crossed over at the next block tower, and when we arrived there we would find the cross over all lined up and the signals set at proceed and we would slow down just enough to take the cross over at a safe speed.

Now the most of those fast passenger trains in those days made that one hundred and forty- five mile run over the Hudson division in about two hours and forty-five minutes without a stop,[7] as near as I can remember from the schedules in the employes' official time card, as they scooped their water on the fly and the one tank of coal was enough to take them through, and I have been told by some of the firemen on those fast runs, that they never left the deck to climb upon their seatboxes to sit down for a moment, for they were kept busy shoveling coal into the roaring hot fire box in order to keep the engine hot so that the engineer could make the time, and the best they got was to step to one side of the gangway and suck in a few breaths of cool air between fires, until they reached the end of their runs.

Now about all the brakemen had to do on these fast freight runs was to set up there and ride, except when we stopped at Poughkeepsie, and while the fireman was taking coal, we brakemen had to look our trains over for hot boxes, and to see if everything was running all right, and although it was true that we brakemen did not have much to do, it was also true that we did not get much at that time for doing it, for in those days we only got two dollars and seventy cents for making that one hundred and forty-five miles, or five dollars and forty cents for the round trip. Of course I know that they get more than that there now, but the time I am speaking about was away back in 1906, and the difference between the eastern roads at that time and the western roads was that the most of the eastern roads paid by the trip or so much a month, while the western roads paid mileage and overtime except on some of their passenger runs.

Now you very seldom saw a boomer working on the eastern roads, for the railroad men in those days held down their jobs pretty well, and I had some of the boys that I worked with while I was there to tell me they did not understand how I got a job there, as I was a western boomer, for they had never heard of the New York Central hiring an experienced man before. I remember of working partners with one brakeman there, who told me that he had been braking there for sixteen years, and his regular partner who was laying off, and whose place I was taking had been there twelve years as a brakeman, but I suppose it is different there now in these days, but at that time I found those old timers to be a fine set of fellows, and most all of them were good brotherhood men too, and they were always ready to give a boomer a feed and a lift anytime that he was traveling through and ask them for a favor, I know, for they carried me and they fed me.

Now I remember once while I was there, they deadheaded me up to a place called Croton on the Hudson[8] to work on a work train, which tied up there every night, and we used to come down as far as Tarrytown[9] and pick up a string of loads, and take them back up to a place between Ossining[10] and Croton where the New York Central Company was building a big electric power plant, and when we passed through Ossining I could stand on top of a box car and look over the walls into the prison yards of the great Sing Sing prison that you read and hear so much about.

Well after I worked there in the road service for some time, they transferred me into yard service along the Harlem River at One Hundred and Fifty-fifth St. near what was called High Bridge, north of Monthaven Junction and boy, I want to tell you right here that they had more ways of killing a man there in those yards than any other yards that I ever switched cars in, no foolin'. I thought Green River, Wyo., and the St. Louis Terminal was bad enough, but this New York Central yard had anything skinned that I had ever seen or heard of.

Now in the first place not only the main line tracks but all of the yard tracks were too close together, for if a man happened to be hanging onto or climbing up a side ladder of a car, he was in danger of being swiped off by something projecting out from a passing train or another car, such as the big wooden false stakes that is used on flat cars loaded with lumber, or open doors on reefers, and if a man was riding on top of a boxcar, there were many things to look out for, such as low bridges of streets that went over the top of the tracks, and also some of the local passenger stations that were built up over the tracks, of course I suppose those things are all changed by now, and again there were the big steel third rails, that carried hundreds of volts of electric current, from which the new big electric locomotives and the electric trains took their juice, and these third rails hung suspended on goose-neck brackets, which were bolted down on the ends of the cross ties, and stood up about sixteen inches above the track and the tops and sides were covered with a wooden shield about one inch thick, but the bottoms were bare, for the electric locomotives and the local passenger trains made contact with the bottom of the third rails through sliding shoes instead of [overhead] trolleys, and a man sure had to be careful when he swung down off a moving train or engine, so as to not get tangled up with those third rails, for if he happened to fall or slip under the rail and make contact with it and the ground, it was just too bad, for it sure meant a halo and a harp for him that's all.

Now I remember one cold rainy day while I was switching there, I had on a pair of shoes with brass tacks in the soles, and I stepped upon top of the wooden shield that covered the third rail which was wet, and reached over and took hold of the pinlifter to make a cut, and man oh man, when I took hold of that piece of iron, I thought I had been struck with lightning, for enough current leaked through the wet covering of the third rail and the brass tacks in my shoes to give me an awful shock when I took hold of the iron lever which grounded me, and it knocked me back into the middle of the next track, and although I was not hurt I sure was almost scared out of my wits. And there was another time that a gang of Italian trackmen were working nearby, and one of them let one end of the lining bar that he had in his hands come in contact with the underside of the rail, and it killed him right now, and the iron bar fell from his hands across one of the track rails, and it was melted just like a piece of solder.

Now while I was braking in the yards as they call switching there, I lived in the railroad Y.M.C.A. at Monthaven Junction, and one night while I was setting in one of the lounging rooms reading a book, I overheard a yard brakeman talking to a rough looking fellow, and from the tone of their conversation, I took the tough looking guy to be a member of the great noted Lake Shore gang, a bunch of crooks and thieves that operated on the New York Central and Lake Shore & Michigan Southern,[11] in those days, all the way between New York and Chicago, and it was said that the gang was made up of underworld crooks, railroad men, and railroad detectives, but they were so well organized that it was almost impossible to catch any of them, for it was also said that they would not hesitate to murder a man if he got in their way. I was told that members of the gang would be planted in the cars while they were being loaded there at the docks on the North River [in New York], and while the train was speeding along through the country on its way, at certain places along the route, these crooks would open the doors and throw out the most valuable merchandise, and some other members would be there with wagons or trucks to pick it up and take it away, then other members of the gang would dispose of it.

Now I remember the first trip that I made out of New York City on a fast merchandise train known in those days as A.R. One, the conductor told me before we pulled out of the Seventy-second yards, that when we stopped at Poughkeepsie to take coal, for me to look the train over, but if I saw any tough looking guys hanging around the train, for me to just go on about my business and let them alone, for if they were members of the Lake Shore gang, and I tried to interfere with them, they might sap me on the bean and dump me into the Hudson River, and believe me any time I was looking the train over I never bothered any body, for I was only pulling down two dollars and seventy cents a trip for doing a job of braking, and not catching members of the Lake Shore gang, for from all I heard about them, they sure were a lot of tough hard-boiled yeggs.

Well I worked there for the New York Central all winter, and up until about the middle of March 1907, when I bunched the job and headed back for the west, and I remember that I rode with different train crews over the N.Y.C. in their cabooses until I reached Buffalo, then I stopped for a day and took a run up to Niagara Falls, and I want to say right here that those Falls were one of the most wonderful sights that I ever saw in my whole life. I will not try to describe it for I can't, but I remember that I stood there at a place that they called Lovers' Leap, and I was so fascinated by watching the falling water pouring over that cliff that I could not understand the funny feeling that crept over me, then I went across over on the Island, and took a good look at the big Horse Shoe falls on the Canadian side, and I sure would not have missed seeing the Niagara Falls for anything.

Well I came on back down to Buffalo, and that evening I took a lake steamer on Lake Erie and crossed over to Cleveland where I arrived the next morning, and the next day after I left Cleveland I landed in Danville, Ill.,[12] where my folks now lived, for my stepfather had sold out his tin and plumbing shop in Hoopeston and they had all moved down to Danville, where they and my brother Tom and his wife and baby were all living together and brother Tom was braking out of there on the C.&E.I. road between Danville and Chicago.

And a few days after I landed in Danville my brother Tom took me over to the trainmaster's office and introduced me to the chief clerk, and he gave me a job of braking right on the spot, for they were needing men at the time, and the chief clerk sort of broke the company rule by putting me on the same car with brother Tom, and we broke partners for a boomer conductor by the name of Charlie Keatly (which was not his right name for he was working under a flag on phoney references) and he liked Tom and I for we were boomers like himself, and he was a doubleheader too, for he belonged to the big O's and the B. of R.T. both and believe me he was some guy, and I got a big kick out of him, for one of his outdoor sports while out on the road was that of fighting with the engineers that happened to be pulling us. Gee, that guy would rather kick up a rumpus with a hoghead than to eat when he was hungry.

Now one trip when we were going north on an extra with a drag of coal, my brother Tom had layed off a round trip, and we had an extra man on the head end in his place, and after we had got quite a ways up the line, it seems like the coal was getting back so far that the fireman could not reach it very easy any more, so the hoghead told this extra brakeman to get upon the tank and shovel down some coal for the fireman, but the head shack told him nothing doing, for if he wanted to shovel coal he would have got a job of firing instead of braking, then the hogger told him that he would shovel down coal or get off, for no shack could ride on HIS engine unless they shoveled down coal, so when we headed in at a little place called Wellington[13] for No. 4,[14] the head man dropped back and caught the caboose, and Keatly asked him why he did not stay over ahead so that he could head us out as soon as No. 4 went, and the brakeman told Keatly that the hogger had made him get off because he would not shovel down coal for the tallowpot, and man oh man, that was all Keatly wanted to hear, and he started beating it right over to the engine. And of course we brakemen tagged along after him for we wanted to see the fun, and when we all got over to the head end, Keatly asked the hoghead what was the big idea of telling the brakeman that he could not ride on the engine? and the engineer says to Keatly, well any time a brakeman refuses to shovel down coal, he don't ride on MY engine, and then Keatly says YOUR engine? why I thought that the engine belonged to the company, but if it belongs to you, I will cut it off and send for one of the company's engines, so then he told the head man to cut the engine off, and he started over to the telegraph office, and the hogger who was already down on the ground started to follow him, and kept asking him what he was going to do? and Keatly told him that he was going to send a message to the train dispatcher and tell him to send one of the Company's engines to pull us on into Dalton Yards[15] at Chicago, for the engine that was pulling us now belonged to the engineer, and he refused to let the head brakeman ride on HIS engine. Boy, you should have heard that hoghead beg, and he had a heck of a time trying to talk old Keatly out of it too, and he, the hogger, told Keatly if he would not send the message, that he would shovel down the coal himself for his fireman, and Keatly says all right if you will let my brakeman ride on your engine the rest of the trip we will call it square, and as No. 4 was showing up I went up ahead to be ready to open the switch as soon as she went, while the head man coupled the engine back to the train, and soon as No. 4 went by we pulled out, and boy, I sure had a good laugh, for it was too funny for anything, but everything was jake on the head end for the rest of that trip.

Now this conductor Keatly that my brother Tom and I were braking for was pretty hard boiled with the engineers, but he was a prince of a fellow with us boys, and he would always carry a brotherhood man on his caboose, and feed him, and if the fellow was broke, he would slip him a piece of change. I remember one trip we were going south out of Dalton yards with a long drag of empty coal cars, and it was after dark when we reached Chicago Heights,[16] and while we were pulling up through the city an air-hose blowed out some place along in the train, which set the brakes and stopped us, and we had about three or four of the street crossings blocked, and the street traffic was all tied up, and the City cops there at Chicago Heights were hard boiled and hostile toward the train crews when they blocked the street crossings very long, and in some cases they had pinched the train conductors and took them over to jail and made them pay a fine before they would let them go. So on this occasion when we stopped so long, before my brother Tom who was the head man could find the leak in the train-line and put on a new air-hose, the City bulls were right over there raising all kinds of heck, and one big flannel mouth flatfoot was running all around there asking everybody if they had seen the train conductor, for . . . he would be after runnin' him in if he could find him, and Keatly the conductor had doused his glim (put out his lantern) and hid it in one of the empty cars, and then he took his conductor's badge off his cap, and put it in his pocket, and he was running around there raising all kinds of heck helping the Irish cop to find the conductor, and I sure got a good kick out of it when Keatly and Tom told me about it afterwards, as I did not know what was going on up ahead for I had to stay back and flag.

Now this Keatly sure was some booze hound, and if there was anything that he liked better than booze, it was more booze. I remember a story some of the other boys told to me about Keatly getting canned. Of course I was braking for him at the time but I did not see what happened, but I will tell it as I heard it. Now it seems as though that old Keatly went down town there in Danville and got pretty well likkered up, then he went into a Jew [clothing] store and bought his wife a house dress, after which he went back into a saloon and got a quart bottle of booze, to take home with him, and he had wooled the package that his wife's dress was done up in, around so much that the string and paper had come off, so he thought about the best way to carry it to keep from losing it was to put it on, which he did. That is he slipped the dress on over his clothes, and took the quart bottle of booze by the neck in one hand and got on the street car and started for home, and this car run up to the Junction which was the end of the line, and while on the car Keatly had one heck of a time, for he was wanting some of the C.&E.I. boys that were on the street car to drink with him, and he was a regular show, and kept all of the passengers hollering and laughing, and when the car reached the end of the line and stopped, it was right in front of the main office building of the C.&E.I. road, and Keatly got off still wearing the dress and carrying the bottle of booze by the neck, and he run right square into old man Huffman, the C.&E.I. trainmaster, who had just come out of the office building, and as Keatly did not know what else to do, he offered old man Huffman a drink out of his bottle, but that was his finish, for old man Huffman called him in the next day and tied a can on him.

Well when Keatly got fired, that left our car vacant for a conductor, and there was an old conductor by the name of Dave Wheeler who was assigned to the car, and although he had a few funny ways of his own, he was not a bad old fellow to brake for.

Now the C.&E.I. was principally a coal road, and had branches scattered all around here and there, which went to the different coal fields around through that part of the country, and when we chain gang crews left Danville our home division, sometimes we would be gone a week or ten days, before we would get back home again, for we would go to Dalton Yards just out of Chicago with a drag of coal, and then instead of going back to Danville, maybe they would send us down the Brazil branch with a long drag of empty coal cars, for the mines at Brazil, Ind.,[17] and then we would get a drag of coal for Chicago and go back to Dalton.

Well after we got into Dalton Yards again, the chances would be that when we were called again we would be sent down the St. Louis branch with a drag of empties to Villa Grove,[18] and then we would have to take our turn out of there, and get a drag of coal and go back to Dalton Yards again, and if we were lucky when we were called again, we might get a drag of empties and go to Danville, so all of we train crews lived in our cabooses away from home. We had our bed clothes on the car, and most all of us brought big baskets of groceries and done our own cooking on oil stoves on our cabooses.

Now most of the time while I was there on the C.&E.I., it happened that I nearly always had to brake behind, and be what was called the parlor brakeman, that means that I was the chief cook and dishwasher, and general housemaid on the caboose, but I did not mind it much, as I sort of liked to mess around in the kitchen anyway, and I got the name while braking there on the C.&E.I. of being a pretty good caboose cook, and I had three or four conductors who wanted me to come on their caboose and brake for them and do the cooking.

Now I remember one time that we had been away from home so long that our groceries had all run out, and we were all broke as most railroad men are just before payday, and we were headed for Villa Grove down the St. Louis Branch with a mile of empty coal cars, and when we stopped to take water at some little place along the route I was standing back aways behind the caboose with my red flag in my hand, and it was winter time with snow on the ground, and I saw some rabbit tracks in the snow, so I followed them a little ways along the road bed. Just ahead of me I saw old Mr. Rabbit setting in a bunch of grass, and I picked up a good sized lump of coal that was laying there on the ground, and I throwed it down on him, stunning him so that I could catch him, and boy, by the time we got into Villa Grove I had him all stewed up for supper, and the extra conductor that was running the car that trip went out there in Villa Grove and rustled around and borrowed enough money to buy some bread, coffee and sugar, and boy, we sure filled up on stewed rabbit, bread and coffee before we went to bed that night.

Well along in the fall of 1907 while going south out of Dalton yards to Danville one trip after being away from home about two weeks, the dispatcher sent old Dave Wheeler our skipper a message that when we arrived at Rossville Junction,[19] for us to set out about half of our train of empties and proceed to Villa Grove by the way of the Sidell branch with the rest of our train, instead of coming on into Danville, and that made my brother Tom so mad that he flew up and bunched the job right there at Rossville Junction, and we had to lay there for sometime waiting for them to deadhead a man up from Danville to take Tom's place on the crew before we could proceed, and I would have quit too, but old Dave Wheeler talked me out of it, so when the extra man came we started out over the Sidell branch for Villa Grove, but just before we left Rossville Junction, we got a message to stop at a little burg out on the branch, and pick up an extra gang of Italians and move them to another place further down the line, so old Dave rode the engine out of Rossville Junction in order to be on the head end to help the brakeman pick up the extra gang's bunk cars. When we arrived at the place and stopped, the head man cut off the engine and brought her into the spur track to couple onto the string of bunk cars, while old Davie had climbed up on top and was letting off the binders, but when the engine went to couple on to them, the coupling failed to make, and as old Dave had let off most of the hand brakes, the string of cars started rolling down the spur track until the one on the end run off the end of the track and turned over on its side, for at that place the ground sloped off down into a little gully. And from what old Davie told me afterward, when the rest of the Wops heard their fellow countrymen hollering in the car that had turned over, about half of the mob started for the engine with pick-handles, shovels, and anything that they could get their hands on, and when old Dave and the head brakeman saw them coming, they climbed over the right-of-way fence and started running across a corn-field, just as fast as their legs could carry them until they reached a safe distance before they stopped, but the engineer and firemen did not have time to get away before the mob had the engine surrounded, and these crazy Wops were hollering and waving their clubs, and some of them started to climb upon the engine, but as it happened the fireboy had just put on the injector, so he grabbed the squirt-hose and opened the valve and began to spray the Wops with hot water and steam, and as they were not used to this way of fighting, they beat a hasty retreat right now.

Well the foreman of this extra gang was a big double-jointed Swede, and old Dave told me that the way he and his interpreter tore into that mob of Wops was a sight for sore eyes. Old Dave said the Swede waded right into those crazy Italians and knocked them right and left with his bare fists, and he and his interpreter soon had the riot quieted down, and it turned out that the Wops that were in the car when it turned over were more scared than hurt, and the big Swede foreman and the interpreter got the whole gang around the car and soon had it straightened up on its wheels, after which it was easy to pull back on the track.

Well I broke for old Dave Wheeler up to the first part of November of that year [1907], then I ask for a transfer onto another car, as I wanted to brake for a boomer conductor by the name of Charley Coddington who used to work out of Rawlins, Wyo., on the Union Pacific back in 1900, when I first went firing out there, so the chief clerk told me all right that he would transfer me onto Coddington's car which he did, and I broke for Coddington all of that winter, and up to some time in March, 1908.

Well shortly after I was transferred onto Coddington's car, we were assigned to a regular coal run, hauling coal from Danville up to a place called Whiting, Indiana,[20] to the Standard Oil Company's big refining plant, just east of South Chicago on the shore of Lake Michigan, and we held that run all winter, and up to some time in the spring when it was pulled off.

Now as there was no place at Whiting for the engineer and his fireman on this coal run to board, they brought their bed clothes and slept in our caboose and eat with us at that end of the run, and I done all of the cooking for the whole crew, Coddington and I furnished all of the groceries, and we charged the engineer, fireman, and head brakeman two-bits a meal, and they said they sure got their money's worth, for we sure did feed good on that caboose. Now the C.&E.I. did not run to Whiting, so we would branch off at Chicago Heights onto the E.J.&E. belt line[21] and run over their tracks to Whiting.

And I remember one cold winter night when there was snow on

the ground and it was raining and sleeting to beat the band, we were coming south from Whiting with a drag of empties about a mile long, and just about the middle of the train there were two old Trojan-couplers[22] that kept slipping by which caused the train to break in two each time, and I think we must have broke in two at least a half a dozen times by the time we reached a place called Coaler[23] where we stopped for coal and water, and my conductor Charley Coddington was not in any too good a frame of mind when we stopped there, for he and the head man had been having a pretty tough time of it walking over there to couple up each time we broke in two. So, the red board was out when we pulled into Coaler and Charley went over to the office to see what it was, and the operator had a message from the train dispatcher wanting to know why all the delay and why we were not making better time, and Charley told the operator to tell him that we had a bad pair of couplers in the train that kept slipping by and breaking us in two, and that he and his head man had carried scrap iron and spiked them each time but they would work loose and fall out, so the dispatcher asked Charley why he did not bring a switchchain from the caboose and chain the cars up, and then Charley asked the dispatcher if he ever carried or drug a switch-chain about fifteen feet long and weighing half a ton for a half of a mile on a cold winter night through the snow when it was raining and sleeting, and the dispatcher said no and then Charley told him that he never did either, and that was not the half of it, he never would, and he also told the dispatcher that it was easy for him to set up there in a nice warm office and tell us how to railroad out here in the cold and snow, then the dispatcher asked Charley if he did not think it would be better to chain the cars together and get his train over the road, and Charley wired back and says . . . stop your kidding, I will meet you in the Logcabin saloon on north Main St. there in Danville tomorrow afternoon and let you buy me a drink of old Crow, good night.

Now I'll never forget the story I heard the switchmen tell about Coddington there in the switch shanty at Danville of the time when he had charge of the pusher engine that used to couple in behind the cabooses of the coal drags and help them up the hill out of Danville yards, and it went something like this as near as I can remember it. There was a fellow by the name of Fred Freese who was assistant trainmaster there at that time, so he came up to the yard office one afternoon and saw Charley's pusher engine standing on the spot nearby, while Charley was in the switch shanty listening to some of the yard snakes[24] . . . , so Freese came in and says to Charley, what's in sight, Coddington? is there any trains ordered that you will have to push up the hill anyways soon? and Charley says no none that I know of, then Fred Freese says to Coddington, all right, we will take your pusher engine and I will go with you, and we will take a string of empty coal cars down to the Grape Creek mines,[25] and then Charley asks Freese who the other brakeman was going to be? and then assistant trainmaster Freese says, why we don't need any other brakeman, and Coddington says, Oh yes we do, the law calls for not less than two brakemen when running on the main line with a train of cars, so Freese got busy with the telephone and called up old man Huffman, the trainmaster, and told him that Coddington refused to go down to Grape Creek with the empties unless he had two brakemen, and then Freese says to Huffman over the phone, I told Coddington that I was going with him, but he insists on another man, so then old man Huffman phoned back to Freese, and said that he would be the other man and go with them, so Freese hung up the phone and turned to Charley and says, Mr. Huffman is going with us, then Coddington says all right fair enough, but I want you to understand that I will be Conductor Coddington, and instead of it being Trainmaster Huffman, and Assistant Trainmaster Freese, it will be Brakeman Huffman and Brakeman Freese, and we will railroad right up to the book of rules, and both of you will wear brakemen's badges, and you will also ride out on top of the train and decorate, leaving town, for that is one of the company's rules, and as you know, you and Mr. Huffman always insist on us trainmen living right up to the book of rules, so then Freese grabbed the phone and called up old Huffman again, and told him what Coddington had said, so Huffman told Freese over the phone, to just forget it, and cut it out, for they would call a crew and run an extra down to Grape Creek with the emptys later on, so Coddington had out smarted them at their own game, and bluffed them out, which was the cause of an extra crew being called to make the trip and pulling down pay for the mileage.

Well, in the spring and summer of 1908, during the great panic of that year, the bottom dropped right out of business,[26] and the C.&E.I. road began to pull off crews, cut the boards, and lay off men, and conductors who had been running trains, had to go back braking, and engineers who had been running engines, had to go back firing.

Now when the cut and lay-off came, of course everything was governed by seniority rights, and the old heads on the road held all of the jobs, but there was lots of bumping done, before everybody got straightened around, and by the time they got down to me with the bumping, they just simply bumped me clear out of Danville altogether, and I had to go over on the St. Louis Branch and do some bumping on my own hook, so after I got bumped there in Danville, I went over to Villa Grove and had to bump another poor fellow who did not have as many whiskers as I did, off of a regular freight run between Villa Grove and Chicago, known in those days as No. 41 and 42.

We would leave Villa Grove one day and go to Chicago, on No. 42 and return the next day on No. 41. Now you could not call this run a hot shot, red ball run, for we always pulled more or less of a drag, but it was a second class scheduled train on the time card and that was better than running extra, for we had a better chance to get over the road, and we made every day in the month, and the run paid me just one hundred dollars a month, that is if I did not lay off a trip.

Now at the time that I took this run, I was braking for a young conductor by the name of White, and he was a good scout, only he was foolish about hot boxes,[27] and was always looking and smelling for hot ones, and he kept us brakemen pretty busy some trips carrying water to cool them off, and we would also lug the dope [grease] buckets over and repack them, in order to run the cars in, for he hated to set a car out along the line because of a hot box.[28]

Well, I worked out of Villa Grove all of that summer, and in the fall when business picked up again, I bid in a fast-freight-run between Danville and Chicago, known as No. 55 and No. 56, and we worked twenty days a month on these runs, and laid over at home ten days a month, but the run only paid a brakeman eighty dollars a month, but at that, the difference in the work, and the advantage of living at home with my folks there in Danville, more than made up the differences in the wages, for there were dances and shows, and many other places to go to in Danville, where on the other hand Villa Grove was just a little country town with nothing there but the railroad division point, and about a dozen fellows for every one girl which was not so good.

Now this new run that I had bid in (No. 55 and No. 56) was a fast freight run, and when we were going north out of Danville on No. 56 we used to pick up a few cars of livestock at different places along the line and take them into Chicago (I will mention here that these runs were night runs) and when making the return trip coming down from Chicago on No. 55 our run was called a peddler, for we would leave the C.&E.I. freight house there at Twelfth street in Chicago about six P.M. in the evening, with a train of cars loaded with [less-than-carload] merchandise and peddle them out all along down the line, setting out one and two cars here and there at different little towns, and we always made our last set out at a place called Rossville, which was about twenty miles north of Danville,[29] and as a rule by this time our train would be reduced down to about eight or ten cars, and as we were most always late on our time card schedule leaving Rossville, it gave us a chance to wheel them down over that last twenty miles into Danville our home division where we most generally arrived at about three A.M. in the morning.

Now at a little place called Alvin[30] just about six miles south of Rossville there was a branch of the Illinois Central[31] that crossed the C.&E.I. and the crossing was controlled by an interlocking system, and as the branch did not run any trains at night time, the operator on duty up in the tower house would always line up the derails and set the semaphore signals at proceed giving the C.&E.I. trains a clear track over the crossing, so one night after we had made our last set out at Rossville, when we were coming down on No. 55, we had eight cars left in our train and I was braking ahead, so the little Dutch engineer says to me, Brownie, I'll bet you a can of beer that I can go to Danville in twenty minutes, and I says you're on, hop to it old head, for I can ride as fast as you can, then we pulled out of Rossville and went tearing down a five mile grade, and when we hit the big curve that run through a deep cut just about a mile north of Alvin, we saw that the outlaying distance semaphore signal showed clear, which indicated that the home signal was all clear with the derail lined up, giving us the right of way over the crossing, so Louis, the little Dutch hoghead did not slow down, but kept right on rambling and when we swung around the curve through the cut, we could see the green light on the home signal which indicated all clear, and Louie gave two long, and two short toots of the whistle for a wagon road crossing. The only thing that we could figure out afterwards was that the operator up in the block tower must have been asleep and when he heard the engine whistle he must have forgotten for a moment that he had everything lined up for us, and thought we were calling for the crossing, for all at once the green light on the home signal changed to red, and we could see the open derail in the gleam of our headlight about a hundred yards ahead of us, and boy, what I mean my hair stood straight up on my head no foolin', and as I was sitting upon the fireman's seat box with the cab window wide open, I jumped up into the open window and was hanging outside of the cab ready to unload any moment, and Louie the little hogger plugged her, and gave them the works, and jumped up in his window ready to unload also and the poor fireman who was down on the deck putting in a fire at the time, did not know what it was all about, but when he heard Louie big hole the brake valve [set the airbrakes], and saw me hanging out of the cab window, he was just in the act of landing a scoopful of coal in the fire box, so he dropped the whole works, scoop, coal and all down on the deck, as he made a dive for the gangway at the left side of the cab and swung down into the steps ready to unload too, and in another second or two we would have joined the bird gang and flew off of that engine, but just at that moment the red light on the home signal changed back to green, and a few seconds later we shot over the crossing like a cannon ball, and boy, I am telling you right here we had one close shave no foolin', and it all happened about a hundred times faster than I am telling it believe me. After we got over the crossing Louis released the air brakes and we kept on going, and the fireman asked Louie and I what the heck it was all about, as he had not seen what had really happened, then we told him all about it, and then we all doped it out among ourselves something like this. We figured that when the operator heard the engine whistle, that he jumped up about half asleep and grabbed the interlocking lever throwing it over, thinking that he was lining up the derail for us, but instead he had opened it almost in front of us, causing the green light to go red, but at the same moment he saw his mistake and slammed the lever right back over again, just in time to save us, for boy, if we had hit that open derail at the speed we were going, we sure would have piled them in the ditch, no foolin'.

Now I want to state right here in my story that a fireman on a coal burning engine stands a pretty slim chance of getting out in case of a wreck or a head-on collision, for the most of the time he is standing down on the deck behind the boiler head where he can't see out ahead, and besides he is so busy shoveling coal into the fire box especially on a fast run, that he has not got time to think about anything else, for his business is to keep the old mill hot so that the engineer can make the time, and another thing that I would like to mention right here, is this. When you read in a newspaper about an engineer dying at his post with his hand on the throttle in a train wreck, about nine times out of ten it is a lotta bunk, for most any railroad man will tell you that these so called brave engineers that sticks to his post and dies with his hand on the throttle when he had a chance to jump would sure be an awful sap, and the truth of the matter in most cases where a poor unfortunate engineer is caught in a wreck and gets killed, is because that things happened so quick and fast that the poor fellow did not have a ghost of a show to jump or get out, and save himself before the crash came. For dear readers I want to tell you that in ninety-nine cases out of a hundred when train wrecks happen they always happen without warning to the train crew or anybody else, and they happen so quick and fast that nobody hardly knows what has happened until they have stopped piling up and it is all over but the cleaning up the wreckage, and as I said before the fireman has not got as much chance to get out as the engineer, for the engineer has always got his eyes peeled for danger ahead for that is part of his business as he sits upon his seat box with his eyes glued on the track as his engine goes sailing along over the road, but compared with the engineer the fireman works under a handicap, especially at night time, for after closing the door after putting in a fire he is to a certain extent blinded for several seconds from looking into the gleaming bright hot fire.

Now I remember at times when I was firing coal that after closing the fire door I would be as blind as a bat for a few seconds, and could not even see the steam gauge or the water glass, but of course it is different when you are firing an oil burner, for the fireman does all of his firing while sitting upon the seat box where he can see just what is going on all around him the same as the engineer, and the worst drawback that I found while firing oil was trying to keep awake after I had been out on the road for some time and was tired and sleepy, for firing an oil burner requires close attention, and the fireman has to keep his eyes on the [oil-injector] gun, or his steam will go down or the engine will be popping off which is not so good.

Well I worked there on the C.&E.I. road up until the first part of May, 1909, when the feeling come over me that I wanted to travel again, for I kept hearing the call of the west so I made up my mind that instead of quitting my job this time, I would use my noodle and work the C.&E.I. for a bunch of transportation which would allow me to ride the cushions on passenger trains instead of having to ride cabooses with my worthy brothers, for I was figuring on making a long jump out into the Rocky Mountains, for as I said before the west was calling me, so I applied for a sixty day leave of absence, and asked for transportation from Danville, Ill., to Frisco, Los

Angeles, El Paso, Texas, and back to Danville, for I figured if I happened to change my mind about staying in the west that I had a job to come back to, and I would have a nice trip of about five thousand miles around the country anyway. Of course in asking for this transportation I had everything to gain, and nothing to lose, and when I told some of the boys there on the C.&E.I. what I had done, they gave me the horse laugh, and said I would never get it, but about two weeks after I made the request for all of this, I was called into the trainmaster's office one day and handed a letter which granted me the sixty days off, and an envelope which contained passes over foreign roads.[32]

Now I remember the first pass was over the Rock Island from Chicago to Denver, Colo.,[33] and the second from Denver by way of Cheyenne, Wyo., and to Ogden, Utah, over the Union Pacific,[34] and the third from Ogden to El Paso, Texas, via Frisco[35] and the fourth from El Paso to Santa Rosa, New Mexico, over the El Paso & Northeastern,[36] and the fifth from Santa Rosa back to Chicago over the Chicago, Rock Island & Pacific,[37] and of course I had a round trip pass from Danville to Chicago and return over the C.&E.I., and boy, when I showed this bunch of passes to some of the guys that had given me the big ha ha it sure made them look like thirty cents, for some . . . had told me it could not be done.

Well a couple of days after I got my passes, I packed my little old traveling bag and bid my mother and the rest of the folks goodbye and headed west for the Rocky Mountains, and after arriving at Denver I layed over there for a couple of days and took in some of the sights as it had been ten years since I was there before, for I passed through there one time when I was a kid hoboing around over the country, so when I left Denver I took a train on the Union Pacific and went up to Cheyenne, and from there I headed west for Ogden, Utah, and when my train arrived in Rawlins I got off to stretch my legs and to take a look around while they were changing engines and crews, and I am unable to express my feelings and the thrill I got as I looked upon old familiar scenes. It was the same old town, same old mountains, and there stood the big brick round house that I had helped to build ten years before. Gee, the sight of all these things brought back to my memory and made me think of the time that I worked there as a laborer and as a machinist helper in the round house, and then of the time that the round house foreman sent me out on an engine with her crew to be their engine watchman, and how I got my first chance to go firing on the road. Gee, it seemed to me just like I had been away from home for a long time, and had just got back, for there stood old Elk Mountain just the same as she looked to me ten long years before.

Now I am unable to explain what it is about the west with its mountains and deserts that seems to get a fellow, but whatever it is, it gets right in under the skin and stays there too, or it has mine anyway, . . .

Well to get back to my story, when my train arrived at Evanston the next morning, and while they were changing engines there I was out on the depot platform walking up and down to stretch my legs and breathing the fresh mountain air, and an old friend of mine by the name of Mike Loam came walking by (if you remember further back, I told you of Kid Mike Loam that I used to brake partners with out of Evanston for old Bill Berry). So he and I talked about old times until my train pulled out, and along about noon we arrived in Ogden, and there the beautiful little city nestled in the great Salt Lake Valley at the foot of a range of the Wasatch Mountains and looked just the same as when I last saw it with the exception of many City improvements.

Well I stayed there in Ogden for a day and night, then I took a run down to Salt Lake City,[38] as I had not been there since the summer of 1902, and when I landed there I met some boomers who told me that the D.&R.G.[39] road was hiring brakemen, and as I felt so good because I was back in the west, I went to the D.&R.G. trainmaster's office, and got a job of braking out of there, working between Salt Lake City and Helper, Utah,[40] over old Soldier summit, so I returned the unused passes that I had left, and resigned from the C.&E.I. by mail, and asked them to send me a service letter which they did, but they sort of give me a bawling out for quitting them that way, but I could not help it, for I could not leave this wonderful country and go back there where they pulled a mile of cars, for out here the trains were lighter in tonnage, and shorter in length, which suited me O.K.

Now the railroad men's wages had been raised out here in the mountain country since I left the Union Pacific back in 1902, and the brakemen on the D.&R.G. between Salt Lake and Helper, were now getting three dollars and sixty cents a hundred [miles], and that was quite a raise for me, as I had only been getting two dollars and forty seven cents a hundred back on the C.&E.I. out of Danville, Ill., and we were making lots of overtime out here, for they were trying to do too much business on the D.&R.G. for a single track road, and the trains were so thick that you could not get very far at a time, for it kept you busy meeting freight trains, and getting into clear for passenger trains, and the passenger traffic was pretty heavy too.

I remember we used to leave Salt Lake City and proceed as far as a place called Thistle,[41] where we picked up our first helper [or pusher] engine, after which we went on up to Tucker[42] at the foot of Soldier Summit grade,[43] where we took coal and water and got our second helper engine, which coupled in behind our caboose, and the three engines would take the train of about six to eight hundred tons up Soldier Summit grade, which at that time was from four to five per cent, but since that time they have cut the grade down to about one percent (or at least that is what I have been told).[44]

Now while I was working on that division, it was there at Tucker where I met old Charley Bordner, the old boomer engineer that I had worked with out of Springfield, Mo., on the old K.C.F.S.&M. [Kansas City, Fort Scott & Memphis] road, down through the Ozark mountains who told me that he did not need any retainers turned up while going down the hills, that was away back in the winter of 1903 and 1904 and here I met him again running one of the helper engines pushing trains up Soldier Summit grade on the D.&R.G. in the summer of 1909.

For the old grade that I speak of was the steepest piece of standard gauge main line railroad in the United States according to the dope given out by the D.&R.G. as I heard it at that time, and I was told that a train dropped down eighteen hundred feet from the time it pulled out of the snow sheds[45] up at Summit until it reached Tucker in the short distance of seven miles.

Well I'll tell the world that I will never forget the first trip that I made down there on a freight train. We had went to Helper, the first division point east of Salt Lake, and were making the return trip, and when we pulled into the snow sheds at the top of Summit, the air brake inspectors fixed a blue flag on our engine, and that means we could not move until they took it down, and gave us a release order which was an O.K. on the air brakes, so we stayed there for some time before they released us, for if there was too much slack in the brake rigging under a car they had to take it up, and the chains and ratchet dogs on all of the hand brakes had to be in good working order, before they would let us go, and if we had more than eight hundred tons, we would have to reduce by setting out some loads, for eight hundred tons was the limit from the Summit down to Tucker, seven miles below where we most always had to fill out again if there was anything to go, for these loads were brought down from Summit by the swing crews and the helper engines.

Well when the air inspectors got everything all fixed up they took down their blue flag and gave the engineer his O.K. and while we were there we two brakemen had gone over the top of the train and turned up all of the pops, and when we started down we brakemen were out on top with our brake clubs ready to catch them up just as soon as the hogger made his first application of the brakes, which he did just as we tipped over the crown of the hill at the west end of the snow sheds, which at that time looked to me like going down the incline of an old time coal chute, if you get what I mean, for boy, it sure did look down hill from the top of that head box car where I was standing and the hind man was back about the middle of the train, and just as soon as the engineer set his brakes, we went right after the hand brakes with our brake clubs, and set them up as tight as we could. I worked back from the head end, and the hind man worked back from the middle of the train, and we kept the train under control while we crept down the hill at a speed of about six miles an hour, until we reached a place half way down known as Midway, where we had to come to a full stop, and let the wheels and brake shoes cool off a bit.

Now at this place called Midway there was a spur track took off from the main line and run about three miles from the way it looked to me, up the incline of another hill, and the switch that connected this spur track to the main line was always set or lined up for the spur, and if a train came down there out of control it would run off up the spur track and stop, so after stopping there and allowing the wheels to cool, the engineer would call for the switch with four blasts of the whistle, then the operator who lived there in the telegraph office would come out and line up the switch for the main line, and give the hogger a highball. Now when a train stops like that with all of the pops turned up and the hand brakes all set up tight, it is a heck of a job to get it started again, for as we used to say in the mountain country, the brakes are froze, and the brakemen in this case work from the hind end by letting off the hand brakes until the train starts, and believe me they start dang quick sometimes, no foolin', for sometimes after you have let off a few brakes and then let off one good tight binder, the whole works starts with a run and jump, or that is the way it seems anyway, and then the brakemen have got to hop to it and get the brakes set up again before they lose control of the train, for if you ever lose control after passing Midway, you might as well unload, for the only thing that will stop them then would be when they went into the ditch when they struck the sharp curve just above Tucker, and now I am going to tell you about a runaway train that did that very thing while I was working there. It happened along in September, 1909, as near as I can remember, after I had been there a little over three months, and the only one of the crew that I ever knew was the engineer whose name was Eddie End, and I met him again afterwards and fired for him on the Santa Fe out of Needles, Calif., and although I had heard all about it while I was working there on the D.&R.G. at the time that it happened, I got the first hand true story from Eddie one trip while I was firing for him on the Santa Fe . . . and it went something like this. Eddie told me that after they had stopped in the snow sheds at the Summit, and the air brake inspectors had fixed up the train and took down the blue flag and give him his release O.K. then he started out and everything was working fine and dandy, and the brakemen were out on top giving him good support with the hand brakes, so they slipped down to Midway, and made their stop as per rule, and he tooted four times for the switch, and the operator came out and lined it up and give him a highball to come ahead, then Eddie said that he whistled off and got a highball from the conductor back on the caboose, so he released the air and tried to start the train, but as everything was froze, he did not have any luck, until the brakemen let off several hand brakes on the rear end, and they did start, they started all at once with a run and jump as it were, and he said that he set the air, but he saw right away that it did not have any effect, so he gave one short toot of the whistle, which is a call for brakes and at the same time gives warning to the trainmen that the train is out of control, and he looked back and could see the two brakemen hurrying over the tops of the swaying cars setting up the brakes as fast as they could, but it was too late, for the train was gaining speed every minute, and by this time the conductor was out on top doubling up on the brakes with the hindman and the fireman got out on top and coupled up the the headman, trying to set the brakes up tighter, but it was no use, for by this time the momentum of the train was so great, that the brakes could not hold them, and Eddie had the engine in the back motion on sand,[46] so the conductor and his two brakemen and the fireman beat it back to the caboose and pulled the pin cutting the caboose off from the train and by setting the brake up as tight as they could caused it to slacken speed enough to drop back about fifteen car lengths from the rest of the train, and all of this time Eddie stuck to his engine and kept blowing the whistle to warn other crews down around the curve at Tucker. And I asked Eddie why in the heck he did not unload, and he told me that if he had jumped off into the rocks at the speed that they were going, he would have been just committing suicide, so he just took one chance out of a thousand and stayed with her, and when she hit the sharp curve just above Tucker she left the rails and plowed along in the dirt for a little ways, and then she turned over on her side in the middle of the east bound track and skidded along endways just like a log on a pair of skids (I will state here that it was double track from Tucker up over the Summit) and as luck would have, she skidded far enough ahead after turning over to keep out of the way of the cars that were piling up behind her, and Eddie said after everything stopped he crawled out from under what wreckage had piled up over him, and he was not much hurt, except a few cuts, bruises, and burns. But it turned out that the rest of the crew back in the caboose did not fare so well, for when the train went into the ditch and stopped, the caboose came sailing down and slammed into the wreck and dang near finished the conductor, fireman, and two brakemen, for they all had to be taken to the hospital, but Eddie did not, but as I said before, he only had one chance in a thousand to get out alive, and he just got a break, that is all, and he told me that the reason he stayed with the engine was because by the time he saw that he could not get stopped, it was too late, for they were going so fast by that time that if he had jumped he sure would have been killed.

Now the Western Pacific, a new road at that time and belonging to the Gould System just the same as the D.&R.G. did, had just finished building between Salt Lake City and Frisco,[47] and they were bringing the new rolling stock from the east over the D.&R.G. for the Western Pacific with which they were equipping the new road, and I remember one trip we were coming west out of Helper, and we had two new Western Pacific engines in our train, known as dead engines, that is they were not steamed up, and when we stopped for water at a little place called Colton[48] just about ten miles east of the Summit, the operator had a message from the dispatcher for our conductor and also for the man that was traveling along with the new engines known as an engine messenger, to fill up the tanks of the two new engines with water there at Colton, for the traveling engineer was supposed to meet us up at Summit where he was going to cut in the air brakes on the engines so that we could use the brakes going down the grade, and the reason for filling the tanks with water was to give them more weight on their wheels so that the wheels would not be so apt to slide and wear flat spots on them. So after our engine took water, we pulled up and spotted the first new engine at the water tank so that the engine messenger could fill her tank with water, and a few seconds after he had started the water running into the tank, all at once a man's head popped up through the manhole and he looked like a drowned rat, as he crawled out and hollered at the messenger to please stop the water, and he gave the messenger such a scare at first, that he let loose of the valve rope and was just about to jump down off the tank when the fellow crawled out, for it was just after midnight and was pretty dark, and I guess the messenger thought that he was seeing things, so he asked the fellow what he was doing down in there? and by this time the poor fellow was standing out on top of the tank bare headed, and in his shirt sleeves, and sock feet, and soaked to the skin, and he was shivering and his teeth were chattering so bad that he could hardly talk, for it was in the month of October and believe me at that time of year up there in the Wasatch mountains it sure was pretty crimpy at night time, for there was ice froze all around under the water tank, and the fellow finally says to the messenger, where is this? Is this Helper? and by this time I had climbed up on the tank, and I told him no, this was Colton about thirty miles west of Helper, [49] and he says why I wanted to get off at Helper, and it sounded too funny, for you would think he was a paid passenger, and we had carried him by his station, and the poor fellow was such a funny looking sight standing up there shivering and his wet socks froze to the top of the steel tank, that the conductor who was standing down on the ground, and the messenger and I all bust out laughing, for the whole thing seemed so funny that we all got a good laugh and a big kick out of it, and finally the messenger says well why didn't you get off at Helper? while the train was standing there in the yards? and the fellow says well I guess I was asleep, and then he says, say mister, will you wait until I crawl down in there and get my bed of blankets, coat, hat and shoes? and he told him yes, to go ahead and get all of his things out of there, so I held my lantern down through the man hole so he could see to get his things, and he handed everything out to us but his shoes, and he could not find them as the water had covered them over, then the conductor told him to bring all of his things and come back to the caboose where it was warm so that he could dry out, and we proceeded on up to the Summit, but the traveling engineer had failed to show up, so my skipper wired the dispatcher at Salt Lake, and asked what he should do about the dead engines, and the dispatcher wired back and told him to set them out, which we did, and the engine messenger promised the fellow that just as soon as he got into Salt Lake he would drain the water out of the tank and get his shoes for him, and the fellow told him that he would be there waiting for them, for he had just bought the shoes new and paid seven dollars for them.

Well we came on down from Summit to Tucker, and filled out there by picking up three or four hundred tons, after which we headed in and met a couple of eastbound extras, and it seems to me that we got stuck there for a couple of passenger trains too, for I remember by the time we got down to Thistle and got stuck there for some more trains, that our sixteen hours were up, and the dogcatchers (a relief crew) had to come out and get us and take our train on in to Salt Lake. (I will mention here that my crew got paid at the rate of twelve miles an hour while dead heading from Thistle on in to Salt Lake, just the same as if we were working, in other words we got paid just the same as the relief crew that were taking our train on in, for riding in our caboose, but our eight hours rest started at the moment that our sixteen hours were up, and it did not matter when we got into Salt Lake, they could call us again for duty at the end of that eight hours.)

Well while we were laying there in Thistle waiting for the relief crew to come, our engineer and fireman had come back to the caboose, and we all cooked up a big feed, and the young fellow that we had got out of the engine tank at Colton had a bunch of jack, so he went over to a saloon there in Thistle and bought two quarts of whiskey and brought [it] back to the caboose, and we all had a regular picnic while dead heading on in to Salt Lake, and the hobo told us that he had paid the brakeman on the division east of Helper one dollar to hide him away in the new engine tank, and the shack told him to go into the hay if he wanted to, for he would wake him up when they pulled into Helper yards, but it seemed like when they arrived in Helper, that the brakeman forgot to play bell hop and call the sleeper in No. 723,[50] for that was the number of the engine tank that the dollar guest was sleeping in, and that was how he come to be in the engine tank where we had drowned him out at Colton, but he was a good sport anyway, and got as much kick out of the joke as we did, but I don't know if he ever got his seven dollar shoes or not.

Well I had lots of fun while working out of Salt Lake, for I used to go out to Salt-Air Beach[51] about twelve miles west of the city, and go bathing in the great Salt Lake, and I'll never forget the first time that I went into that salty water, for I had been told how a body would float on the surface of the water, but I thought it was a lotta boloney, so I went wading out until I got over waist deep, and all at once my feet come up, and my head sort of ducked under far enough so that I got my eyes full of the salty water, and snuffed some of it up my nose, and there I was floating just like a cork, but gee, when I tried to rub the water out of my eyes with my wet hands, it made matters all the worse, for they smarted something awful, and I began to think that the lining was being torn out of my nose, and I was in one heck of a shape, when a fellow who was floating right near me saw what I was up against, he told me to put my fingers in my mouth and lick all of the salt off of them before rubbing my eyes, so I did as he told me and after a while I was all right again. Boy, it sure was fun to lay on your back with your feet crossed and your arms folded back under your head, and float around like a piece of wood, but it was almost useless to try to swim, for the water was so heavy that you could not make any headway, but if you wanted to move about, you just stretched out on your back and used your hands as paddles, and you could go anywhere you wanted to, and if you did not want to lay stretched out, you could draw up your knees in a sort of setting position and your head and shoulders would be out of the water, and you can believe me or not, when I tell you that I saw men sitting in the water like this with a big sunshade hat on, reading a newspaper and smoking a cigar.

Now I remember one time when I was out there, that another fellow and I were floating around, and we met two pretty Mormon girls, and we floated around and talked to them, and it turned out that one of them had a brother firing on the D.&R.G., so she and I got pretty chummy, and I finally got to stepping out with her, and I used to go with her to choir practice up to the Mormon Tabernacle[52] as she was one of the five hundred singers in that wonderful Mormon Tabernacle Choir, and I used to set back at the further end from the great pipe organ and listen to the wonderful music, and it beat anything that I had ever heard in the way of church music. Now the shape of the Tabernacle was oblong, and the roof was a sort of concave affair, which one of the guides told me was ten feet thick, and the trussed arches that made it self supporting were pinned together with wooden pins, and not a nail was used in it, and there was not a single post to hold it up, for it was just like a lid set upon top of the outside brick walls and the nearest thing that I can compare it to, would be if you took a cocoanut and cut it half in two length ways, and used one half of the shell for a roof, and the under side of the roof was shaped so that it deflected the sound evenly to all parts of the building, and acted as a sounding board, as it were, and I have set in the back part of the Tabernacle and heard one of the guides speak in a whisper while he was standing away up in front by the big pipe organ, and if we take into consideration the time that this Tabernacle was built, which was right after the Mormons settled in the great Salt Lake Valley it is a most wonderful building.

And then there is the great Mormon Temple, which I was told that they were forty years building,[53] and I want to say right here that I always have been stuck on Salt Lake City, for it is a beautiful place as it nestles at the foot of a range of the Wasatch mountains.

Well I worked there on the D.&R.G. up until the first part of November [1909], when it began to get pretty cold, and as the traffic on the road was so thick it was getting to be a heck of a job to get a train over the road, so as I had a good stake saved up, I bunched the job and headed for Frisco.

Chapter VIII

*W*ell when I reached Reno, Nevada,[1] I stopped
off for a couple of days and took in some of the sights,
and I sure got stuck on that little town located there
on the Truckee River, just a few miles east of the
boundary line between Nevada and California at the
foot of the Sierra Nevada Mountains, then I took a
train out of there on the Southern Pacific which climbs
right up and goes over the top of the Sierra Nevada
range, and the train wound its way up the steep grades
until it reached the top, and then for forty-two miles
it runs through the snow sheds,[2] after which it started down the
western slope toward the Pacific Ocean. I was told that these snow
sheds were mostly all snowed under during the winter months, and
if it were not for them the line would be tied up most of the time
in the winter, for as it is they have to use the big rotary snow plows
to keep the road open on both the east and west slopes of the range,
and I have been told that the snow gets from six to eight feet deep
down as far as the little town of Truckee,[3] which is on the Truckee
River down on the eastern slope, and it keeps the big rotary snow
plows pretty busy clearing the line. Now it is a wonderful sight to
see one of these snow plows in action, for it wades right through
the snow and makes a cut just wide enough for a train to pass through,
and the solid packed walls of these snow cuts are as high as the tops
of box cars at some places, and the big rotary on the front end of
the plow, which looks something like a big fan wheel, is what cuts
the snow and throws it away out clear of the track, and it is driven
by big powerful engines which are within the plow itself, and the
plow in turn is pushed along by a big locomotive which also pulls

a short train behind it, which is made up of the supply, dining, and sleeping cars of the snow plow crews, and the caboose on the rear end for the train crew.

Well this trip up over the hump, as the railroad boys call the mountain range, is sure some trip. I know, for I made it myself three different times, and I have seen some of the most wonderful mountain scenery while going over this division between Reno, Nevada, and Sacramento, Calif., that I ever saw any where, and I have been in every state west of the Mississippi River excepting Louisiana.

Well I finally reached Frisco, and stopped there for a couple of days, but I was not much impressed with the town at that time. (I will tell later on of working out of Frisco on the coast line of the S.P. railroad.) So I left there and came on down to Los Angeles, and I fell in love with the City of the Angels at first sight, and I stayed here for two whole weeks, and took in some of the sights, and then I made the rounds of all three of the railroads that run into Los Angeles[4] but they were all full up and did not need any more men just then, so I got a ride out of here with a Santa Fe crew on an orange [citrus] train to San Bernardino,[5] and with another crew to Barstow,[6] and from Barstow to Needles[7] with a well known conductor on the Santa Fe at that time by the name of Dudley, and I remember that he carried his big, white bulldog on the caboose with him all of the time, and the boys used to say, here comes Dudley and his dog, for everybody working out of Needles in those days knew Dudley's dog.

Well when I landed in Needles I got a job of firing oil on the Santa Fe, and this was along in December of 1909, and believe me it was some dandy job of firing too, and the pay was good, for the divisions both ways out of Needles were long, which paid us lots of mileage, and they had some of the biggest engines there that I had ever seen up to that time, but they were oil burners and all a fireman had to do was just to set up there on the seat box and watch his water and steam gauges, and operate the firing valve, which was a lot better than standing down on the deck heaving in the black diamonds.

Now when I got this job I was required to fill out the book with the five hundred questions, just the same as I did when I went to work for the Santa Fe down in Temple, Texas, back in the spring of 1906, so when I got it filled out, I took it back to the master mechanic's chief clerk, and he looked it over then he says to me, boomer where did you get the book of rules to copy these answers from, and I says to him, now listen chief, you are talking out of your turn, for I was not lucky enough to get hold of a book of rules, and besides it would be too much trouble to keep turning through the book looking for the answers anyway, then I told him if he would look at my application, he would see that I had worked for the Santa Fe once before, down in Temple, Texas, and then I says to him, if you don't think I know my book of rules, just go ahead and ask me something, and I will show you that I have done passed out of the A B C class, and then he laughed, and says no Brown, I am not going to waste any time asking you questions, for I guess you know your rules all right.[8]

Well I was marked up on the fireman's extra board, and I'll never forget the first trip that I made as an oil burner fireman. It so happened that I got out on my first trip with a young engineer who had just been set up [promoted], and he was making his first trip as an engineer, and to make things all the worse, we caught an old tramp engine which should have been in the back shops being overhauled instead of trying to pull a train over the mountains, and as near as I can remember, we were called for an extra east around about eight P.M. that evening, and we got one of the 900 class engines[9] which was a decompound or a tandem compound,[10] but better known by the Santa Fe boys as a Mike, and all of the 900's and 1600's there at Needles were of this class engine,[11] and they were regular mountain whales, and carried a working pressure of two hundred and twenty pounds of steam. Now a tramp engine is one that has no regular assigned crew, and is run and handled by first one extra crew and then another, and the last crew that comes in on her figures that they will not catch her again soon, and they don't care if there is any repair work done on her or not, and as a rule, the round house force only does enough work on her to keep her from falling to pieces while she is in the round house, so these poor old tramp engines go from bad to worse, and the one we caught that night was worse. So when I went over to the round house, after being called, I met the young hoghead who was all ready there, and we introduced ourselves to each other, and he told me that this would be his first trip as an engineer, and I says well you haven't got anything on me buddy, for this will be my first trip as an oil burner fireman, then he asked me if I had ever done any firing before? and I told him yes, but with coal, not with oil and he says well I guess we will get through some way or other, and I says let us hope so, for if we don't it sure will be a long trip, then he laughed a sort of a nervous little laugh which sounded like he was trying to kid himself along, and then he says well we will have to kinda help each other along, and I says all right brother I am with you, so we were still busy trying to get the old scrapheap ready when the brakeman came after us. And we finally got over in the yards and coupled onto the train, and I was trying to get all of the cab lights filled and lit before the conductor came with the order, for I don't believe that I ever saw a conductor when he came with the orders but what he was always in a heck of a hurry to get out and get over to some other place for some other train, and sure enough when this skipper showed up he was running true to form, for he was in one heck of a hurry to get out so that we could make Topock,[12] the second station east of Needles, where we crossed the silvery Colorado [River] over into Arizona for No. 9, a westbound mail train.[13]

Well we started out and the young hogger was a little bit nervous and excited, but he did not have anything on me, for this was one time that the old boomer did not seem to just fit in somehow or other, for I did not know just where to grab ahold at, for there were so many little valves to be twisted, turned and set, such as the valve on the steam heating plant that heated the oil inside of the oil tank, and there was the atomizer valve that allowed the steam to go to the oil burner in the firebox which sprayed the oil into the fire, and then there was the firing valve which controlled the flow of oil to the burner, and which looked something like the handle on the engineer's brake valve, and all in all there were so many little doodads to fool around with that it kept me guessing where to grab next.

Now if the engine had been a coal burner, I would have known just what to do, for I would have grabbed the old scoop shovel and went to heaving the black diamonds into the fire box, but when it come to shooting the oil in there I sure was in the kindergarten, no foolin'.

Well we finally got the train out on the main line and the rear brakeman closed the switch and gave us a highball, and the young hogger whistled off and went right after her, and the way he grabbed that throttle and yanked it open, I thought he was going to take it off and lay it back on the tank, and when he yanked the throttle open I should have yanked my firing valve open and give her more oil, but I did not know right then that the fireboy had to sort of watch the hoghead and operate his firing valve along with the throttle, so the hogger hollered across the cab and told me to give her more oil, so I grabbed the firing valve and jerked it wide open, and boy you should have seen the beautiful smoke screen that I was laying down. Man, it would have hidden the whole Pacific Fleet, then the hogger jumped down off his seat and come over and says to me, you are giving her too much oil and not enough atomizer, then I eased off on the oil and he opened the atomizer valve a little bit more, and he took off one of his gloves and touched the front part of the oil tank with his bare hand, then he says you have got your oil too hot, and that is what is making her smoke so bad, then he closed the heater valve, but still she smoked, and every time I would cut down on the oil feed to cut out the smoke, my steam would drop back, for she was a bum steamer. (Now I will state here that if an oil burner engine is right, you will only see just a good dark color coming out of the smokestack, and you can't beat them out of steam, and all oil burner firemen watch the smokestack as much as they do the steam gauge, for they can tell what kind of a fire they have got by just watching the color coming out of the smokestack.)

Well we rambled over to Topock and headed in for the passenger train, and the young hogger told me to put on the blower and the injector and get her hot and the boiler full of water and then we would blow her out. . . . the water in the west is bad for use in boilers, on account of the alkali and soda that it contains, and in these days much of the water used on western roads is treated and besides they carry a chemical compound on the engines that the fireman puts into the engine tank everytime that he takes a fresh tank of water, and this helps to keep the water from foaming while it is being generated into steam in the boiler, but after the water has been in the boiler for some time, the compound seems to lose its effect, and then the engine crews have to open up the big blowout cocks,[14] and blow out as much of the dead water as they dare to.

Well after No. 9 arrived and departed, we pulled out of Topock and proceeded on our way toward Seligman, Arizona,[15] the next division point one hundred and fifty-three miles east of Needles, Calif., and from Topock it is all upgrade to the top of old Yampai mountain, which is about twenty miles west of Seligman, so we had a steady pull all the way, and by the time we got up to Kingman[16] it was midnight, and all trains going east stop and take water, and the freight crews all eat there in the Harvey lunch room, so we pulled up and stopped, and after taking water, we went into the lunch room and put a good feed under our belts, then we pulled out of Kingman and went on over to a little place called Hackberry,[17] where we took both water and oil, and from there we proceeded up through Crozer's canyon, to Peach Springs[18] where we took water again, and from there we went up through Nelson's canyon,[19] and then up over Yampai mountain, and then down across a beautiful valley, where you could see for miles and there were thousands of range cattle scattered all up and down the valley, then just east of there we pulled into Seligman, which was the end of our trip, and I sure was ready to hit the hay after getting something to eat.

Well when our eight hours rest was up, they called us for an extra west, and we started out and got as far as Hackberry, and I remember it was along in the morning when we stopped there for water, so the operator came out and gave my engineer a message from the train dispatcher at Needles, informing us that we and our engine were assigned to work train duty there at Hackberry, on the gravel run, hauling gravel from the gravel pit out on the main line and unloading it, and that the engine that was now on the gravel run and its crew would bring our train on to Needles, so she took our main line train and went on, and we were stuck for the work train so the work train crew coupled us on to a string of dump cars loaded with gravel there at Hackberry, and away we went back up to Peach Springs where we stopped and picked up the gang of Mexicans that done the unloading, and then we proceeded on up into Nelson's canyon and unloaded the train and went back to Hackberry, and got another train of gravel and took it up into Nelson's canyon, but this trip we got two or three cars off the track and we did not get back into Hackberry until about ten P.M. that night. My engineer and I had not eat a bite since breakfast early that morning, so we asked the engine watchman that was taking care of our engine and also the gravel pit engine, if he could tell us where we could get something to eat, and he said no, that there were not a dozen houses in the whole town and everybody was gone to bed, and he happened to be a fireman, and belonged to the brotherhood, so he made us take his midnight lunch and eat it, for he said that he could stand it until morning, then he took us over to where he roomed, and woke the people up and they fixed us up with beds for the night, so we paid our four bits apiece and piled into the hay, and at four A.M. in the morning they sent the engine watchman to call us, and we got up and went over to the engine and he had her all steamed up and all ready for us to go, and as there was no place to get anything to eat at that time in the morning, there in that burg, we had to do without our breakfast.

Now the conductor and his two brakemen slept, cooked, and eat in their caboose, so they were all right, but it was tough sledding for my engineer and I, for we were not getting our three squares a day. The train crew coupled us on to a train of gravel, and we started for Nelson's canyon, and by the time we reached Peach Springs it was daylight and the Mexicans were waiting for us, and after unloading we beat it back to Hackberry and grabbed another train and brought it up and unloaded, and when we started back we had to get in the clear there at Peach Springs for No. 10,[20] an eastbound passenger train, and while we were waiting there in the passing track, the engineer run over to a little one-horse makeshift of a store, and bought a can of corned beef and some crackers, for that was all he could get, so we eat that up and as soon as No. 10 went, we pulled out and went down to Hackberry and grabbed another train. After getting laid out for other trains, it was late in the afternoon when we got back up to Nelson's canyon to unload, and of course we had to go and get some cars off the track and by the time we got them back on and got back to Hackberry it was late in the night, and the watchman wanted us to take his lunch again, but we would not do it, so we went over to the place and went to bed on empty stomachs. The next morning they called us just before daylight, and when we got over to the engine the conductor was hopping around like a chicken with its head off, and he was trying to hurry everybody up so that we could get out ahead of an orange train that was coming east, and in the meantime the head man had coupled us onto the train of gravel, so the conductor came rushing up to the engine with the orders, and says to the engineer, come on let's get out of here ahead of that orange train that is coming, but I balked and tied up the whole works, for I says to the skipper, say listen bo, I don't go one foot out of here until I get some breakfast. He flew up and got sore, and then he says, what in the blankety blank heck, aint you eat yet, and then I blowed up and I says you know danged well we haven't eat yet, for where in the heck are we going to get anything to eat in the burg, and I says that is not all we haven't eat for two days, so you go tell that dispatcher that Fireman C. P. Brown has tied up until he can find a place to get some breakfast, and he says you are danged right I'll tell the dispatcher, and I'll tell him plenty too, and I'll sure put the delay where it belongs, then I says I don't give a dang what you tell him, but be sure and tell him this for me, that if I can't make arrangements here some place to get my eats, that he can send another fireman to take my place for I am through. So he went into the telegraph office and sent a message to the dispatcher at Needles and told him that Fireman C. P. Brown had tied up the works, and the dispatcher asked him what for, and he answered back and told the dispatcher that I refused to go until I got some breakfast, for I had said that I could not find any place to eat, then the dispatcher asked him why the engineer and fireman did not eat where he and his two brakemen eat at, and the conductor told him because that he and his brakemen cooked and eat on their caboose, and then the dispatcher asked him where did the gravel pit crews eat at, and the skipper told him that they eat in a boarding car over at the gravel pit, but the cook and his wife did not have any orders to feed any road crews, and besides they only served regular meals at meal time. The dispatcher must have got busy there in Needles, for pretty soon here came a message addressed to the cook in charge of the boarding car, instructing him that hereafter that he would feed the engine crew on the gravel train, at any time that they came in off their run and wanted to eat, so the conductor came back to the engine with the message and told the head man to cut us off and head out on the main line, for we had to take the engine and go over to the gravel pit (which was about a mile west of Hackberry). When we got over there the train and engine crew and steam shovel crew was eating their breakfast, so we all went in and when the conductor gave the cook the message from Needles instructing him to feed my engineer and I, he got pretty sore and said that he and his wife had their hands full now as it was, much less getting up at all hours to feed the extra engine crew, but we got our breakfast just the same, and we were all ready to follow the orange train out of there when it pulled out, so we went up and unloaded and came back and set our empties in the gravel pit and lined up another train of loads and as it was about eleven A.M., I told the conductor that I would not go without my dinner, and that burned him up for he was a mileage hound, and was trying to get in all of the mileage he could regardless of whether the engine crew got anything to eat or not, but his mileage did not bother me, for I told him that any time that I could not eat on a job, I would not work on it either, so he rushed us over to the boarding car and fixed it up with the cook to let us eat before the pit crew came into dinner, which the cook did. Then we took our train of gravel up and unloaded it and got back to Hackberry about three P.M. in the afternoon, and the operator came out and gave my engineer a message stating that we were to change off with another engine and crew that were coming west on an extra, and boy, I sure was glad to get out of that hole, so when the extra pulled in, we took the train and came on into Needles, and I expected to be called upon the carpet and get a bawling out for the stand that I took out at Hackberry in regards to laying out the gravel run when I refused to go until I got my breakfast, but I never heard a word about it after that.

Well I was marked up on the extra board again, and the next trip I made I caught a regular engine for thirty days, as the regular fireman had laid off and went into Los Angeles, and this engine belonged on the one hundred and seventy mile division that run west out of Needles across the great Mojave desert, to Barstow the next division west . . . and she was the old 940 . . . (nine forty)[21] and her engineer was a prince of a little fellow by the name of Eddie Murray, and the thirty days that I fired for him passed before I hardly noticed it, and besides I had put in a good full month that put me on my feet (I will tell later on how I bid the old 940 in for my regular engine about a year after that).

Well by this time I had been there about six weeks, and it was around about the last of January, 1910, and one morning I went into the Harvey lunch room there at Needles, after being on the road all night coming from Barstow on an orange train, and who do you suppose I saw waiting on the boys at the lunch counter, and handing out the same old bush-wah? I will give you one guess, yes you are right, for it was nobody else but our own little Billie, the blue-eyed blonde that I had known down in Texas, when I was switching cars for the Santa Fe at Summerville back in 1906, and when she came over to take my order, she says, say fireboy, where have I seen you before? and I says why Billie don't you remember Brownie that was switching in the yards at Summerville, Texas, when you had charge of the night lunch counter down there in 1906, and she says why Brownie, sure I remember you now, you and Johnnie Johnston and a little boomer from El Paso was on the night engine in the main line yards, and I says you are right, that's me kid, and she reached over the counter and grabbed both of my hands, and told me how glad she was to see me, and we were there holding hands and talking about old times when a brakeman says, hey break away there Billie, and give me another cup of coffee, then a young conductor says yes and if you are through holding that tallowpot's hands, you can come and hold mine for a while or bring me something to eat for I crave service, and she laughed and says, oh you boys are only jealous, but Brownie and I are old friends for we used to know each other down in Texas.

Well she gave the brakeman his coffee, and took the conductor's order, then she came back to me and says well Brownie, what are you going to eat? so I gave her my order, and after she got everybody waited on at her station of the counter, she came back to me, and says listen Brownie, what are you doing tonight? and I told her that I did not know if I would get out or not, but the first thing that I was going to do was to go to my room and get some shut eye, as I had been on the road all night coming from Barstow on a fruit train. Then she says gee, I don't like Barstow, for they had me over there for a while last summer, and then they sent me to Bakersfield for a while, then on up the Valley to Fresno, and from there to Oakland,[22] and as I did not like the weather up there, I put up a holler to be transferred here to Needles. And I says why did you leave Oakland? for that and Frisco are two good towns, and she says because it is too cold and rainy up there at this time of the year, and besides I like this place in the winter time, and I says why have you worked here before Billie? and she laughed and says why sure Brownie, this will be my second winter in Needles, and I laughed and says why Billie you are a worse boomer than I am, then I says gee, Billie, you must have some drag to go traveling around over the whole Fred Harvey System, and she smiled and says well Brownie, you know I am an old head with the Harvey System, for I have been slinging hash for them now almost six years, and I sure take advantage of my seniority rights, which gives me a chance to travel and see the country, and then I says you are right Billie, I don't blame you for being a boomer, for that is about the only way a poor working guy can see some of the country, and I says well Billie, I have got to go and get some sleep, but if I am not called to go out, I will see you tonight over at the recreation hall[23] in the library reading room. Then I picked up my roll of overclothes and my gloves, and says well adios Billie until tonight, then I beat it up to my room and piled into the hay, and after sleeping good for four or five hours, I got up feeling fine, and went down to the lunch room and eat some supper, then I went over to the round house, to see how many times out I was, and they had me marked up on a tramp engine with an extra engineer by the name of Monk Haggard, and we were due to go out on a work train at five A.M. the next morning, so I went over to the recreation hall and waited for Billie. And pretty soon here she come, and she asked me if I thought I was going to get out? and then I told her that I was marked up for a work train for the next day, and would get out at five A.M. in the morning, and then she says Oh fine, now we can have a good long talk about old times down in Texas, and then she asked me to tell her where all I had been since she last saw me, so I told her that sometime after she left Summerville, I bunched the job and went down to Galveston, and layed around there for a while, then I took a steamship out of there and went to New York City, and when I told her how seasick I got a couple of times while making the trip she sure did laugh, and then I told her about some of the wonderful sights that I had seen, and also about working on the New York Central road up and down the Hudson River, and how the trains all scooped their water on the fly, and of the four main tracks, and of the fast freights that I had run on, and then of being transferred into the yards at One Hundred and Fifty-fifth street at High Bridge. She says, Gee, Brownie, I wish the Harvey System extended further east than Chicago, for I would like to travel and see the east, and I says yes Billie it sure is a nice trip, but I did not get to see one hundredth part of what I would like to have seen, and then I told her about going to Danville Ill., where my mother lived, and of working out of there up until some time in May 1909, and then of working out of Salt Lake City on the D.&R.G. over Soldier Summit, and then of bunching the job and going to Frisco and Los Angeles, and then out here to Needles about six weeks ago, and here I am, and she says how come you went firing out of here, Brownie? and I told her that I used to fire years ago, and loved an engine, but the railroad companies got to building the engines so big that it was a man killing job to fire them with coal, so I had got wise to myself and cut it out, and had been following braking and switching until I blowed into Needles, and when I saw all of the engines were oil burners, out in this part of the country I went back to my first love, the locomotive. Then she told me after she left Summerville they sent her down to Galveston, and after staying there for a while, they sent her to Kansas City, and from there she went down to Springfield, Mo., on the Frisco System, as the Frisco road had the Fred Harvey eating houses also,[24] and I told her yes that I knew that, for I had worked out of Springfield and St. Louis on the Frisco system myself, and she looked surprised, and says you did, when was that Brownie? and I told her it was away back in 1902, . . . then I asked her if she ever worked in Chicago? and she says why sure, I worked there in the lunch room in the old Dearborn St. Station and then I says well Billie, I run out of that old Station for sometime myself. I worked as flagman on passenger trains for the Wabash railroad back in 1905 and part of 1906, when I quit and went down into Texas, where I was switching cars for the Santa Fe when you blowed into Summerville, and now we both meet again on the Santa Fe in Needles, Calif., then we both laughed, and she says, gee, Brownie, isn't it funny how boomers meet each other again around in different parts of the country? and I says yes Billie, for it don't make any difference where I go, I most always meet some old timer that I have worked with or known on some other railroad, in a different part of the country. So we set there and talked until eleven P.M., when the lady librarian says, well it is time to close up everybody out, so I walked over to the Harvey House with Billie, and bid her adios as she went up the stairs to the rooms where all the Harvey House girls slept, then I went on up to my room and hit the hay until I was called to go out on the work train the next morning.

Now this work train was to work up at a passing track called Klinfelter, about twelve miles west of Needles, and after working all day, we would return to Needles and tie up for the night, and boy, it was some swell job, three squares every day, and every night at home in the feathers, and the hoghead Monk Haggard and I held down this job on the work train for about three weeks. It sure was easy pickings, for all we had to do was stand in on a spur track, with two flat cars coupled ahead of the engine, while a gang of Mexicans loaded them with rock, and then when the two flats were loaded, we would pull out on the main line, and go up a little ways to a trestle bridge that spanned across over a dry wash, and the Mexicans would dump the rocks down into the wash at the ends of the trestle, where they were used to bolster up the embankment around the abutt- ment to keep the trestle from being washed out, as it had been before during a big storm in the mountains up above there, by the flood waters that came rushing down through the canyons.

Now this little town of Needles is located right on the banks of the Colorado River, and at that time consisted of about three thousand population, by counting the white people, Mexicans and Indians, and besides being a division point on the Santa Fe railroad, it was a sort of headquarters for some mining districts around in the moun- tains and deserts, and the climate out there in the winter time sure is delightful. I remember the first winter that I was there, one day there came a light snow storm, and it snowed just enough to make the ground white a little before it melted, and as this was the first snow that anybody had ever remembered of seeing there in Needles, they turned the school children out so that they could see it, and there was a flock of Kodak nuts who were running around taking snapshots of the big feathery snowflakes as they fell, and the Mojave Indians, who always go barefooted the whole year round, did not know what to make of the snow, for they would walk for a short distance, then stop and hold up first one foot, and then the other, and they would look at their barefoot tracks in the snow, and then grunt and shake their heads, and say no savvy, for they were born and raised right there in the desert, and all of the snow that they knew anything about was what they could see away off on the tops of the snowcapped mountains.

I remember I used to take Billie or some other of the Harvey House girls over across the tracks to Indian Town on the banks of the River, and watch the Indians working and making the different things that they peddled to the passengers.

Now as I said before, Needles is a fine place in the winter time, but oh boy, she sure is a bearcat in the good old summer time, one hundred and twenty-five in the shade, and no shade. I remember one afternoon in August, 1910, I was called for an extra east, and it was an orange train, and when the head brakeman come and took us over into the yards, and coupled us on to the train which was being re-iced at the ice house, the thermometer stood at one hundred and twenty-five as it hung on the side of the ice house, and I have seen the time there in Needles when it was one hundred and ten at the hour of midnight, and a great many of the people used to bring their pillows and come down and sleep on the recreation hall lawn during the hottest nights, and all of the railroad men that can afford it, always send their families inside, that is they send them into Los Angeles, or to the beaches during the hot summer months.

Now the first summer that I was there, I remember that I caught a passenger engine firing for an engineer by the name of Charley Bert, and I held his engine for sixty days on account of his fireman getting overcome by the heat coming down the mountain from Goffs[25] one afternoon on No. 4,[26] a fast eastbound passenger train, and the company had to send him into Los Angeles to the Santa Fe hospital,[27] where he stayed for two months before returning to Needles. But winter or summer we used to have our dances over in the recreation hall, and in the summer time after each number of a dance we would all flock around the two big water coolers and drink ice water and sweat until our shirts were wringing wet, and the ladies shirtwaists would be the same, but we did not care as long as we could dance and have a good time.

Now this recreation hall was built and kept up by the Santa Fe company for the benefit of the railroad men and their families. It was something on the same order as the railroad Y.M.C.A. institutions back east, for it had a nice library and reading room, and a lounging room where the boys could play cards and many other games, and downstairs there was a bowling alley, and then there was a big inside plunge swimming pool, and all kinds of tub and shower baths, then there was the big gymnasium hall which we used to dance in two nights a week, and they also used it as a show house when the many traveling entertainers came along the line and put on their little shows. I give the Santa Fe all due credit for the way that they tried to make life as pleasant as they could out there in that scorching desert for their employees and their families,[28] and in the Harvey House lunch and dining rooms they served everything that was in season, that you could get in Los Angeles at any time of the year, and I want to say right here, that I have regretted it many times that I acted a fool and quit there, for outside of the heat, it was one of the best railroad jobs that I ever had in all of my railroad career.

Now I remember on the night of the Fourth of July, in 1910, the day that James J. Jeffries and Jack Johnson fought their championship battle at Reno, Nevada,[29] that I was called to go out on No. 8, the eastbound fast mail,[30] firing the engine 1275,[31] for old Tom Gallagher, and those 1270 class engines were new super heater simple passenger engines,[32] and they only carried one hundred and eighty pounds working pressure of steam, where the old compounds carried two hundred and twenty pounds working pressure, and it was said that these new super heaters could pull as much tonnage with one hundred and eighty pounds steam pressure as the old compounds could with their two hundred and twenty pounds steam pressure, but if the fire-boy let his steam drop back five or ten pounds on these new simple engines, it sure made a big difference in her pulling power.

Now I had never been out on one of these new super heaters yet, and this old hogger [age 42] Tom Gallagher that I was called to go out with, had the name there on the road of being a hard boiled old wampas cat to fire for, and none of the extra firemen would go out with him if they could help it, and after the call boy had called two different firemen and they both laid down on him and said that they were sick after he told them they were to go out on the 1275 with old Tom Gallagher, then he came and called me and told me that I had to go, so I went over to the roundhouse and was getting the 1275 ready for the trip when old Tom showed up. The first thing that he said to me was this, well Brownie I suppose you know your business, or they would not have you on here? and I could see that he was sore about something, and I says, I think I do, for I have been here over six months now, and I worked a couple of places before I came here, and then he says have you ever fired one of these super heaters before? and I says no, for this is the first time that I have caught one of them, and he says, well they are not like the old compounds, and No. 8 is a fast, hard run, and we are expected to make the time, and you want to keep your eye on the gun and keep her hot, for if she gets away from you and drops back five or ten pounds I won't be able to make the time, and I told him that I would do the best that I could.

Well the engine herder [roundhouse "hostler" or attendent] came and took us over to the station to wait for No. 8, and pretty soon she come pulling in right on time, and after the herder cut her engine off and headed her through the cross over, he backed us up and coupled us on to the train, and as No. 8 stopped there twenty minutes for supper we finished getting ready for the trip.

Now old Tom Gallagher had a young nephew [age 22] there and his name was Tom Gallagher also, and they were called by everybody there on the Santa Fe old Tom and young Tom Gallagher, and young Tom fired the 1275 regular for his uncle, old Tom, but from what I heard it seemed like that the two Toms had had a family quarrel on the engine while coming down from Seligman the day before on No. 9, the fast mail, and young Tom refused to go out with old Tom on the run any more, so while we were waiting there for the passengers to eat their supper, young Tom came strolling by with a little Harvey House hashslinger on his arm, and old Tom jumped down off the engine and began to bawl young Tom out something fierce, until young Tom walked away with his girl and left old Tom standing there, and boy, when he got back up on the engine he sure was spitting fire, no foolin', but I had all ready made up my mind, that if he hopped onto me, I was going to hop right back at him, and tell him where to head in at, so pretty soon here came the conductor with our train orders, and he got my name and set it down in his train book, then we all compared time, to see how our watches were running, for the conductor has always got to get the correct time from the regulator [clock] in the dispatcher's office before leaving a division point, and then the rest of the crew have to compare time with him before leaving.

Well when it came time to leave, the conductor hollered all aboard, and gave us a highball with his lantern, and we started out, but just before that old Tom had come over on my side of the cab and opened up the oil heater valve a little more than what I already had it open, and when we started out old Tom went right after her, and while he was making the air brake running test, he kept working the engine so hard that he knocked me out of five pounds of steam before I could say scat, and after he released the brakes and we got going, he looked up at the steam gauge and when he saw that she was five pounds shy, he let out a bellow, and says what in the blankety blank heck, there is something rotten somewhere, and then he stuck his head out of the cab window and kept it there until we reached the River bridge at Topock, and when he shut off rounding the curve onto the bridge, I put on my blower and by the time we had pulled across I had her back up to one hundred and eighty pounds again, and I held her there but she was smoking to beat the band, and old Tom was still hanging his head out of the window, but I could see that he was so mad that he could bite a nail in two.

Well the only thing that I could figure out was that the oil was too hot, so I reached over and closed the heater valve a little bit, and pretty soon the smoke began to clear up, then I hopped down on the deck and grabbed the sand funnel and put about three or four slugs of sand through her, to clear out the [boiler] flues, and boy, after that she laid right up there against the peg. Old Tom was sure taking it out of her, and he was right, for No. 8, was a heavy train and her time was fast and hard to make, so we rambled on up to a little place in the desert called Yucca,[33] where we stopped and took water, and as I was going back over the tank to take water, I almost fell over three or four hoboes, who were laying on the back of the tank near the manhole, so I told them to keep down flat and to keep quiet, so that the engineer and conductor could not hear them, and I also told them when we pulled into Kingman which would be the next stop, for them to get back on top of the train and keep out of sight, for there was a railroad bull that watched the trains at Kingman, and after we pulled out of there, they could come back over on the tank again.

Well after pulling out of Yucca, old Tom came down off his high-horse and come over on my side of the cab, and says well Brownie; you are doing fine since you got the hang of it, and I says yes and I would have done fine right out of Needles too, if you had not come over and opened up that heater valve so much, just before we pulled out of there, for the oil was getting too much heat, and that was what made her smoke so bad. Then he says, well that is where I thought Tommy always worked the heater valve, and he says besides Tommy got me so mad just before we pulled out, that I was sore about everything, and then he says you know Brownie I have been a father to that boy, and when he treats me like that it breaks me all up, and I says yes, I guess it is pretty tough all right. Then old Tom went back across the cab and crawled up on his seat box, and kept his eyes glued on the track ahead, but I could see that he was doing some heavy thinking, so when we pulled up into Kingman and stopped I went back to take water, and my hobo friends had taken my tip for they were out of sight. After leaving Kingman we proceeded on up to Peach Springs, where we made another stop for water, and when I went back to take water there were my hoboes again, and I told them that the next stop would be Seligman, the end of our run, and they had better crawl back on top again while they changed engines there, for the yard bull at Seligman was tough and hard boiled, and he carried a gat as big as a young cannon, and one of the fellows was just a kid, and he says gee, Mr. Fireman, it sure is good of you to tell us all these things, and I says that's all right kid, for I used to go hoboing around over the country myself before I went railroading.

Well we dragged our train up through Nelson's canyon and on up over the top of old Yampai mountain, and then down through the beautiful cattle country and on to Seligman where we arrived on time about two thirty A.M. in the morning, at the end of our run. Old Tom and I washed up on the deck of the engine, then we went over to the Harvey lunch room and took on a light lunch before piling into the hay, and I slept until I was called for No. 9, which was due to leave there around about twelve noon as near as I can remember, so as soon as No. 9 pulled in from the east, we were soon on our way back to Needles.

Well I fired the 1275 for old Tom Gallagher on No. 8 and No. 9 for about two weeks and by that time the two Toms had made up, and young Tom came back on the engine and fired for his uncle until he, young Tom, got set up, and became an engineer himself, after which old Tom sure was proud of his kid as he called young Tom.

Now by this time I was the oldest man on the extra board, and they kept me on passenger runs most all of the time, so instead of bidding in a regular freight engine I stayed on the fireman's extra board, for I made just as much money, and I had more time to myself there in Needles to attend the dances and to play around with the little Harvey House hashslingers, and there was also little Billie, the blue eyed blonde, who I played around with until she left there.

Now I remember one time I was firing for old Smokey Wallace, and we were pulling No. 3 and No. 4, the Chicago and Los Angeles limited between Needles and Seligman. Old Smokey had the reputation of being a fast rambler, so we left Seligman about one A.M. on No. 3 one morning, and we were about thirty minutes late, but the dispatcher did not bother us by putting us on a time order, for he knew that old Smokey would bring No. 3 into Needles on time if he let him alone. So when we pulled out of Seligman, old Smokey hollered across the cab to me, and says, well Brownie you had better tie your hat on, for here we go, and the next stop is Kingman, and I hollered back and says to him, go to it old head I am with you, for I can ride just as fast as you can. And man oh man, we sailed across the valley, and up over old Yampai mountain, then down through Nelson's and Crozer's canyon, and across Hualapai valley, and boy, the way that old engine rocked and swayed as she shot around one curve after another, almost made me dizzy. When we pulled down into Kingman and stopped, we got down and while old Smokey dropped some oil on the guides, I screwed down the dope plugs on the main-pins,[34] and as the order board was clear, the captain gave us a highball with his lantern, and we were off again down across the desert for Needles, where we arrived right on the cat-hop. Our running time down the mountains, through canyons, around curves and across the flats, was just three hours and eighteen minutes for the one hundred and fifty-three miles from Seligman to Needles.[35]

Well along in the afternoon, I was setting down in front of the Harvey House Hotel there in Needles, and the passenger brakeman whose name was Art Ruelon (the poor fellow got killed there afterwards) that was on No. 3 coming down from Seligman with us that morning, came and set down beside me. And I says well kid how did you like the ride we gave you this morning coming down on No. 3, and he says gee, Brownie, my conductor who is an old head here on the road, and I, were sitting back in the parlor car, as all of the passengers were in bed, and when that old car swung around some of those sharp curves, my conductor would grab the sides of the big arm chair that he was sitting in and hang on to beat the band. Then I laughed and says to him, well if that old parlor car was swaying around on the tail end, what do you think that old engine was doing on the head end, then I told him if he ever wanted to get a real thrill, to just come over and ride with us on the engine some time, and he says, no thanks, if I have to take mine, I will take it back in the train.

Now I remember another time, I was firing passenger for engineer Charley Bert, on the west end between Needles and Barstow, and it was in 1910, while the revolution was going on down in Old Mexico,[36] and one morning we caught a soldier train east out of Barstow, for the United States Government was rushing soldiers from the Presidio at Frisco,[37] down to El Paso, Texas, on the border, and we were running extra as a soldier special from Barstow to Needles. And when we arrived at Goffs, at the top of the hill thirty miles west of Needles, the order board was out, so we stopped, and the skipper beat it into the telegraph office and came out with a message addressed to the engine crew of soldier special, stating that on account of an engine being off in the turn table pit at Needles, they were unable to get another engine out of the roundhouse, and our engine would have to go through to Seligman with the soldier special, and the dispatcher wanted to know if we wanted to go through with our engine, or to be relieved in Needles. So Charley and I told them that we would go through with our engine, and when we pulled into Needles about eight A.M. that morning, Art Sheen the hostler and his helper were there at the depot waiting for us. They took our engine over to the roundhouse, and filled up her water and oil tanks, and put on the regular allowance of other supplies, and refilled the lubricator[38] for us, and they brought her back and coupled her onto the train, while Charley and I went into the lunch room and eat our breakfast. And we layed there for one hour, for the Harvey House had to feed the whole train of soldiers, and then we were off on our way to Seligman, and old Charley danced a jig on the deck of the engine, and I says what in the heck is the matter? are you glad that you are going through so that you can make a lot of mileage today? and he says heck no, I am not thinking of mileage Brownie, it is my wife and baby that I am thinking about, for they are up at Seligman visiting with my wife's people, and I will get to see them. But for my part I was glad to make the extra mileage, for that one hundred and fifty-three miles added onto the one hundred and seventy miles that we had made from Barstow to Needles would make me three hundred and twenty three miles for that trip, which would look good on the old paycheck.

Well we arrived at Seligman at about two P.M. that afternoon, and Charley Bert and I had completed a three hundred and twenty three mile run with a train load of soldiers, which was a record for an engine crew for one continuous trip on duty.

Well after putting a good feed under my belt, I piled into the hay and pounded my ear until I was called for second No. 3, which was due to leave Seligman at twelve forty A.M. in the morning, and boy, it was so foggy that we could only see two or three car lengths ahead of the engine, and old Charley and I sure kept our eyes pealed for first No. 3, which we knew was running just ten minutes ahead of us. As there were no automatic electric block signals[39] on that part of the Santa Fe in those days, it sure made a fellow feel creepy riding in the cab of an engine on a fast passenger run, going it blind in a dense fog, when he knows there is another train just ahead of him. Well by the time that we got down to Kingman we had run out of the fog, and it was clear sailing on into Needles.

Now I remember another time I was called to go out on the old 1010 (ten ten),[40] a tramp passenger engine which they used out of Needles to double head and help heavy passenger trains up the mountains, and the engineer was an extra man who had come there just a short time before off of the Great Northern at Minot, North Dakota, but I can't think of his name just now. Well anyway we went over to the roundhouse to get the old 1010 ready for we were going to double head No. 8 out of Needles that night as she was an extra heavy train this trip, and old Tom Gallagher and his 1275 had to have help up to the top of Yampai mountain. But before the passenger engine herder came to take us over to the depot, I took a look in the fire box, and I noticed that several of the flues were leaking pretty bad, and then I told the hogger about them, then he took a look, after which he beat it into the roundhouse, and got hold of the night roundhouse foreman, and brought him out to the engine and let him see for himself just how bad she was leaking. Then the engineer told the foreman that the only way that we would take her out in that condition would be by order from the mechanical department, and the foreman says O.K. go ahead and if you have any trouble or delay, I will stand behind you and release you from all blame. So when we got over to the depot and coupled on ahead of the 1275, I put on the blower and kept her good and hot, with plenty of water in the boiler, and when we pulled out and got going, the hogger worked her pretty hard, and I kept a good hot fire in her. After we had gone several miles, the flues took up and stopped leaking, but the engineer seemed to be having trouble with her from some cause or other, for she was not working just right. And when we pulled up in the desert and stopped at Yucca for water, he told old Tom Gallagher about it, and old Tom says, well you go back and run the 1275 and I will run the old 1010 up as far as Kingman and see if I can locate the trouble, for this old girl used to be my regular engine, and I run her for four or five years. So after we pulled out of Yucca old Tom fussed around with her for a while, and by the time we reached Kingman she was working fine and pulling her share of the train. Old Tom told me while we were going from Yucca up to Kingman that he had pulled Death Valley Scotty's special from Barstow to Needles with her,[41] and that he had given old Death Valley Scotty and his bunch a ride for their lives, and that old Death Valley Scotty was such a hound for speed that he came over on the engine and rode with old Tom and his fireman and patted them on the back for the speed that they were making, and he was so tickled that he gave each one of them a twenty dollar gold piece. He says that was back in 1905, so I told old Tom that I remembered the time, for I was working out of Chicago at the time on the Wabash, and was right there in the old Dearborn Street Station when old Scotty's private special pulled into the depot.

Well after we pulled out of Kingman, we proceeded on up to the top of the hill at Yampai where the negro train porter cut us off and backed us into the passing track, and then No. 8 went on her way, and then the hogger and I took our old tramp engine around the wye, and turned her nose back toward Needles. While the engineer was over in the telegraph office getting running orders for us to return to Needles, I was sitting up in the cab, for it was pretty crimpy up there on top of the mountain, with plenty of snow on the ground, and the first thing I knew there was a young negro hobo climbed up into the cab. And he says to me, "say mistah, does yoal mind ef ah stays heah til ah gets wham? ahs been up heah all night, and ahm jis erbout froze," so I told him sure stay and get warm until the engineer comes with the orders, and I asked him where he was headed for? and he told me that he was trying to get back to Los Angeles. I asked him how he come to be up there at Yampai? and he told me that he had got kicked off of the blind of No. 7 that afternoon and had not been able to get out of there since. So when the hogger came back to the engine with our running orders, and climbed up into the cab, he says to the little coon, say boy where are you going? and the coon says, boss ah don't ceah weah ah goes, jes so ah gits down ofen this heah mountin, away from dis heah cole snow, so the hogger says well stay right on here and we will take you down into the desert where it is lots warmer, and the little coon sure was glad to get to ride down out of there, for he had been having a tough time of it.

Santa Fe Mainline in Eastern California and Western Arizona, 1910. The distance from Chicago, Illinois, is given in parentheses.

Well we sure had our troubles making that return trip running light with that old tramp engine, for the flues let loose again and went to leaking to beat the band, and I had to keep the blower working all of the time to keep a good hot fire in her, for we wanted to get back to Needles before she died on the road with us, so we came on down to Kingman where we took water, and got some breakfast. The engineer brought the little coon a couple of sandwiches when he came back from the lunch room, and he sure was tickled, for he told us that he had not eaten for some time. We pulled out of Kingman and proceeded on down to Yucca where we had to head in for some eastbound train. Before we got out of there it was daylight, so the engineer told the little coon that he was sorry but we could not take chances on letting him ride any further in the day time for it might get us into trouble, and the little fellow thanked us for letting him ride this far. After the train that we were to meet there arrived, we pulled out and beat it for Needles, and when we got there the old girl was just about dead, for we did not have steam enough to work the injectors any more, and Jim Flynn the traveling engineer on the east end was there at the roundhouse when we pulled in, and he says that was good work boys, for we were afraid that you were not going to make it.

Chapter IX

*W*ell after I had been firing out of Needles for about a year, one day I got a letter from the master mechanic's chief clerk and he wanted to know why and how come, that I had not bid in a regular freight engine before this, for I was plenty old enough in the service. He went on to state that there had been a big squawk from some of the younger boys on the fireman's extra board that I was staying on the extra board and getting most of the extra passenger work to do, when I was old enough to hold a regular freight engine, and he gave me a gentle hint that to keep peace in the family that I had better do my stuff and bid in a regular engine.

Well as luck would have it, the "old" 940 [2-10-2] had just returned from San Bernardino where she had been in the big back shops and had been overhauled, and she was in fine shape. As she had no regular fireman she was up for bid, and of course me being the oldest extra man, I bid her in for my regular engine, and little Eddie Murry of whom I have spoken of before was now my regular engineer. As I have said before, he was a little prince, so I fired the old 940 for Eddie up into the summer of 1911 when there was a vacancy showed up on the east end out of Needles, between there and Seligman on account of an east end engine blowing up and killing her engineer and fireman.

And the east end out of Needles was preferable between there and Seligman by the old heads there on the Santa Fe, for after you get east of Kingman, Ariz., it is much cooler, and a person can always get a good sleep there in Seligman.

And when the vacancy showed up on the east end out of Needles, and was posted for bids, of course Eddie being the oldest engineer on the west end, he bid it in and took the old 940 over on the east end with him, but I could not go with him and the "old" 940, for I did not have whiskers enough to hold an engine on the east end.

And the outcome of it was, they assigned the "old" 1657[1] in the "old" 940's place on the west end, and I had to take her for my regular engine.

Now the west end division across the great Mojave Desert between Needles and Barstow is one hundred and seventy miles long, and working in the cab of an engine across that one hundred and seventy miles of hot burning desert sand in the summer time is something fierce on the engineer and fireman. I remember many times that I had been all night coming from Barstow to Needles on a fruit train, and would be all in from the want of sleep, so I would go to bed there in Needles in the day time and try to get some sleep, but it would be so hot that I would just lay there and sweat. All the sleep that I would get would be just little cat-naps, which did not do me much good, and maybe I would be called again to go out that evening, and boy, I want to tell you that it sure was torture to sit up there in the cab of a big hot engine and watch the steam and water gauges, and keep everything just right when you was so sleepy that you could hardly keep your eyes open another minute. I also remember that in the hot summer months while I was firing fast passenger runs across the desert, we would have to keep all of the cab windows closed, and keep the deck of the engine wet down good with water so that we would be able to stand it as we went rushing through the hot desert wind which came off of the burning hot sands.

Now as there was a vacancy on my engine (the old 1657) for an engineer, she was bid in by a hoghead by the name of Charley Westor, and he had been made right there on the Santa Fe, and he was what we call a homemade home-guard. He was a sort of a high-hat surly cuss who had refused to join the firemen's brotherhood when he was firing an engine. As he had only been running an engine extra for a few months, he sure had lots to learn yet about the railroad game, but after bidding in this regular engine, he had swelled all up like a poisoned pup, and you could not hand him an orange on a fishing pole.

Well, I had heard all about this guy before, but I did not know him until we met over at the roundhouse when he was called to make his first trip on the "old" 1657, after bidding her in for his regular engine. So he wanted to know how long I had been firing her? and what kind of shape she was in? and was she any good when it come to pulling on the hills? and then I told him that I had not been firing her very long, and that she was in bad shape and a bum steamer, and could not pull the hat off his head, for she had been a tramp engine, and the extra crews had not taken much interest in her, and nobody had kept her up. He tried to appear tough and hard boiled before me, for he says, well when I report work on her, they will do it or I will find out the reason why. And after we pulled out of Needles on this, his first trip, and got as far as Bagdad[2], about half way over the road, I saw that this swell head and I were not going to love each other any too well, for after leaving Needles we pulled up to the top of the hill at Goffs, and stopped and took a tank of water, then we started down the other side for Bagdad, and after we had gone five or six miles, he came over to my side of the cab and I had about three inches of water showing in the glass [boiler-water indicator], which any mountain railroad man knows is enough water in the western country where the water is bad, for when you get down on the flats and the engine levels up she will have plenty of water in the boiler. Well anyway he says to me, listen Brown, I want you to carry more water in the boiler while going down hill, and he pointed to the water glass with his finger, and showed me where he wanted me to carry the water, which made it over two thirds full, and I told him all right that I could carry the water wherever he wanted it, but if we kept her that full going down hill, when we reached the bottom and started across the flats, the water would level up in the boiler and she would be almost chuck full, and he says that's all right, I am the engineer and my fireman will always carry the water where I want it, so I says all right old head, its jake with me, for I can carry her chuck full just as easy as half full.

Well things went along so-so, until one night we were coming down the hill from Goffs to Needles on an orange train, and I was carrying the boiler full of water as he told me to on his first trip, and while coming down this hill the brakeman always had to ride out on top and turn up the pops (retainers) on the cars to help the engineer to hold the train while coming down the heavy grade, so when we reached a little place called Java, where there was nothing but a passing track and a section house, just above a big horseshoe curve, this wiseacre of a hoghead of mine, whistled into the station, and I saw him keep looking back and leaning out of his cab window, and finally he hollers across to me and says, hey did you see any highball from the hind end? so I leaned out my window and looked back, then I hollered back and told him no, and I also says why the heck worry about a highball, for everything is coming all right. Then he slammed on the air and come grinding down to a stop, and I says what is the big idea of stopping here? and he says why the book of rules says when an engineer whistles into a station that he is to get a highball from the conductor or somebody else on the caboose, or to stop and find out the reason why, and I says well what the heck, everybody knows that, but how come that you just now took the notion into your head to start living right up to the book of rules? and then he says well, when I am pulling a train crew they have got to hit the ball with me, and railroad right up to the handle, and I says, Oh you are one of those book of rule railroaders are you? and then he grabbed the whistle cord and give four short toots calling for a signal, and just then they gave him a highball from the rear end. He whistled off by giving two more toots from the old foghorn, then he released the air and tried to start the train, but he could not budge, for the brakes were froze, and the train was tied down as solid as a rock, for the retainers that the brakemen had turned up back on the cars were holding the air brakes set, and they could not be released until the brakemen went along over the top and turned the pops all down again. But this swell headed sap did not know that much, so he kept slacking her back, then he would hoss [start] her over into the forward motion, and try to get them started, and he opened the throttle so wide that the drive wheels would lose their grip on the rails and she would just stand there and spin them around, and the boiler being so full of water this caused the engine to prime and churn water through the cylinders and throw it out the smoke-stack. So this book of rules dumbbell says to me, if you did not have her so full of water, I might be able to get her started, and boy, when he said that my Irish blood began to boil, and I says to him, say listen you blankety blank home-made scissor bill, it is under your orders that I am carrying this boiler full of water, going down these hills, and besides if you was a railroad man and knew the first thing about running an engine, you would not have stopped here in the first place, and in the second place, if you knew anything about han-dling air brakes, you would not be trying to start the train now, but you would just let them stand here until the brakemen got enough of the retainers turned down so that the train would start itself down this hill, but you don't know that much you swell headed sap. Then he says to me, where in the heck do you get all of your railroad knowledge? and I says why you big dumbbell, I was railroading while you was down on the farm following an old mule down between two corn rows.

Well by that time the two brakemen had turned down enough retainers to release enough brakes while he and I were having our chewing match, and the train started off down the hill before he knew what was doing, and by the time that he got the brakes set up again and slowed the train down a bit, we hit the big horseshoe curve. Boy, the way we shot around that big circle was enough to make a fellow think that he was riding on a merry-go-round, and looking back I could see the two brakemen's lantern bobbing around, and I knew from experience that they were hurrying over the top of the train going from car to car turning up the retaining valves again. And it was a good thing that they did too, for otherwise the train would have gotten away from that brainless excuse of an engineer of mine, and we sure would have run away down that mountain grade, and we would have went tearing right down through Needles if we had not went in the ditch before we reached there.

Well we finally pulled down into the yards at Needles and stopped, and the head brakeman come over and cut us off, and while we were backing down the lead to the roundhouse, the brakeman climbed up into the cab and says to Westor the hoghead, what was the matter up on the hill at Java passing track? what did you stop for? And Westor says because I did not get a highball when I whistled into the station, that's why, and then he says to the brakeman, I guess the next time I am pulling you guys you will all know what to do. And the old boomer brakeman says to him, you are danged right we will know what to do, for if you ever pull that stunt with us coming down hill again, I'll come over and tear your can off, and kick you off the engine besides. And I says to the brakeman, yes and if you can't do it I will help you.

Well we were called the next day for an extra west, and we proceeded as far as the two twin horseshoe curves, just a few miles west of Bagdad, and we had just pulled around the first horseshoe and I was down on the deck putting a slug of sand through the flues to clean them out, for the "old" 1657 was not steaming any too well, and I had to smoke her a bit in order to keep her hot, and when you smoke an oil burner too much it sort of stops up the flues with a gummy soot, and the engine will not steam very freely, so you have got to sand her out every once in a while.

Well Mr. High Hat Westor the book of rules engineer, could not find anything else to crab about, so he says to me, say listen, I don't want you to be using so much sand, for pretty soon you will have the flues all cut out. Then I says to him you should worry about the flues, for if I cut them out the company will put in some more, and I says besides I am getting paid for firing this engine, and I will sand her out whenever I think she needs it, for that is what they put this box of sand on here for, and as long as I keep her hot and you have your two hundred and twenty pounds of putty, and a boiler full of water, you have not got any squawk coming. So he and I kept raving at each other off and on until we got over to a place called Daggett,[3] where we had to stop so that the conductor could check the register, for the Union Pacific trains used the Santa Fe tracks from Daggett to San Bernardino, and all trains had to stop there and check the register against the Union Pacific passenger trains. While we were standing there, Westor says to me, say listen Brown when we get back to Needles you get off this engine, and I says what do you mean, and then he says I mean for you to go and turn yourself in, for if you don't I will turn you in myself. And I says is that so, well I am telling you right now that you can go to heck, and go jump in the lake, for this engine suits me all O.K., and I am not going to let the likes of you run me off of her, for she was my regular engine when you came on here, and if you don't like it when we get back to Needles, you can get off yourself, and he says well you or I one will get off, for this cab is not big enough for you and I both, and I says well it will be you, for I was here first. So when we got back to Needles he went and turned me in, but I did not know anything about it until the next day when the call boy came after me and told me that I was wanted at the superintendent's office. When I got down to the office, the superintendent was out of town, but the east end trainmaster was going to hold the investigation in his place, and he says to me, what is the matter Brown? don't you know that we have been waiting for you? And I says waiting for me? what for? and he says why to hold your investigation of course, and I says my investigation, and he says why yes, don't you know that your engineer, Mr. Westor, has turned you in for insubordination? I says no, this all news to me, and then he says, well let's get started, for Mr. Westor is here with his witness, then I says well Mr. Westor can just stay here with his witness, and we will not start this trial until I can go and see the chairman of the firemen's adjustment board[4] for I was not duly notified and have not had a chance to have my witness called so I walked out on them, and went over to the chairman's house. As luck would have it he was at home, so I told him what was doing, and he went back over to the office with me and he told the trainmaster that he was the chairman of the grievance board from the brotherhood of locomotive firemen and enginemen, and that he was there to see that I got a fair deal, and that the investigation could not proceed until they had called in what engineers that I wanted for my witnesses. So I gave them a list of names of engineers that I had fired for, but I only remember a few of the names at this time such as Charley Bert, Monk Haggard, old Daddy Sheen, Eddie Murry, Jerry La Duke, Simon Renaud, and old Smokey Wallace, and I could have called many more, for I had fired for almost all of the engineers running out of Needles, at one time or another. So they sent the call boy out and all he could round up was Charley Bert and old Smokey Wallace, two passenger engineers, and Monk Haggard and Jerry La Duke, two freight engineers, and as soon as the four men got there, the trial started. And oh boy, what we did to Mr. Westor and his witness, who was a little square headed Dutchman by the name Bergerman, and all that he could say about me was that I talked back to him one time when he hopped onto me because he thought that I used too much time screwing down the dope plugs on the side rods when we stopped at Hackberry for a red order board one time when we were coming down from Seligman on No. 7 which had been almost a year before this time.

Well all four of my witnesses told the trainmaster who was acting as the judge that when I was on their engines with them that they found me to be as good as any of the rest of the firemen working out of Needles, and that they would take me for their regular fireman any time that I was old enough [enough seniority] to bid their engines in. So the trainmaster after hearing both sides of the story told Mr. Westor that all he could do was to dismiss the case, for it looked to him like that one was just as bad as the other, and we would have to fight it out between ourselves, and Mr. Chaney, the master mechanic. So Mr. Chaney called me over to his office near the roundhouse, and told me that he knew that Westor was as much at fault as I was, for his record as a fireman was nothing to brag about, and that I was entitled to hold the engine if I wanted to, but he says if I were you Brown, I would get off of the engine for the chances are if you stay on the 1657 with Westor, you and him will get into a fight, and maybe both of you will get canned and you don't want to do that, for you will soon be old enough to bid in a passenger run. So I told Mr. Chaney that I would give up the 1657, and go back to the extra board for a while, so the next day I caught a passenger engine for thirty days.

Now at this time I owned a little short order restaurant there in Needles,[5] and had a woman running it for me. I had a pretty good trade among the railroad boys, but Westor knew that I was the silent owner of the restaurant, and he was not satisfied that I had got off of his engine, but the dirty stool-pigeon had to go and tell the Superintendent about me. I was called up on the carpet in the superintendent's office, and he told me that he understood that I owned the Star restaurant, and he says don't you know Brown that it is against the Santa Fe company's rules to own and operate a business when you are in their employ. And I told him that I did not own it any longer, for I had sold out to the woman that had been running it for me, then he says well, I am going to have our chief special agent to investigate the matter, and if I find out that you have lied to me, I will discharge you. So then I beat it back to the restaurant and told the woman that Westor had tipped me off to the old man, for I had just come from his office and he had told me that he was going to have their chief flatfoot dick to look me up, and I told her what I had told the old man about me selling out to her, and if the dick came to her, for her to tell him the same. I thought everything was going to be jake, but a few days later when I came in off my run, I went into the roundhouse to register in the rest book, and I saw this little message from the old man written across the enginemen's call board, take Fireman C. P. Brown out of service until further notice. The next day the old man sent for me again, and he told me that his chief special agent had found plenty of proof to convince him that I still owned and operated the restaurant, and that he was going to hold me out of service until I disposed of it, so I flew up and got sore and told him that he and the whole Santa Fe system could go and take a run and jump into the lake, for I was through. Then I went over to the master mechanic's office and told the chief clerk to make it [final check] out for me for I had bunched the job, and I also told him to fix me up with a service letter, and just then Mr. Chaney called me into his private office. He says Brown I think you are making a bad mistake, the thing for you to do is to get shut of that restaurant even if you have to give it away, for you will be ahead of the game in the long run.

Now I was bullheaded at that time and could not see it that way, but I want to say right here that I have regretted it many of a time since that I did not take Mr. Chaney's advice, for I almost gave the dang restaurant away after all later on when I got ready to leave Needles, and come in here to Los Angeles.

Well after I got in here to Los Angeles I was so sore at myself for what I had done that I made up my mind to quit railroading, so I got me a job as engineer out at the McKinley Orphans Home between Los Angeles and San Pedro, and my job was to take care of the electric light system, keep up the plumbing, fire the boiler and oversee the laundry machinery, and also to operate the big twenty horsepower gas engine that drove the big centrifugal pump to pump the water into the big plunge [pool] for the boys to swim in, after which the water was used to irrigate the farm with. And when I was working there among all of those boys, it made me think of the time when I was a kid in an Orphans Home away back in Crawfordsville, Indiana.

Well after working there for a couple of months, I quit and come back into Los Angeles, and then I got a job of firing the boilers on a dredger down on the Santa Ana River, when they were building the big levees down there. My pay was fifty dollars a month and board and room, and I saved up a stake and came back to Los Angeles, and ragged myself out with a new suit of clothes, new shoes and hat, and had a nice piece of change left to hit the road with. For by this time I was homesick to go back railroading, and I had my dues all paid up for three months ahead in both the B. of R.T. and the B. of L.F.&E.[6] brotherhoods, for I was a double header and belonged to the trainmen and fireman both. I figured on blowing in a few days here in Los Angeles before I started traveling looking for a railroad job.

Now while I was firing for the Santa Fe, I had met old Fuzz, a Texas longhorn boomer who I had worked with while I was switching cars for the Santa Fe down in Summerville, Texas, back in 1906, and at that time old Fuzz was night yard master out at Barstow for the Santa Fe, and I was figuring that when I left Los Angeles that I would go to Barstow and hit old Fuzz up for a job of switching in the yards. The night before I was going to leave town, I got robbed of everything that I had that was of any good. Some thief had come in through the fire-escape window, while I was asleep in my room near Eighth and Spring Streets and took my new clothes, my money and my railroad watch, and all of my railroad letters, and my brotherhood receipts and traveling cards. And boy, what I mean they put me on the hummer just about right, for they sure made a bum out of me, for all I had left was some old working clothes. When I woke up the next morning and found out that I was cleaned, I put on my old overalls and jumper and other things that I had in an old suitcase, and started out to see if I could mooch some breakfast. I had walked up Spring street as far as Second, and I had to stop to let a yellow [trolley] car come around the corner out of Second street into Spring street. As the rear end of the car went by me, I heard somebody holler, hello there Brownie, and I looked up and saw it was the street car conductor who had hollered at me, and I remembered him as a boomer brakeman by the name of Charley White that I worked with out of Decatur, Ill., on the Wabash railroad back in 1904. He motioned for me to come and get on, so I run and caught the car and got on, then we shook hands, and he says to me, what in the heck are you doing out here in Los Angeles? for the love of Mike, Brownie, I thought you were still back in Decatur on the Wabash, and then I told him how I come to be out on the coast and what had just happened to me. He belonged to the B. of R.T. the trainmen, so he reached into his pocket and gave me a dollar, and I rode out to the end of the line with him and back, and I remember that his run was out West Pico street and back up Broadway to Second street and then around on Spring street again.

Well we had a good talk about old times back in Decatur, and just before I got off his car at Second and Spring, he says now Brownie if you go hungry it will be your own fault, for you can catch me here at Second and Spring at this same time any day in the week until you get on your feet, so I thanked him, and says don't worry for I will be back. (But I never saw him again until in 1915.) So when the car reached Second and Spring again I got off and walked east on Second and crossed over Main street, and went into a little restaurant that used to be on the corner of Second and Main streets in those days, and put a feed of ham and eggs under my belt. Then I went into one of the employment offices that used to be on Second street between Main and Los Angeles streets, and was looking over the jobs that were marked upon the boards, when one of the clerks came out of the private office and hollered out that he had a short job good for a couple of days, who wanted it. And as nobody else made a move like they wanted it, I asked the clerk what kind of work it was and how much was the office fee, and he told me that it was a pick and shovel job, and the office fee was two bits, so I says all right I'll take it, then he filled out a card and gave it to me with instructions how to get out to the job, then I grabbed a P.E. Red car[7] and beat it out to Avenue something over toward South Pasadena where the job was at. The boss was a plumber, and he was connecting up the bathroom of a new house with the city sewer out in the street, so I gave him the card from the employment office, and then he put me to work digging the ditch from the house out through the front yard and into the street so that he could lay the sewer pipes. I remember I worked nine hours for which he paid me two dollars and twenty-five cents a day, and I got in five days with him altogether, and boy, I'll tell the whole world that I never had a job that I appreciated any more than I did that one right at that time, for it sort of put me on my feet and helped me to get a start to make another stake.

Well the first day that I worked for the plumber I told him what had happened to me the night before, so at the end of that first days work he gave me two dollars so that I could eat and get a flop that night, but he made me promise that I would be back on the job the next morning. I told him not to worry for I needed him worse than he needed me, so when we got all through with the job, he paid me off and I went to a Jew second hand store where I bought me a cheap second hand suit of clothes, and just had enough money left to buy me another job at the employment office, which was known as the Humle Brothers employment office.[8]

Well this time I got a job as a waiter slinging hash behind the counter of a little restaurant down on East Third street, for eight dollars a week and my meals, and right at that time I sure was glad to get it too, for it set into raining as it was along in March which is part of the rainy season here in Los Angeles and I was sure glad to have this little old job inside where it was dry.

Well I stayed there and worked in the little restaurant for about six weeks, and I saved up a small stake. In the meantime I had written back to some of the railroads that I had worked for in different parts of the country, and asked them if they would send me duplicate service letters as I had lost the original ones, so some of the roads answered my request and sent me duplicates, and some did not. By this time I had received my duplicate brotherhood receipts and new traveling cards, so I bunched the little restaurant job and beat it out of Los Angeles and headed north for Sacramento.[9]

Now this was along in the first part of May 1912, and by the time I got to Sacramento I was just about broke again, so I had to go to work at anything that I could get to do, and I finally landed a job as a helper on the new M-street bridge that was being built across the Sacramento River at that time. I batched with a fellow worker who had a little houseboat which was anchored out in the River almost right down under the new bridge.

Well sometime along in August I quit the job on the Sacramento River bridge and got a ride with a Southern Pacific Passenger conductor up over the hump [Sierra Nevadas] and went to Reno, Nev., and stopped off there for a day, and then I went over to Wadsworth[10] about thirty miles east of there on the S.P. road where they were building a new line from Wadsworth up north into Oregon,[11] and I was told there in Wadsworth that there was all kinds of work at the different camps strung out along the new line north of there, so I made up my mind to go to work there some place and save up a good stake and then head back to Salt Lake.

Now it happened that the first camp just about a mile out of Wadsworth was a big steam shovel camp, where they were digging a big cut through a young mountain, and making some big fills across a deep canyon, so I walked out to this camp to see if I could pick up some kind of a job, and when I got up there I went into the commissary office and asked the Swede walking boss if he could use another man in his outfit. He says to me, well what are you, a mule skinner, donkey skinner, or a steam shovel man? and then I says, well in fact I am a railroad man, but I have done some mule skinning, but it was many moons ago. There was a big fellow standing there leaning against the railing of the office, who was dressed in overalls and jumper, and when he saw my fireman's brotherhood pin on my coat, he says where do you belong to the firemen at brother? and I looked at him sort of surprised, and says, why I belong to Silver Mountain lodge No. 327, at Needles, Calif., and then we shook hands and told each other our names. He told me that he belonged at Sparks, the S.P. division point near Reno, for he was off the S.P. at Sparks, on account of a wreck that he had been in, and he was expecting to be called back and reinstated, for the Firemen's brotherhood was working on his case then at the time, so after we talked for a while, he turned around and says to the walking boss, Pete, I want you to give this brother a job, for any man that wears that kind of a pin on his coat is jake and O.K. The walking boss says well Jack, I have not got any opening right now, in the train service, until we get your engine fixed up and the new parts won't be here until tomorrow, and Jack says, well put him on as my fireman (his name was Jack Doalon), and when the new parts come for the engine, he can help me fix her up, for that big mule skinner that I have got firing for me now don't know anything about an engine any way. So Pete (his name was Pete Peterson, the big Swede) says all right, Jack, for we would much rather have experienced railroad men to operate our

[203]

engines and trains, when we can get them, than to have to use mule skinners and shovel stiffs. So I got a job as Jack's fireman, at seventy-five dollars a month and board and room, or rather a bunk in the engine men's and Steam Shovel crew's bunk house to sleep in, for the mule skinners and shovel stiffs all bunked in big tents. So Jack took me over to the bunk house and showed me an empty bunk with a new mattress in it, then I went back to the commissary and bought a couple blankets and fixed me up a bed. About that time the supper bell rang, which was an iron bar bent into a triangle form and was having a tune played upon it by the cook who used another small piece of iron which he held in his hand, and I says to Jack if that guy is as good at cooking as he is of pounding on that triangle, he must be jake.

Well you could see the poor working stiffs coming from all directions, to the eating shack to get their mulligan and java. In this dining shack there were two tables about seventy five feet long, and there was a flunkey waiting on each table, keeping the big platters and bowls and other dishes filled up with good hot food right from the kitchen, and also passing around the big hot pots of coffee, which in such camps is always called java, and bread is punk, butter is salve, milk is cow, sugar is gravel train, and potatoes is spuds.

Well the food was very good in this camp, and plenty of it which cannot be said of all such camps, and this outfit was owned and operated by the Palmer, McBride, and Quail construction company of Frisco. The steam shovel and the engines of this camp were new, but the cars had been used for some time before. But they were standard gauge and up-to-date, with airbrakes, and airdumping equipment, and there were eight cars and an engine to each train, and the engines each carried a nine and half inch airpump, and the dumps and brakes on the cars were all Westinghouse equipment, and the whole train of eight cars could be dumped at one time by the engineer from the engine by operating an air valve, but at this time one of the trains was laid up on account of Jack's engine jumping the track and breaking off one of her eccentric straps and blade,[12] and those were the new parts that they were waiting for. So, the next day the new parts came and Jack and I set to work fixing up the engine, for at this camp the enginemen had to do all of their own repair work and keep their engines up as far as they could, and Jack's brakeman on his train was a little old boomer conductor off of the big trunk lines throughout the country, but who could not hold the main line jobs any more, because he was a booze hound and could not keep sober, and the engineer on the other engine was also an outcast on account of drinking too much giggle water, but they were all good fellows and brotherhood men.

Well I had been firing there about two weeks for Jack when he got word from the chairman of the grievance board there in Sparks that he had been reinstated as an engineer, as everything had been all straightened out, and for him to come on back and go to work, so Jack went to old Pete Peterson the big Swede as he was called, and asked old Pete to let me take charge of the engine, and old Pete asked Jack if he thought that I could handle her on these hills? and Jack says why sure he can, for he done all of his firing in the Rocky Mountains, then old Pete said all right that he would give me a chance, and I was promoted to be an engineer, and now my wages jumped up to one hundred dollars . . . and besides I made lots of overtime which run me up to about one hundred and twenty-five dollars a month.

Now the steam shovel was digging a cut through a big hill, and our two work trains were hauling the dirt away and dumping it down into a deep canyon to make a fill across it, to build the new road bed on, and the way that they done this at first, to get the fill across, was to build a false trestle works across the canyon just strong enough to hold up the empty cars which were shoved out onto it after they had been dumped at the end of the fill, which buried the trestle works under as the fill proceeded across the canyon. So, one night we were working overtime as we were in a hurry to get the job done, for by this time winter had set in and it was very cold and it was snowing and blowing, and the gang boss who had charge of the dumping, and his gang of about six men, had all throwed in and made up a jackpot and the gang boss had sent one of his men down town to Wadsworth and he brought back a gallon of booze and every time that we would come down from the steam shovel with a train load of dirt, my brakeman the little old boomer conductor would take a big shot of firewater out of their jug. Pretty soon the whole gang were all likkered up and feeling pretty good, so they got the idea into their heads that dumping one car at a time at the end of the fill was too slow, and they were going to speed things up a bit by running the whole train of loads out on the trestle and then having me to dump the whole works for them from the engine with the air-dumping system, and as it was dark and I could not see just where I was at, and besides I did not know what they were trying to do, but as my brakeman kept giving me a back up signal with his lantern, I kept backing up slow and began to wonder what was going on, for what little I could see of the landmarks it looked to me like that we were getting too far out over the canyon. But I kept backing up expecting to get a stop signal any moment, when all at once I heard a noise like breaking and crashing timbers, and just then I saw the front end of the head car that had been coupled to the engine, rear up above the hind end of the tank and disappear into the darkness as it went plunging down into the dark canyon with the rest of the train, and Shorty, my brakeman who was now running by the engine hollered up to me and says get out of there Brownie, get out of there. I hollered to my fireman to unload as I jumped through the cab window, while the eight cars loaded with dirt went roaring down into the canyon below, but as the knuckle of the coupler on the head car slipped out of the coupler of the engine as the car reared up, that left the engine standing alone right at the edge of the canyon as the air brakes had set automatically when the air hose parted, and my fireman who was asleep at the time did not jump and get out until everything was over.

Well there was my whole train of eight cars down in the canyon, for the false trestle works was not strong enough to hold up the train of loaded cars, and down everything went but the engine, and the noise that it made was so loud that they heard it clear up at the camp and there came men running down from the camp, bosses, cooks, flunkeys, mule skinners and all, and some had lanterns and others were bringing big open air torches. Mr. Quail, one of the owners of the outfit happened to be in camp that night, and he and old Pete came running down to the engine, which by this time I had run about a hundred feet from the rim of the canyon and stopped, and they asked me what had happened, and I told them that the whole train of eight cars had went down into the canyon, and they asked me how it all happened, so I told them that they would have to talk to the gang-boss, for all I knew about it was that I kept getting a signal to back up, and the first thing that I knew the whole works except the engine went down with the trestle. And Mr. Quail said to me, well I am glad that you saved the engine anyway Brown, and I told him that I did not save her, for she had saved herself as the air brakes had set when the train line parted, when the head car come uncoupled as it tipped over the rim of the canyon, and to save myself, I had unloaded by jumping through the cab window. When old Pete saw that the whole gang were pretty well stewed up except my fireman and I, he lit into the rest of them and what he told them was a plenty, and he canned the whole works right there except Shorty, my brakeman, as Shorty told him that he was working under orders of the gang boss, then old Pete told Shorty that he would let him go this time, but the next time that he caught him drunk he would tie a can on him so big that they could hear it rattle all over the camp.

Well that tied up the works for that night, and the next day each engine took four cars and we hauled the dirt from the steam shovel and throwed it down a waste dump, so that they could keep the shovel going, and they took a bunch of men and went down to the mouth of the canyon near the Truckee river, and began to lay a track up the canyon to where the cars were at, so that they could get them out, for the way they had gone down did not wreck them up very much, as the trestle had sort of broke the fall, and in about a week they had them all out of there by building a track around the point of a hill and up a steep grade to the main line, and when they would get a car all fixed up and on the track that they had built up the canyon, they would hitch a big bunch of mules to it, and then pull it out and up to the main line.

Now while I was working there that fall and winter, I attended some of the dances that the town folks give in the school house there in Wadsworth, and I got to know some of the girls, and some of them used to ride out to the camp on their broncos, and then I would take the girls on the engine and let them ride, and they thought it was great fun to get to ride in the cab of an engine, and there was one that I sort of got stuck on, and we wrote to each other for some time after I left there.[13]

Now I remember that some of us boys would go down town after supper if we did not have to work overtime, and the sights that I used to see down there in the saloons and on the streets of drunken mule skinners, shovel stiffs, and all kinds of other working men, reminded me of the time that I first went railroading out of Rawlins, Wyo., back in the days of 1900, for I was told that there were all kinds of camps strung out for sixty miles north of Wadsworth, and the working men all had to come through Wadsworth going out and coming back, and there was a stream of men coming and going all of the time, the most of them would go out and work for a month or two, and then come back into Wadsworth to blow in their stake, and it did not take some of them long, but they thought that they were having one heck of a time while it lasted.

Now the whole job of construction was leased to the big Utah construction company of Salt Lake, and they in turn subleased to all of these other outfits, but when a man quit his job at any one of these camps along the line, the boss would give him an identity which he would have to take to the main office of the Utah construction company there in Wadsworth and get his check, and then he would go busting over to a saloon to get it cashed, and I have seen fellows come into a saloon and slam their check down on the bar, and holler, "Fire in the headin," which means in the lingo of the hobo camp follower, for everybody in the saloon to come up to the bar and have a drink on him, and that is the way their money went until they were broke, and then they would lay around town for a week or two mooching their eats and drinks off of the next live ones that kept coming in off the jobs, and there were drunken fights, knock down and drag outs, and you could see drunken stiffs at all times laying around in the saloons on the floor asleep, and some had black eyes, and skinned and bruised faces from the fights that they had been mixed up in, and the most of them went broke before they even got a shave or a hair cut, or any new working clothes to wear.

Well we worked there until the first part of February, 1913, when we finished up the job and moved our outfit over to a little town called Baypoint, Calif.,[14] just thirty miles east of Oakland, where our company had a contract of building a stretch of new track for the Oakland, Antioch & Eastern,[15] which was a new Electric railroad, and at that time was building from Oakland to Sacramento, and which already had been finished as far as this little town of Baypoint, and our company were to build the road from Baypoint on up to a little town by the name of Pittsburgh,[16] where the new line crossed the Sacramento River, and by the time they got the outfit moved over to Baypoint and got going again, it was around about the first of March [1913]. I remember that after we got everything loaded and ready for shipment over there at Wadsworth, Nev., Charley Green, the other engineer and I and our firemen all got passes from our company over the Southern Pacific and went to Frisco to kick up our heels and play around a bit while we were waiting for the outfit to be shipped over into California.

And I remember when we got to Frisco, we all went to the Golden Eagle hotel which was on Third street near Howard, and got rooms, for the Golden Eagle was a sort of headquarters for steam shovel men and dinky skinners, (as locomotive engineers are called when running an engine for a construction company outfit,) and in a few days more some of the steam shovel boys came dropping in, and boy, I want to tell you that we had some good times there in Frisco, but after we had been there about three weeks, we were called up to

Palmer, McBride & Quail's office there on Market street, and told to report out at Baypoint for duty in the next day or two.

Well we all had had a good time in Frisco and now we were all ready to get into the collar and go to work again and as our headquarters were right there in Baypoint, we train crews and the steam shovel men all boarded and roomed in a hotel at the company's expense, and they also had a big camp about five miles east of there, where they were digging a subway through in under the S.P. and Santa Fe tracks which run along side by side at this place, and the Electric road had to go under them, and they had all of the shovel stiffs and mule skinners up at that camp.

Well we finished up our job there in Baypoint, along about the first of July, and the Palmer McBride & Quail company were figuring on another big job that would be coming up in about six weeks or two months, so they layed us all off for the time being, and the most of us went back into Frisco, and after we had been there for two or three days, my fireman, a young fellow by the name of Dick Avery, came to me in the [Golden] Eagle Hotel, one day and says Brownie I just saw some fellows that are going up to a place called Wheatland[17] just north of Sacramento to pick hops in the big hop yards, and they say a fellow can make five or six dollars a day, and have all kinds of fun just like camping out, and we can fill in the time that way until Palmer, McBride & Quail company gets ready for us again. So I told him that it was jake with me, for I would like to take a vacation and go camping out for a spell anyway, so he and I took our suit cases and went down to the boat landing just north of the Ferry building there in Frisco, and boarded a Sacramento River steam boat and enjoyed the trip up the river to Sacramento where we took a train from there up to this little town on the Shasta Route [Sacramento to Portland] of the Southern Pacific. When we arrived in Wheatland, there were hundreds of people coming in there by train and wagons and buggies and some of the old boys with their blanket rolls on their backs were walking in, so Dick and I followed the mob which was headed out to the Durst Bros. Co. about one half mile east of town, where they had a big camp, and we got a job of picking hops, and the company furnished us with a tent to sleep in which we pitched down in one corner of the camp grounds, and then we went to a big straw stack and got a big bunch of straw and fixed us a bed, for we had taken our roll of bedding with us when we left Frisco. And after we got our camp all fixed up we went to picking hops which were more like feathers than anything else when it come to weighing the dang things in at quitting time, for we got paid one cent a pound for picking them, and boy, it looked to me like that it took a wagon box full of them hops to weigh one hundred pounds, and Dick and I could not have made five or six dollars a day in those hops if we had pulled up the vines and all and throwed into our sacks, for about the best we could do was a couple of hundred pounds each in one day. But we did not care for it did not cost us much to live up there, and as long as we made our expenses we did not give a dang, for we were sure having one heck of a good time, for the Durst Bros. Company had built a big dancing platform right in the center of the big camp grounds, and they had also strung electric lights all around so that we had plenty of light, and boy, we used to dance our fool heads off, gee but we had lots of fun, for there were hundreds of men and women, and boys and girls, and all kinds of music, and they would pass a hat around and take up a collection, . . . to pay the musicians with, and we would dance until they turned the lights off at midnight.[18]

Well we picked hops up there until along about the first of August [1913] when a fellow they called Blackie Ford,[19] who was an I.W.W. (better known by the hobo working stiffs as wobblies)[20] speaker, and another fellow, who was an I.W.W. organizer, came up there from Frisco and tried to organize the hop pickers into the wobblies, and this made the Durst Bros. sore. One Sunday morning while Blackie Ford was using the dancing platform for a hall to speak to the mob of hop pickers, one of the Durst Bros. went down town and come back with the town marshal who tried to arrest Blackie, but the I.W.W. hop pickers would not let the marshal take him, so that afternoon while Blackie was speaking to a big mob from the dancing platform, here came the sheriff and a whole flock of deputies, and also the district attorney of Yuba county who had just drove down from Marysville,[21] and they started to break up the meeting, and tried to arrest Blackie Ford and the organizer, and that started a big fight, and I says to Dick, come on let's get the heck away from here, and we were running to get away from the mob when the shooting started, and after the battle was over and the smoke cleared away, Blackie and the organizer had made their escape while the mix up was going on, and the district attorney and one deputy sheriff and two hop pickers lay dead on the field of battle, and a number of other people were badly wounded from being hit with clubs and stray bullets, and we saw one poor fellow with his right hand shot off by one of the deputy sheriff's sawed off shot guns.[22]

Well after this trouble Dick and I pulled out of Wheatland and went over into the Santa Rosa country in north of Frisco on the Russian River, where the hops were just beginning to get ripe enough to pick, and we got a job of picking over there. This part of the country was much nicer than Wheatland, for it was cooler, and our camp was right on the River banks, and we could go swimming, boatriding, and do all kinds of fishing, so my buddy Dick Avery and I spent five weeks up there before we came down to Frisco, and besides having an outing and lots of fun, we each one had saved up a small stake. So when we got back into Frisco we went to the Golden Eagle hotel, and got a room, and the next day we called up the construction company and asked what was doing, and they told us that they would have things lined up in about another month, but that was too long for us, as we had just came back off of a vacation and was ready to go to work. That night we met some more of the boys that we had worked with in the steam shovel outfit, and they had just blowed into town off of some little job, so we all made up our minds to whoop it up and raise a little heck for a few days before we tried to get another job, and every night for about a week found us up in Chinatown, and at Barbary Coast on Pacific street, which was claimed to be one of the fastest, toughest, and most wicked places in the country at that time, with its saloons, cafes, dance halls, and painted women. And boy, if those painted gold diggers that worked in the dance halls could not separate you from your jack, you sure would have to be a Scotchman, and if they could not get your money, their lovers would waylay a fellow if they got half a chance, and sap him over the bean and take it away from him, and I'll tell the world that it was no place for a gay cat, or greenhorn scissor bill that did not know his onions, for they would have him cleaned before he reached the first whistling post.

Well after we had been there about a week Dick got him a job out at the World's Fair Grounds[23] where they had just began to start getting it ready for the World's Fair which was held in 1915. By this time I was getting homesick for the railroad again, so I went up to the trainmaster's office there in the old Town Station[24] of the S.P. Coast line and landed a job of braking, and I run on through freight from Frisco down the coast line to San Luis Obispo.[25] But I only worked there for a short time, for I think it was some time in October that a forest fire came down the side of a mountain and set fire to the wooden frame work of tunnel number five, just a few miles north of San Luis Obispo which tied up traffic on the Coast line of the

Southern Pacific, and they assigned me on a work train there at the tunnel, and I held that job down until I got bumped by an older [more senior] brakeman than I was, then they dead headed me back to Frisco and I was marked up on the brakemen's extra board. I was second out, so that night when I went to bed, I was sure that I would get out before morning, as all of the Coast line traffic was being routed from San Jose east over the cut off to the San Joaquin Valley Route, which run down through Fresno, Bakersfield and up over the Tehachapi Pass and then on down to Los Angeles, but I was not called that night, so the next morning after I eat some breakfast, I went down to the yard office to see what was the matter. When I took a look at the names marked up on the extra board, I saw that instead of being two times out, I was five times out, or in other words where there was one man ahead of me the night before, now there were four men ahead of me on the slow board, and I was going down toward the bottom instead of going up to the top, and I thought that there might be some mistake, so I got ahold of the call boy and asked him what was the big idea of running all of these other men around me on the slow board? and he says because those guys are older than you are [in seniority], and I says what difference does that make on the extra board? for I came in ahead of those fellows. Then he told me that the oldest extra men done all of the extra work, so I went up to the trainmaster's office there in the depot, and asked the chief clerk how come I was second out last night and now I was five times out? then he says to me, why you know we use the strict seniority rule here on the Coast line, and I says what do you mean strict seniority rule? don't you work the extra men first in first out on the extra board? And he says why no, now listen and I will explain it to you, now we will say that you was first out on the board and an older extra man than you came in off the road after you did, but you are not called to go out before his eight hours rest is up, then he is marked up ahead of you on the board and gets out ahead of you, and so on down the line. Then I says to him, do you mean to tell me that the guys that are working extra the same as I am but older in the service than I am, can come in off the road after I do and if their rest is up before I get out, that they are entitled to run around me on the extra board, and go out before I do? And he says yes that's it, that is what we call strict seniority, the oldest extra men do all of the extra work. Then I says to him, well brother, I have worked for several railroads throughout these United States, but I have never got up against anything like this before, so you can just make it out for me for I am through, and you don't need to mind about a service letter, for I don't want anybody to know that I ever worked on a pike like this, so you can give me what little I have got coming to me, and I will be on my way, then he says all right but first you will have to turn in your company property. So I went to my room and got my lantern, book of rules, brakeman's badge, and switch key, and brought them back to him and then he gave me my check, and after sticking around Frisco for a few days, I took a River steamer and went to Sacramento, and from there I went up the Shasta Route of the Southern Pacific to Portland, Oregon[26] . . . where I stayed for a day and a night.

. . . and when I got to Seattle[27] I stopped there for a couple of days taking in the sights, then I headed for Butte, Montana[28] over the Chicago, Milwaukee & St. Paul road, . . . where I stayed for a couple of days, but I was not much impressed with the town of Butte itself, so I went to the office of the Oregon Short Line, and got a pass down to Pocatello, Idaho, as I had been told that the O.S.L. was hiring some brakemen at that place. But when I got down there to Pocatello, the Oregon Short Line had all of the night yard masters and brakemen that they needed, so they passed me down to Ogden, Utah, and I went up to the Union Pacific office there in the depot, and they gave me a pass out to Rawlins for they were wanting some brakemen there, to help them move their trains as there was a rush of business on at the time. And I remember that some more fellows and I landed there on a Sunday morning, and the trainmaster was there waiting for us, so he rounded us all up and told us to go and get some breakfast and then come over to his office, for he had made arrangements with the company doctor to put us through the physical examination, for he wanted to use some of us that night.

Well here I was back in Rawlins, Wyo., after all my years of booming around over the country, and I had just got a job of braking on the same division between Rawlins and Green River where I started railroading several years before, but I did not know at that time that this was to be my last job of railroading, but it seemed like fate had decreed that I was to come back and finish my railroad career where I had started it several years before.

Well after I had made out the application and filled out the book of questions, I went over and passed the doctor, and that night I was on my way to Rock Springs where I was to be assigned on a crew to work between Rock Springs and a little coal mining town by the name of Superior[29] which was seven miles off the main line up in the hills just north of Thayer Junction, where we branched off of the main line to go up to the mines.

Well I remember that we would leave Rock Springs at about six A.M. in the morning, and run caboose bounce (with just engine and caboose) out to Thayer Junction and pick up a drag of empty coal cars, and shove them ahead of the engine up to the mines at Superior, after which we would distribute them around to the different mines, and then we would pick up the loads and bring them back down to the main line and set them out there at Thayer Junction in the storage tracks for the main line crews to pick up. Then we would take another string of empties up and peddle them around to the mines and then bring the rest of the loads down and set them out at Thayer Junction and then return to Rock Springs and tie up for the night. And boy, as jobs go on a railroad, this was some swell job, for a brakeman could knock out around about one hundred and fifty dollars a month, with three squares a day, and every night at home in the feathers, and as we nearly always got back into Rock Springs around six P.M. in the evening, it gave me a good chance to play around and have a good time, for I belonged to two different dancing clubs, and I went to the roller skating rink once or twice a week, and the rest of the time I went to the picture shows, and boy what I mean I sure was having the time of my life, but we never know what is in store for us, and it is a good thing that we don't.

Well after I had been there for about two months, that is to be exact, it was on the night of the twentieth of December, 1913, at about six P.M. in the evening, that I met with the greatest tragedy of my life. Now just before this time there had been some pretty severe blizzards and snow storms all through the Rocky Mountain section of the country, and the snowfall at some places was pretty deep, and I remember at that time, that all of the papers stated that the snow was about four feet deep in Denver, Colo., and before they could get the streets cleared so that they could get around with delivery trucks, many people suffered from hunger and cold.

Well, anyway, the coal cars began to arrive at the Superior coal mines full of snow, and most of them looked like the snow had been shoveled into them, while cleaning up the railroad yards east of there, and when we would take these cars up to Superior and spot them at the mines, they had to be cleaned out before they could be loaded with coal, so the company had a gang of men there shoveling the snow out of these cars. The boss who had charge of this gang, that was shoveling the snow out of the cars, disregarded the rules and regulations of the railroad company, which called for four feet clearance on each side of the tracks, which according to law must be kept clear so as not to endanger the lives and limbs of the train crews while doing a job of switching, or otherwise while working around their trains, but instead of keeping this four foot space clear, the boss in charge of these snow shovelers allowed them to throw the snow out all along the sides of the tracks which piled up so high that it would roll back against the sides of the cars, in many places and froze there like so much ice, which made a solid bank right up against the cars.

Well, on this twentieth day of December, 1913, we had been working all day in a fierce Wyoming blizzard and snow storm, and the thermometer stood down twenty below zero, and as we had been working at a handicap all day, we were away late and it was after dark when we shoved our last cut of emptys into mine E before starting back to Rock Springs, and the mine tracks were built on heavy grades around the mines, and we had to leave the cars tied down with the hand brakes.

Well, while the rest of the crew pulled up over the mine lead switch, I dropped off and walked across and lined up the switch for an empty track and when they came backing down in there I swung onto the first car and had just started to climb up with the intention of setting up the hand brakes, but as I had my brake club in one hand, and my lantern in the other, I was taking my time about climbing up. Before I knew what was happening, with my feet still in the stirrup on the side of the car, the car plowed right into one of these frozen banks of snow and dragged me off the side of the car with such force that I was slammed down face first into that frozen sharp jagged pile of snow, and besides having my face all cut and bruised, I was knocked partly unconscious and the fall had broken my nose. Then I got wedged in between the car and the bank of snow and was dragged, rolled, and tumbled along until I came to a place where the snow was not up against the car, and as I could not roll out from the car on account of the pile of snow, I was rolled in under the train, and I have a faint recollection of being rolled and tumbled around under there until the wheels went over my legs and cut off both of my feet just above my ankles. Then I became unconscious, and the other boys told me afterwards that my clothes had caught on the brake rigging underneath the cars, and that I had been dragged for about eight or ten car lengths before the train stopped, as they did not stop until they had shoved into clear.

Well, the swing man was on top setting brakes at about the middle of the cut, and the head man had cut off his engine, and then climbed up and set up some binders on the head end, and the swing man after setting a few brakes, had got down and walked up to the engine and they were waiting for me to come up, for I was supposed to be setting brakes on the rear end, so after they waited for some time, and I failed to show up, they came back looking for me. It was so cold and the wind was blowing so strong that it was hard for them to keep their lanterns lit, but they finally found me under the train, for I had come to myself and was hollering for help as best I could, but which was not loud enough to be heard above the howling wind and storm, then after they got me out from under the cars, they could not pick me up in that condition and take me on the engine, so they had to cut the engine off and go back down about a mile where we had left the caboose, and bring it up there so that they could pick me up on the stretchers. While they were gone, one of my partners, the swing man by the name of Shirly, had cut the bell rope off from the engine bell, and cut it into two pieces and then he took the pieces of rope and tied them around my legs just above each knee, making a tourniquet by twisting them up tight with a couple of brake clubs, and while I was lying there in the snow gasping for breath, he took a little book and pencil from his pocket, while he was kneeling down beside me, and he says now Brownie I don't know how long you are going to live, so you had better give me the names and addresses of some of your people, then I gasped out the best that I could my mother's name and address, who at that time lived in Cleveland, Ohio, and he wrote it down in the book. Then he tried to encourage me by telling me to buck up for they were coming back with the caboose and they would soon have me in where it was warm, and then I would be all right, and he told me that he was going to quit the game, for he had seen too many of his brother workers all cut to pieces, and if they were not killed outright, they were crippled for life.

Well, they finally got there with the stretcher, and picked me up and took me into the caboose where it was warm, and they told me that it had been the biggest part of an hour that I had laid there in the storm and snow, and in the meantime the conductor had stayed down at the depot and wired the train dispatcher as to what had happened, and asked him to have a clear track for us when we got down to the main line at Thayer Junction. When we got down to the Junction the dispatcher had everything lined up for us so that we

[216]

could make a fast run into Rock Springs,[30] and they had also wired the hospital there in Rock Springs and when we arrived there, they had the ambulance waiting for me, and they drove the horses at a fast run. The wagon road up to the hospital was rough and rocky, and I thought that I would die before I got there, and when we arrived, the doctors and nurses were all waiting for me, and I remember that the first thing that they did after getting me inside, was to cut all of my clothes off of me. Now just a short time before, I had bought me two new double-breasted blue flannel shirts, with pockets on each side and big white buttons all around, and I sure was proud of those two shirts, and I had put one of them on just that morning, and as I saw them with my one good eye (as the other one was swelled shut) start to cutting my new shirt off of me, it sure made me sore, no fooling, but I could not help myself, and they kept on cutting my clothes to pieces.

Well, after they had put me in bed, they piled on plenty of blankets and also put many hot water bottles all around me, to try and get me warm again, and then one of the nurses took some warm water and a cloth and washed my face and cleaned the cinders out of the wound of my broken nose. Then they examined my eye, for they thought it was knocked out, but it was all right except a bad cut above and under it, which caused it to swell shut, so after I had been there for about an hour or so, they came into the room where I was at, with a sort of a stretcher on wheels and put me on it and wheeled me out into the operating room and laid me on the operating table, and the doctor in charge says to me, Now, Mr. Brown, we are going to do the very best we can for you, and I says all right doctor, that is all you can do, and I can still see the cluster of three big powerful electric lights right above me as one of the doctors told me to take a long deep breath as he poured the ether into the cone-shaped thing, that he was holding over my face, and then I seemed to float away off up into the great dark unknown where there is no pain, and I knew nothing more until the next day at about noon, when I woke up. Nobody will ever know what pain and torture that I was passing through at that time and the long weeks of suffering after that, but me and me alone.

Well, in the meantime the Union Pacific Railroad Company had sent my mother a message telling her that I had met with an accident and could not live until morning, as they had no hopes for me, but instead of dying, I pulled through, but I will never be able to tell how I did it, for there were times when the pain and agony was so severe that I just thought that I could not stand it another minute.

Well, in the meantime the company had sent my mother transportation from Cleveland and return, and she came out to see me, and before she left home, she had sent a message to my brother Tom who was working out of St. Paul, Minn., at that time on the Chicago, Milwaukee & St. Paul road, and he also came out to see me, and they stayed there about a week with me, and when the doctor told them that I would recover, they went back home, and after I had been in the hospital just a little over eight weeks, the doctor told me that my stumps had all healed up and as far as he and the nurses were concerned, they could not do anything more for me, for from now on, nature would just have to take her own time to make me well and sound again, so I wrote a letter to my brother Tom to come and take me home to Cleveland, Ohio, where my mother lived, which he did, and I remember it was around about the last of February, 1914, when we arrived in Cleveland, and it was snowing and blowing to beat the band.

Well, I stayed there in my mother's home and suffered off and on for three long months or up into the first part of June, when I got up and was able to wear my first pair of artificial limbs, and then I could get out of the house and walk around in the sunshine and breathe the good fresh air, and in a short time I was feeling pretty good again, for I grew stronger as I began to take on more weight, and in the meantime I had got my insurance money from the brotherhoods, and a few months later I was called to Omaha, Neb., and settled out of court with the Union Pacific Railroad Company,[31] and then after going back and bidding my mother and the rest of them good-bye, my brother Tom and I headed for Los Angeles where we arrived sometime in January, 1915, and I bought me a little home[32] and put the rest of the money in the bank. After I had been here for a couple of years I got me a job as an elevator operator and I have worked at it off and on ever since, but as it is a very monotonous job going up and down year after year, I got the notion into my head that I would like to do something else, for being penned up in an elevator cage day after day was just like prison to me, after all of the years that I had been free to go rambling around over the country wherever I wanted to, so along in October, 1928, I started to write the story and memories of my life, and in this story I have tried to give the non-railroading public a look behind the scenes, as it were, into the real lives of the railroad men as they work and live their lives while operating the thousands of trains on the great network of tracks and railroad systems throughout the United States.

And now I want to say to my readers that I have written this life story and memories true to life as near as my memory will serve me, and although at times my memory may have failed me to a small degree, in some few details, the story as a whole is a picture of my life as I lived it while growing up from boyhood to the present time, although I will admit that the last few years have been pretty tame. At first when I came here to Los Angeles to settle down, it sure was hard for me to do, as I had always been of a roving disposition, and I still have the great desire to roam and travel around and see the country, and to see and learn things that a fellow is not able to see and learn by sitting down in one place all of the time. Now my folks and friends used to tell me that a rolling stone never gathered any moss, and I used to laugh and tell them that was true all right, for not much moss could be expected to stick to a rolling stone, for in many cases the stone was too well polished, and on the other hand in most cases, where a stone never rolled, it generally got so dang mossy that it couldn't roll.

Well my little bungalow home here where I live in Belvedere Gardens on the east side which is known as the industrial district of Los Angeles is right near the Union Pacific yards and roundhouse, and the Santa Fe main line is only about a quarter of a mile south of that, and all day long I can see and hear the switch engines in the U.P. yards, switching and making up trains, and when a road engine comes down through the yards from the roundhouse with her bell ringing on her way to take out a train, the tones of that bell give me a thrill, and a heartache, and it makes me glad and sad in turn, it makes me glad because I am lucky enough to be living close enough to be also to hear it, and it makes me sad because it brings back memories of the past when I was an able-bodied man booming around over the country working as a fireman, brakeman or switchman, first one place and then another, happy go lucky not giving a dang where I was, for if things did not suit me one place I would bunch the job and take a little trip of a thousand miles or two across the country and get me another one. Then again there is the trains going out and coming in on the Santa Fe, and when I hear the musical sound of those big chime whistles, it fairly makes my blood tingle, and reminds me of the days when I worked as a fireman on the Santa Fe firing the big oilburners out of Needles, California, and gee; what a thrill I got one day almost a year ago [1928], while driving in my little old Ford across the New Ninth Street bridge that spans the Los Angeles River, and the U.P. and the Santa Fe railroads, for passing under the bridge on the west bank of the river, was a Santa Fe passenger train coming into town from the east, and the engine that was pulling the train was the old 1275 (twelve seventy five), the very same engine that I had once fired for a time out of Needles on No. 8, and No. 9, for old Tom Gallagher between Needles and Seligman, Arizona, away back in 1910, so I just stopped the old Ford and set there and watched the train and the engine until it pulled out of sight around a curve, for it was just like seeing an old friend that I had worked with years before.

Now, it is hard for me to try to express my feelings about such things, so as to make the public understand, for I guess, it is only we railroad men that do really understand these things after all, for it seems to be in our blood and the engines, whistles, bells, and the different colored signal lights of red, green and yellow that guide us on our way through the dark and many times stormy nights, those things to we railroad men are a part of our very lives as we live them in the railroad game day by day, and year after year, throughout the country on the great railroad's systems.

And even after being retired, and pensioned off on account of the old age limit, or by being maimed and crippled for life, the love for those things is still in our hearts, even on to death when we make that last farewell trip over the dark, mysterious division which lands us in the terminal of that great unknown, at the end of our last highball run where we tie up for an everlasting rest to be called no more.

Appendix

Steam locomotives are commonly referred to by their classification in the Whyte System, developed by F. H. Whyte, an official from the New York Central Lines. Whyte used the number of pilot-truck wheels, drivers, and trailing-truck wheels to identify most kinds of steam locomotives. Thus the "American" or "8-wheeler" locomotive is a 4-4-0, which means it has a four-wheel pilot truck, two pairs of coupled drivers, and no trailing truck.

Wheel arrangements and names for common steam locomotives, 1900–1915:

0-4-0	4-wheel switcher
0-6-0	6-wheel switcher
0-8-0	8-wheel switcher
0-10-0	10-wheel switcher
2-4-2	Columbia
2-6-0	Mogul
2-6-2	Prairie
2-8-0	Consolidation
2-8-2	Mikado
2-8-4	Berkshire
2-10-0	Decapod
2-10-2	Santa Fe
2-10-4	Texas
4-4-0	American or 8-wheeler
4-4-2	Atlantic
4-6-0	10-wheeler
4-6-2	Pacific
4-6-4	Hudson
4-8-0	12-wheeler
4-8-2	Mountain
4-8-4	Northern

Notes

Introduction

1. The leading studies of railroad workers include James H. Ducker, *Men of the Steel Rails: Workers on the Atchison, Topeka & Santa Fe, 1869–1900* (Lincoln: University of Nebraska Press, 1983); Carl R. Graves, "Scientific Management and the Santa Fe Railway Shopmen of Topeka, Kansas, 1900–1925," (Ph.D. dissertation, Harvard University, 1980); Walter Licht, *Working for the Railroad: The Organization of Work in the Nineteenth Century* (Princeton: Princeton University Press, 1983); Shelton Stromquist, *A Generation of Boomers: The Pattern of Railroad Conflict in Nineteenth-Century America* (Urbana: University of Illinois Press, 1987); and W. Thomas White, "A History of Railroad Workers in the Pacific Northwest, 1883–1934," (Ph.D. dissertation, University of Washington, 1981).

2. See W. Thomas White, "Race, Ethnicity, and Gender in the Railroad Work Force: The Case of the Far Northwest, 1883–1918," *Western Historical Quarterly* 16 (July 1985):265–83.

3. Charles C. Shannon to editor, October 12, 1988; hereafter cited as Shannon letter.

4. *The Maize* 1 (December 1912):n.p.

5. Charles P. Brown, *The Life Story of Chas. P. Brown As A Boomer Railroad Man* (Whittier, Calif.: Western Printing Corporation, 1929), 176.

6. Freeman H. Hubbard, *Railroad Avenue: Great Stories and Legends of American Railroading* (New York: McGraw-Hill Book Company, 1945), 186–87.

7. Brown, *The Life of Chas. P. Brown,* 142–43.

8. Quoted in Charles S. Wallace to Frank P. Donovan, Jr., n.d., James J. Hill Reference Library, St. Paul, Minnesota.

9. Jules Tygiel, "Tramping Artisans: The Case of the Carpenters in Industrial America," *Labor History* 22 (Summer 1981):358.

10. Interview with D. Keith Lawson, Rogers, Arkansas, October 18, 1980.

11. Shannon letter.

12. Charles P. Brown, *Brownie the Boomer: The Life Story of Chas. P. Brown As A Boomer Railroad Man* (Whittier, Calif.: Western Printing Corporation, 1930), 150.

13. Hubbard, *Railroad Avenue,* 188.

14. Brown, *The Life Story of Chas. P. Brown,* 2.

15. Brown's list of employers includes Union Pacific Railroad (1899–1902, 1913); Lake Erie & Western Railroad (1902); St. Louis-San Francisco Railroad (Frisco) (1902, 1903–1904); Toledo, St. Louis & Western Railroad (Clover Leaf) (1902–1903); Terminal Railroad Association of St. Louis (1904); Missouri Pacific Railway (1904) [hired but never worked]; Wabash Railroad (1904–1906); Chicago, Milwaukee & St. Paul Railway (1906); Gulf, Colorado & Santa Fe Railway (Santa Fe System) (1906); New York Central Lines (1906–1907); Chicago & Eastern Illinois Railroad (1907–1909); Denver & Rio Grande Railroad (1909); Atchison, Topeka & Santa Railway (1909–1912); and Southern Pacific Company (1913). Brown also worked for a railroad contractor, Palmer, McBride & Quail, in 1912 and 1913.

16. Brown, *The Life Story of Chas. P. Brown,* Preface.

17. Ibid., 3.

18. William Jackson, son of Samuel Jackson who founded the Western Printing Corporation in 1922, speculates that Brown selected the firm because it cost less than printers in Los Angeles, even though it was a union shop. "We charged about 10 to 25 percent less than the downtown L.A. plants because we enjoyed the lower costs of Whittier." Western also was a thriving and well-known operation. "We printed at that time [1929] about 35 city directories and we did an extensive legal printing business. . . . We also published a lot of books." Telephone interview with William Jackson, October 5, 1988.

19. William Jackson recalls that Western typically charged five dollars per page for a press run of 500 to 1,000 books. Unfortunately, a fire in 1958 destroyed any records of Brown's two books.

20. The remaining Union Pacific records of employees for the early twentieth century, including the "Personal Injury Registers," are housed in the Union Pacific Railroad Collection at the Nebraska State Historical Society in Lincoln.

21. Brown's Santa Fe payroll documents are located with the records of the Atchison, Topeka & Santa Fe in the Kansas State Historical Society in Topeka.

22. "Statement of Death and Disability Claims Filed with the General Secretary and Treasurer during the Month Ending February 15, 1914," *The Brotherhood of Locomotive Firemen and Enginemen's Magazine* 56 (March 1914):400.

23. See *Los Angeles City Directory* (Los Angeles: The Los Angeles Directory Company, 1916–1942).

24. Material in the Copyright Office at the Library of Congress reveals

that "Mrs. Charles P. Brown, as widow of the deceased author . . ." renewed the copyright for both the 1929 and 1930 editions in 1957 and 1958 respectively.

25. Brown, *The Life Story of Chas. P. Brown,* Preface.

26. Ibid., 46.

27. Ibid., 1.

28. There is nothing comparable to Brown's autobiography. Perhaps the closest published volume in terms of coverage and spirit is Chauncey Del French's *Railroadman* (New York: Macmillan, 1938). This tale of boomer life was allegedly told to French by his father, Henry Clay French. Their collaborative work covers a railroading career in the Midwest and Pacific Northwest from 1873 to 1930.

29. See Roger A. Bruns, *Knights of the Road: A Hobo History* (New York: Methuen, Inc., 1980), 26–60.

30. Brown, *The Life Story of Chas. P. Brown,* 143–44.

31. Ibid., 183.

Chapter I

1. Lamar, Missouri, with an 1880 population of 907, is the seat of Barton County. This region contained moderately prosperous farms, some of which produced sizable quantities of apples and peaches, for this was part of the highly publicized "Missouri Fruit Belt."

Although Brown was born on February 9, 1879, he and his parents do not appear in the manuscript census taken in June 1880.

2. Brown's father's name is unknown, as is his mother's. Since Brown was the oldest of five children, it can be assumed that his parents married in the late 1870s, and this was probably the time that his father "went railroading."

Railroad equipment was initially braked and coupled by hand. Unfortuantely for workers, carriers commonly used the dangerous link-and-pin couplers on passenger coaches until the 1870s and on freight cars until the 1890s. This type of coupler consisted of a slotted wrought-iron drawbar fastened to the end of the car into which a long, oval link was inserted and held in place by an iron pin that was dropped into a hole in the drawbar after the coupling had been made.

3. Wichita, Kansas, a bustling community of 4,911 in 1880, still retained its cowtown heritage.

Based on Brown's 1929 book, *The Life of Charles P. Brown,* the family never lived in Wichita. Rather the father, a "boomer" brakeman and switchman, worked on a series of jobs in southeastern and southern Kansas. These included the Kansas City, Fort Scott and Memphis in Fort Scott (1880 population of 5,372) and Cherryvale (1880 population of 690), the Atchison, Topeka & Santa Fe in Wellington (1880 population of 2,694), and the Frisco in Wichita. The family, however, apparently lived only in Cherryvale and Wellington.

4. The Brown family moved to Crawfordsville, Indiana, which had a population of 5,251 in 1880. There was a personal connection with that west-central Indiana county-seat: "[My father] had a sister and a brother living [there]." 1929 ed., p. 4.

5. The Indiana, Bloomington & Western, previously the Indianapolis, Bloomington & Western, became part of the Cleveland, Cincinnati, Chicago & St. Louis Railway, the "Big Four," in 1914.

6. Lafayette, Indiana, boasted a population of 16,243 in 1890. According to the 1929 version, Brown's father worked for the "Vandalia Line," the Terre Haute & Indianapolis Railroad, part of the Pennsylvania System, between his jobs on the IB&W and the Monon.

7. The Monon Route, officially the Louisville, New Albany & Chicago Railway, connected Cincinnati and Louisville with Chicago.

8. Brown's father worked south out of Monon, Indiana, a Monon Route division point, with a population of 288 in 1880.

9. Brown's mentions in his 1929 version that his mother "got a job [in Crawfordsville] where she helped out a part of each day in a boarding house where they took in students from Wabash College." Brown himself picked up junk, "old pieces of iron, rags, bottles and bones," and sold these odds and ends to a dealer. Later he became a "boot-black." As he writes, "I would get down on my knees and daub and brush until I had given [the customer] a good shine, after which I would collect my nickle and be on my way looking for another customer." 1929 ed., pp. 6–7.

10. Newspaper coverage of the accident that killed Brown's father is sketchy. The *Crawfordsville Review* of February 16, 1889, mentioned the wreck, three miles south of Cloverdale, Indiana, on February 12, but only that it involved "the loss of human life." The Monon crew member is unnamed.

11. Brown lived in the Montgomery County Orphan's Home. Established in December 1881, the facility was located initially in Crawfordsville. But the county purchased property several miles out of town on the Yountsville Road for a farm operation. When a fire destroyed the house in 1892, the children were moved back to Crawfordsville.

In the tradition of nineteenth century orphanages, the Montgomery County one readily made children available to the community. The *Crawfordsville Review* of March 9, 1889, reported that "The Orphans' Home has 23 inmates, of whom eight are babies. Anyone desiring to adopt a child should call at the home."

12. Knightstown, Indiana, with an 1890 population of 1,867, was located on the Pittsburgh, Cincinnati, Chicago & St. Louis, part of the Pennsylvania System, 34 miles east of Indianapolis.

13. Indianapolis, the Indiana capital, claimed 105,436 residents in 1890.

14. The Peoria Division (or the Peoria & Eastern Division) of the Cleveland, Cincinnati, Chicago & St. Louis or "Big Four Route" extended 351 miles from Peoria, Illinois, to Springfield, Ohio. Brown's run from Indianapolis to Springfield covered 139 miles.

15. Hoopeston, Illinois, with a population of 1,911 in 1890, was served by the Chicago & Eastern Illinois and the Lake Erie & Western railroads. This community grew dramatically during the 1890s and reached 3,823 residents in 1900.

16. Brown, according to the 1929 version, began to work in the machine shop during the spring of 1897. His salary rose from $5 to $6 per week.

17. Brown and his friend, Patrick Kelly, joined Company A of the Illinois militia. But nearby Battery A, destined for action and based in Danville, soon ruined the chances of the Hoopeston unit to enter the war. For one thing, Battery A took the larger men. "[It] would not take a man unless he stood five foot and eight inches high, and weighed at least one hundred and sixty pounds." Clearly, Brown and Kelly were smaller. As Brown relates, "[T]hat was the beginning of the end for our company, for a short time after that our officers give it up as a bad job and disbanded the company, and the heck of it was it was too late now to go any place else and join up with another outfit, for everything was all filed up and awaiting orders to move." 1929 ed., pp. 47–48.

Chapter II

1. The C.&E.I. was a Chicago-based coal carrier, the Chicago & Eastern Illinois Railroad Company. Known at this time as the "Evansville Route," the 625-mile C.&E.I. was affiliated with the 155-mile Evansville & Terre Haute Railroad and the 150-mile Evansville & Indianapolis Railroad.

2. The Masonic Temple, located on State Street in Chicago's "Loop," was a 21-story "skyscraper." Built in 1892, it was demolished in 1939.

3. Ferris Wheel Park, on the northside of Chicago, contained George Ferris's 265-foot high "Ferris Wheel." It had been the great attraction of the Columbian Exposition of 1893.

4. William Frederick Cody, "Buffalo Bill," launched in 1882 what became the best known of the wild west shows of the late 19th and early 20th centuries. A born showman and organizer, Buffalo Bill converted popular interest in the West into a thriving business venture.

5. Annie Oakley (1860–1926) was a renowned markswoman. She joined Buffalo Bill's show in 1885 and remained with it for seventeen years.

6. Johnny Baker, known as the "Cowboy Kid," joined Buffalo Bill's Wild West Show at an early date as an expert marksman. His rivalry with Annie Oakley pleased the show's audiences.

7. The Chicago, Milwaukee & St. Paul Railway, commonly

nicknamed the "St. Paul" (later it would be called the "Milwaukee"), served large sections of the upper Middle West with approximately 4,000 miles of road in 1898.

8. Built to care for veterans of the Civil War, this facility was one of the federal government's first national soldiers' homes. It was located on a 410-acre tract west of Milwaukee.

9. The population of LaCrosse, Wisconsin, stood at 28,895 in 1900.

10. Brown's reference to the "side door Pullman route" means that he and fellow hoboes rode in boxcars and not the posh sleeping cars owned and operated by the Chicago-based Pullman Company.

11. The C.B.&Q., the "Burlington" or the "Q," was the sprawling 7,900-mile Chicago, Burlington & Quincy Railroad. It connected Chicago with the Twin Cities, St. Louis, Kansas City, Omaha, Denver, and Billings, Montana.

12. The first of the northern transcontinentals, completed in 1883, the Northern Pacific linked Minneapolis and St. Paul and Duluth with the Pacific Northwest.

13. Staples, Minnesota, a long-established division point on the Northern Pacific, claimed 1,504 residents in 1900.

14. Traction engines, powered by steam, served as power units for farm chores, including the threshing of grain.

15. Fargo, North Dakota, unofficial capital of the Red River Valley of the North, boasted a population of 9,589 in 1900.

16. In the 1929 version, Brown identifies these "boys" as George Hines, "who was a kid in the Orphans' Home with me," and Hines's friend, Billy Smith. 1929 ed., p. 56.

17. Brown refers to the Fergus Falls Division of James J. Hill's Great Northern Railway, which includes the 78 miles of line between Fargo and Grand Forks.

18. This discussion of railroad "boomers" appears only in the 1929 version as do the previous two paragraphs. 1929 ed., pp. 59–61.

19. The Great Northern called this place on its Fargo to Grand Forks line, Alton.

20. The slip scrapper, a simple piece of construction equipment pulled by horses or mules, was commonly used in building railroad lines at the turn-of-the-century. It contains a large metal (iron or steel) plate that the operator releases to dump the removed earth from each "pass." While moving along the ground, the operator holds onto two big handles like those of an old-fashioned plow.

21. This paragraph of description appears in the 1929 version. 1929 ed., p. 65.

22. Miles City, Montana, with a 1900 population of 1,938, is 745 miles west of St. Paul and served as a Northern Pacific division point.

23. According to Brown's 1929 account, he remained for a week in

Miles City and explored on foot nearby Fort Keough and a Sioux Indian camp along the Yellowstone River. Unable to find a job, he departed for Billings. 1929 ed., pp. 67–68.

24. Billings, Montana, population 3,211 in 1910, by this time had become an important railroad junction. A line of the Burlington, opened in 1894, connected it with Omaha and points east.

25. Huntley is located 13 miles east of Billings, where the Burlington's line to Omaha begins; the Burlington had trackage rights over the Northern Pacific into Billings.

26. Railroads, like the Northern Pacific, built section houses in remote locations to provide housing for maintenance-of-way—"section"—employees and their families.

27. Custer, Montana, named in honor of Colonel George Armstrong Custer of the 7th Cavalry, is 54 miles east of Billings and 41 miles east of Huntley on the Northern Pacific's mainline.

28. Undoubtedly Brown had read the popular "dime novels," which commonly glorified cowboy life.

29. Brown watched the cowboys of the R L Bar Ranch for about a week.

30. In his earlier work Brown explains that a "mucker" is "better known as a shovel stiff" or a common laborer. 1929 ed., p. 77.

31. In 1930, national prohibition remained in effect; the "noble experiment" would be repealed three years later.

32. Brown offers greater detail of his work on the Northern Pacific's Big Horn Tunnel project in the 1929 account, including this paragraph. 1929 ed., p. 78.

33. Forsythe, Montana, with a 1910 population of 1,398, is situated 42 miles east of the Big Horn Tunnel. The town was not incorporated until 1908.

34. Glendive, Montana, a division point like Forsythe on the Northern Pacific, claimed 2,428 inhabitants in 1910, eight years after its incorporation. Glendive is 226 miles east of Billings and 124 miles east of Forsythe.

35. Dickinson, North Dakota, with a 1900 population of 2,076, is a crew-change point 106 miles east of Glendive.

36. Mandan, North Dakota, located on the west bank of the Missouri River and the eastern limit of the Mountain Time zone, is a division point on the Northern Pacific, with a population of 1,658 in 1900. Mandan is 110 miles east of Dickinson.

37. Jamestown, North Dakota, a division point and a junction of two Northern Pacific branchlines, claimed 2,853 residents in 1900. It is 207 miles east of Mandan and 342 miles west of St. Paul.

38. Little Falls, Minnesota, 108 miles west of St. Paul and sporting a 1900 population of 5,774, is a junction point with the Brainerd and Morris branches.

39. This distance between St. Paul and LaCrosse, Wisconsin, on the Burlington is 133 miles.

40. Brown's trip between the St. Paul's North LaCrosse, Wisconsin, yards and Milwaukee covered 196 miles.

41. Chicago is 85 miles from Milwaukee on the St. Paul.

42. The Great Northern Theatre was located at 26 West Jackson Street; it was founded in 1896. In the tradition of the British music halls, the Great Northern catered to working-class audiences.

43. The Dearborn Station, at the corner of Polk and Dearborn streets, served not only the Chicago & Eastern Illinois but also the Chicago & Western Indiana, Erie, Grand Trunk, Santa Fe and Wabash railroads.

44. Apparently Brown worked initially in the Hoopeston, Illinois, machine shop as a stationary engine fireman. Then in January 1899, "I began to travel again, for the wanderlust was in my blood." Brown journeyed to Hot Springs, Arkansas, for a winter holiday. He returned to Illinois about April. 1929 ed., pp. 90–111.

Chapter III

1. Marshalltown, Iowa, a Chicago & North Western division point, was a busy railroad town. Mainlines of the Chicago & North Western, Chicago Great Western and the Minneapolis & St. Louis served this mid-Iowa community of 11,544 in 1900.

2. The Wyoming capital, Cheyenne, with a 1900 population of 14,087, was a center for Union Pacific activities in the West.

3. Brown admits in his earlier version that he participated in this not-so-honest tactic, one that he had used previously to reach Hot Springs, Arkansas.

This paragraph appears in the 1929 version. 1929 ed., p. 113.

4. Pueblo, Colorado, population 28,157 in 1900, was a major point on the Atchison, Topeka & Santa Fe's (Santa Fe) line from Denver to LaJunta, Colorado, and connection there with the Kansas City to California mainline.

5. Crewmen used wooden sticks or "clubs" to turn brake wheels (hand brakes) more easily. Many were made of hickory and were sometimes called "saps" or the "staff of ignorance."

6. In this case Brown literally rode the rods. Hoboes generally used thick boards—their "tickets"—with grooves hewed midway along their lengths that allowed these pieces to slip onto the supporting trusses underneath the cars.

7. Rocky Ford, famous for its "Melon Days" festival and 11 miles west of LaJunta, claimed 2,018 residents in 1900.

8. LaJunta, a Santa Fe division point and shoptown, boasted a 1900 population of 2,513.

9. The "blind" is the recessed front or rear end of a baggage, mail,

or express car. This type of rolling stock commonly contained blinds during the nineteenth and early twentieth centuries. Notes John H. White, Jr., in *The American Railroad Passenger Car* (p. 480), "Many of the earliest R.P.O.s [Railway Post Officees] were built with blind ends; platform steps and hand-rails were retained for the convenience of the brakeman, but there were no end doors. However, the platforms were an inviting place for thieves and hobos, some of whom would actually break through the blank wall in search of plunder."

10. The distance between LaJunta, Colorado, and Coolidge, Kansas, 1900 population of 288, is actually 86 miles.

11. Brown may have been correct to argue that crack Santa Fe passenger trains made the run from LaJunta to Coolidge in about one hour and thirty minutes, yet contemporary public timetables reveal a trip of slightly more than two hours.

12. In his earlier work, Brown says he and Whitie were stranded in Coolidge, Kansas, for nearly three days. As Brownie recalls, "I will hold up my right hand and tell the world that it was the hardest place I ever saw to make a train out of in all of my hobo and railroad days, for it was such an open place right out on the prairie, and between the crews and a half-witted fool of a railroad bull, who kept running around there with a big six-shooter strapped on him, a fellow could not get close enough to a train to land on a car with a parachute." 1929 ed., p. 124.

13. With a 1900 population of 1,942, Dodge City, Kansas, a Santa Fe division point, is 116 miles east of Coolidge.

14. Great Bend, Kansas, population 2,470 in 1900, is 83 miles east of Dodge City.

15. Topeka, the Kansas capital with a 1900 population of 33,608, is 219 miles east of Great Bend and 62 miles west of Kansas City's Argentine Yards.

16. For much of 1899, regular army and state militia units fought against Filipino nationalists, commonly called Insurgents or *Insurrectos*. Although this undeclared war, the so-called Philippine Insurrection, continued until early 1901, most of the major battles had occurred by fall 1899.

17. Argentine, Kansas, location of the Santa Fe's Kansas City area yards, was an unincorporated village in 1900.

18. The Chicago & Alton Railroad, or the "Alton," connected Kansas City and Chicago and operated a line from Chicago to St. Louis.

19. Roodhouse, Illinois, a community of 2,351 in 1900, was a vital junction on the Alton, 251 miles from Kansas City and 237 miles from Chicago.

20. Bloomington, Illinois, a bustling downstate city of 23,286 in 1900, was the junction of the Alton's Roodhouse-Kansas City line and its Springfield-St. Louis line.

21. The L.E.&W., the Lake Erie & Western Railroad or the "Natural

Gas Route," linked Sandusky, Ohio, with Peoria, Illinois. Patrons commonly called the L.E.&W., the "Leave Early and Walk." Brown rode the L.E.&W. for only 72 miles.

22. Burlington, Iowa, with a 1900 population of 23,201, was a division point and shoptown on the Chicago, Burlington & Quincy Railroad. Burlington stands on the west bank of the Mississippi River.

23. "Rip-rap" work involves construction of a retaining wall with large rocks or stones, usually to prevent bank erosion.

24. Council Bluffs, Iowa, 1900 population of 25,802, is on the east side of the Missouri River and is the eastern terminus of the Union Pacific Railroad. At this time six roads, including the Burlington, linked Council Bluffs with Chicago.

25. Edward Henry Harriman (1848–1909) spearheaded rehabilitation of the Union Pacific at the turn of the twentieth century. This "Napoleon of Railroading" maintained that "the way to save money is to spend it wisely and productively." Performance was all that counted with him. In one project, construction of the Sherman (Wyoming) Cutoff, Harriman's Union Pacific ultimately employed 131,332 men.

26. Rawlins, Wyoming, with a population of 2,317 in 1900, is 694 miles west of Council Bluffs.

27. "Second No. 3" is the second section of Number 3, the westbound "Pacific Express." This through passenger train from Council Bluffs to Ogden, Utah, was at this time more of a local (frequent stops) than an express. The better train was Number 1, "The Overland Limited."

28. Brown's reference to a "little old standard eight-wheeler" is to the once ubiquitous "American Standard" or 4-4-0 type locomotive (see also Appendix).

29. Sherman Hill, the summit on the Union Pacific's mainline, is 33 miles west of Cheyenne, with an elevation of 8,247 feet above sea-level in 1869. The company reduced the summit to 8,015 feet early in the twentieth century.

30. Laramie, Wyoming, 57 miles west of Cheyenne, claimed 8,207 residents in 1900.

31. Medicine Bow, Wyoming, an unincorporated hamlet in Carbon County, is 57 miles west of Laramie.

32. This paragraph is found in the 1929 ed., p. 135.

33. Brown held another job before he joined the Rawlins roundhouse crew as a machinist's helper. He worked as a pumper in the company's water service department. 1929 ed., pp. 137–40.

34. Tipton and nearby Red Desert, Wyoming, were both hamlets along the Union Pacific's mainline between Rawlins and Green River. Red Desert is at milepost 764 (from Council Bluffs) and Tipton is at milepost 770.

35. Union Pacific's 1721, a 4-6-0, was built by Brooks in July 1899. Renumbered 1268 in 1915, the Union Pacific junked this locomotive in 1926.

36. The Union Pacific's 1700 Class locomotives were "ten- wheelers," 4-6-0's.

37. Wamsutter, an unincorporated village, is 42 miles west of Rawlins.

38. Green River, Wyoming, population 1,361 in 1900, is 136 miles west of Rawlins.

39. By the turn-of-the-century the Union Pacific and other western railroads commonly hired southern and eastern Europeans—Italians, Greeks, and Bulgarians—to work as unskilled, seasonal laborers. At times these migrants worked directly for private contractors on construction and maintenance jobs.

Chapter IV

1. Every steam locomotive contains two fluesheets or tubesheets. These pieces of heavy metal contain numerous holes and are located at both ends of the boiler.

2. Clean waste is a tangled mass of spun-cotton threads that railroaders used to wipe oil from locomotives and also to pack wheel journals, once it is soaked with oil.

3. Drive-wheels, side-rods, and steam-cylinder jackets are principal parts of steam locomotives. "Drivers" are the large wheels connected to the main or "side-rods" in order to transform power to traction and hence movement. The "jacket," made of heavy steel, covers the boiler.

4. Union Pacific locomotive #1727, a 4-6-0, served the company until October 1925. Designated #1274 after 1915, Brooks built this "ten- wheeler" in July 1899.

5. Union Pacific locomotive #1720, a Brooks 4-6-0, was built in July 1899 and was retired in November 1926. Its number after 1915 became 1267.

6. Flues or "fire tubes," located in the boiler, allow hot gases to pass on their way to the stacks, and in the process convert the surrounding water into steam. At times flues become clogged and must be bored out or replaced.

7. A crownsheet in a steam locomotive is the heavy metal sheeting above the firebox. The crownsheet must be covered by water; if not, an explosion can result.

8. Union Pacific Rule G at this time was known as "General Rule 706": "The use of intoxicants by employees while on duty is prohibited. Their habitual use, or the frequenting of places where they are sold, will be sufficient cause for dismissal."

9. Union Pacific Rule 99 is as follows: "When a train stops or is delayed, under circumstances in which it may be overtaken by another train, the flagman must go back immediately with stop signals; at a point one-fourth of a mile (nine telegraph poles) from the rear of his train, he must place one torpedo on the rail then continue to go back at least one-half mile from the rear of his train and place two torpedoes on the rail, two rail

lengths apart, where he may return to a point one-fourth of a mile from the rear of his train and must remain there until relieved, or recalled by the whistle of his engine. When he returns to his train he will remove the single torpedo.

By night, or when the view is obstructed by fog or otherwise, flagman must place a red fusee on the tracks to assist in protecting his train, while returning.

When a flagman is recalled and there is not a clear view from one-fourth of a mile in rear of train, the train must start immediately on sounding of the whistle recalling the flagman, and be moved ahead, until it reaches a point where the view is clear for one-fourth of a mile.

The flagman must bear in mind that the time of greatest danger is when he is returning to his train. He must be attentive, and should he see or hear a train approaching, must remain and make every effort to stop it in time to prevent an accident. In foggy or stormy weather, and in the vicinity of curves or on descending grades, the distance and number of cautionary signals must be increased.

The front of a train must be protected in the same way, when necessary, by the front brakeman. If the front brakeman is unable to go, the fireman must go in his place.

When a train is flagged, the engineman must obtain a thorough explanation of the cause, stopping if necessary."

10. A *fusee* is a red flare used for flagging purposes. Usually, no following train may legally pass as long as it is burning. Torpedoes, too, are used to protect the rear of a train. Clamped to rail tops, thin, turtle-necked torpedoes explode as wheels roll over them.

11. The company's physical examination included tests for both tuberculosis and syphilis.

12. Union Pacific locomotive 1288, a 2-8-0 or "Consolidation," was a Taunton locomotive, built in April 1883. It was not a "Mogul" or 2-6-0.

13. Creston, Wyoming, an unincorporated hamlet, is 27 miles west of Rawlins and 15 miles east of Wamsutter.

14. Railroads in division and crew-change points employed lads, "call boys," who found employees to tell them to check in for duty. Their efforts were especially needed when men worked on the "extra board" and had no regularly assigned runs.

15. Union Pacific locomotive #642, a 4-4-0, or "American Standard," was built by Rhode Island in February 1889.

16. Wells Fargo Express Company, one of the nation's leading express firms, operated extensively in the West.

17. The Bitter Creek, Wyoming, station was at milespost 787, 75 miles west of Rawlins.

18. Generally Brown's account of the daring robbery of the "Pacific Express" on August 30, 1900, follows national news reports. The loot

amounted to about $100,000 in gold and paper money. According to the *New York Times* of August 31, 1900, "the bandits worked very coolly."

19. Trainmen frequently used heavy toggle chains, carried on the locomotive and in the caboose, to lash freight cars together if couplers failed to hold. Moreover, many industrial plants—for example, sawmills—had sidetracks that were "stubbed" and had extreme curvature. When crew members sought to place or remove a car, coupling was impossible, and so they used chains to connect the car to the locomotive and therefore control it. The "toggle" came into play as a way of keeping the chain from kinking.

20. Point of Rocks, Wyoming, milepost 808, was a station 21 miles west of Bitter Creek.

21. Union Pacific's Number 2, the daily eastbound "Overland Limited," was the company's crack passenger train operated in conjunction with the Southern Pacific and Chicago & North Western railroads from San Francisco to Chicago.

22. Fort Steele, Wyoming, is the first station east of Rawlins, a distance of 15 miles.

23. The "big G" is the Great Northern Railway.

24. The "S.P." is the Southern Pacific Company.

25. Employment on the railroads often depended upon personal connections; nepotism, for example, was rampant at this time.

26. Granger, Wyoming, an unincorporated railroad junction point 30 miles west of Rawlins, was the place where the Oregon Short Line, a Union Pacific subsidiary, left for Portland, Oregon, 945 miles to the northwest.

27. The Oregon Short Line, successor to the Oregon Short Line & Utah Northern Railroad, was part of the Union Pacific System from February 1897 until its dissolution in January 1936.

28. At this time the Union Pacific's Wyoming Division consisted of 515 miles of mainline from Cheyenne to Ogden and another 44 miles of branchlines.

29. The operations of the Oregon Short Line from Granger to Huntington, Oregon, were headquartered in Pocatello, Idaho.

30. The Bear River Valley is located about 15 miles north of Evanston, Wyoming.

31. The "sixteen-hour law" is reference to the Hours of Service Act (or Railway Hours Act) passed by Congress in 1907. This measure, spearheaded by Wisconsin's progressive senator, Robert Marion LaFollette, Sr., guaranteed railroad operating personnel 8 hours of rest after 16 hours of duty.

32. Train Number 4, "The Atlantic Express," operated daily from San Francisco to Council Bluffs, Iowa, via the Southern Pacific and Union Pacific with connection to Chicago over the Chicago & North Western.

33. "Train orders," "waybills," and "switchlists" involve the paperwork associated with the running of freight trains. Train orders (see also

note V:21) inform conductors and enginemen of their travel directions, including "meets" with other trains; waybills are documents prepared by the company that describe a shipment, its routing and charges; and switch lists explain to the conductor the work that must be performed at each station or stop.

34. Altamont, Wyoming, was a station 13 miles east of Evanston.

35. The "branch pipe," "cut-out valve," and "triple valve" are parts of a train's braking system. The branch pipe is a small length of pipe that makes a T-connection with the main line. The cut-out valve is one that a brakeman uses to isolate a defective unit. By adjusting this valve, he can keep the remaining brakes in operation. The "triple valve" is an apparatus connected to the brake pipe, the auxiliary, and the brake cylinder that regulates the intake and exhaust of compressed air in the brake system.

36. A "red board" is a stop signal, in this case probably a station semaphore or "train-order board" attached to a small depot. Crew members needed to stop and sign for their train orders.

37. One of the "Big Four" of the railroad operating unions, the Brotherhood of Railroad Trainmen, dates from 1883, when eight brakemen from the Delaware & Hudson Railroad formed a benevolent association. Later the organization embarked upon trade union activities. Like other fraternal groups, the Trainmen conducted initiation ceremonies.

38. Restaurants commonly sold coupon books, often at a discount, and each coupon was worth a stated amount in food.

39. Carter, Wyoming, was 29 miles west of Granger at milepost 883.

40. Union Pacific's locomotive #1504, a 4-8-0 or "12-wheeler," was Brooks built in May 1899. Renumbered as #1804 in 1915, it was retired in October 1925.

41. Number 8, the "Los Angeles Limited," was a crack train that ran between Los Angeles and Chicago, via the San Pedro, Los Angeles & Salt Lake, Union Pacific and Chicago & North Western railroads.

42. Wasatch, Utah, at times spelled "Wahsatch" by the Union Pacific, was 11 miles west of Evanston, Wyoming.

43. As a courtesy to a fellow trainmen, a fireman or head brakeman commonly covered the electric headlight of his locomotive to reduce the annoyance of its beam.

44. Ogden, Utah, western terminus of the Union Pacific's "Overland Route," is 1,000 miles west of milepost 1 in Council Bluffs, Iowa. This Utah metropolis boasted 16,313 residents in 1900.

45. Brown's reference to "pops" and "binders" is slang for braking appliances. "Binders" are the brakes themselves. "Pops" are retaining valves. These devices, which became commonplace on freightcars in the 1890s, helped to maintain air pressure in the train while the engineer attempted to recharge the braking system. When a brakeman opened a car's retaining

valve, escaping air made a popping sound, hence this nickname of "pops." Brakeman then closed these "pops" at the bottom of the grade. Usually these retaining valves were located next to the brake wheels.

46. Union Pacific locomotive #1664, a 2-8-0, was built by Baldwin in January 1901. The company renumbered it in 1915 as #444 and retired it in September 1930.

47. In his initial work, Brown discusses specifically the Union Pacific's 1600 class locomotives. "[T]hey was compounded on both sides, that is they had two cylinders on each side, the small one was the low pressure, and the live steam came from the boiler and was used in the high pressure, and then exhausted into the low pressure cylinder, where it was used again before being exhausted out through the smokestack to the atmosphere, and they sure was good steamers, and easy on coal and water." 1929 ed., p. 216.

48. The Union Pacific built the 5,900 foot Aspen Tunnel 11.5 miles west of Leroy, Wyoming, where the mainline crosses the Aspen Ridge, a low range of mountains. This bore was opened to traffic on October 15, 1901, two and a half years after the first borings. See W. P. Hardesty, "The Construction of the Aspen, Wyoming, Tunnel on the Union Pacific Railroad," *Engineering News* 47 (March 6, 1902):185–88.

49. The percent grade or gradient of track is the rate of ascent or descent; that is the extent to which the track deviates from a level surface. A vertical ascent of two feet in 100 feet of track is a two percent ascending grade.

50. An angle cock is a valve that is located in the brake pipe under the end of a car, including a caboose, and is immediately in front of the hose connection. It is closed at the rear end of the last car, usually the caboose, but it must be open on all other cars. On many cabooses there is an extender to the angle cock. This permits operating the air hose and thus setting the brakes from the platform of the caboose. (This device also controls a warning signal if the train has to back-up.) There is commonly an extender located over the conductor's desk so he can brake the train in an emergency.

51. The Chicago & North Western Railway, a major midwestern carrier, operated the eastern segment of the famed "Overland Route" between Chicago and San Francisco.

52. The Order of Railway Conductors of America began as a benevolent society in 1868. In that year conductors on the Illinois Central Railroad launched a fraternal association they called the "Conductor's Union." Conductors held a national convention in 1869, where they formally established the Brotherhood of Conductors. Nine years later they changed the name to the Order of Railway Conductors of America.

53. Clinton, Iowa, with a 1900 population of 22,698, has long been a division point on the Chicago & North Western and also the location of the road's carshops.

Chapter V

1. Rankin, Illinois, claimed a population of 754 in 1900 and is 12 miles west of Hoopeston on the Lake Erie & Western Railroad.

2. Lafayette, Indiana, is 56 miles east of Rankin, Illinois, via the L.E.&W.

3. The "Bunn Special" was a popular and high quality railroad watch manufactured by the Illinois Watch Company of Springfield, Illinois.

4. The L.E.&W. did not own a locomotive numbered 335, although it operated locomotives numbered 324, 332, and 334. Acquired from the Lake Shore & Michigan Southern in 1902, these locomotives were 4-6-0's built by Brooks in 1895.

5. The Lake Erie & Western, controlled by the New York Central Lines' Lake Shore & Michigan Southern Railway between 1901 and 1922, was hardly a money-making machine. The company regularly received used equipment from its parent firm. After 1922, the L.E.&W. joined the Nickel Plate Road.

6. Since the Lake Erie & Western crossed the Chicago & Eastern Illinois at Hoopston, an interlocking plant or "tower" protected the crossing. This facility was likely continuously manned by scheduling three eight-hour shifts or "tricks."

7. A Johnson bar is the reverse lever on a steam locomotive. It regulates the direction of motion and the portion of the stroke of the piston during which steam is admitted to the cylinder.

8. Templeton, Indiana, an unincorporated village, is 26 miles east of Hoopeston, Illinois.

9. L.E.&W. Number 3 operated over the 327 miles between Lima, Ohio, and Peoria, Illinois. According to the company's public timetable, it carried "Baggage and Mail Cars, Smoking and First-Class Ladies Coach."

10. At Lafayette, Indiana, the L.E.&W. crossed the Chicago-Louisville line of the Chicago, Indianapolis & Louisville Railway (Monon Route) and the St. Louis-Detroit line of the Wabash Railroad.

11. Frankfort, Indiana, where the L.E.&W. crossed the "Clover Leaf Route," had a population of 7,100 in 1900. Frankfort is 69 miles east of Hoopeston.

12. Tipton, Indiana, a community of 3,764 residents in 1900, is 25 miles east of Frankfort, Indiana.

13. Newburg, Missouri, population 481 in 1900, is 119 miles southwest of St. Louis.

14. The Frisco, officially the St. Louis & San Francisco Railroad Company, operated about 5,000 miles of line in Missouri, Kansas, Oklahoma, Texas, Arkansas, Tennessee, Mississippi, and Alabama. The company's operating center was Springfield, Missouri.

15. Springfield, Missouri, an expanding city of 23,267 in 1900, is 239 miles southwest of St. Louis.

16. Rolla, Missouri, population 1,600 in 1900, was the first station east of Newburg, 111 miles from St. Louis.

17. Dixon, Missouri, population 500 in 1900, was two stations east of Newburg, 106 miles from St. Louis.

18. The Frisco acquired the Kansas City, Fort Scott & Memphis through a 99-year lease on August 23, 1901.

19. Brown is probably referring to the former Kansas City, Fort Scott & Memphis's 4-6-0's, built by the Pittsburgh Locomotive Company in 1901. These locomotives retained their K.C.F.S.&M. numbers, 549–557, on the Frisco.

20. Frisco locomotive #520, a 4-6-0, was built by Baldwin in 1903. Brown has likely misidentified this engine.

21. From the late nineteenth century on, railroads used two train-order forms, a 19 and a 31, to dispatch trains safely. The distinction between the two is that the 31 form requires the train to stop for the signature of the individual to whom it is addressed. A 19 order, however, is given to the crew "on the fly."

22. Brown misidentified Iron Mountain, Missouri. That village was not located on the Frisco but rather on the St. Louis, Iron Mountain & Southern Railway (Missouri Pacific). Perhaps the Frisco had a siding with a water tower and coal chute that it likewise called Iron Mountain.

23. Pacific, Missouri, with a 1900 population of 1,213, is 34 miles from St. Louis.

24. The Frisco's 700-class locomotives were new. These 4-6- 0's were built by Baldwin in 1902.

A compound engine is a steam locomotive that uses steam released from one cylinder into a second cylinder.

25. Number 4 was not the "Meteor," but rather the "St. Louis Express."

26. East St. Louis, Illinois, population 29,655 in 1900, was a major railroad center served by 18 carriers.

27. Brown refers to the "Big Four." Officially, this is the Cleveland, Cincinnati, Chicago & St. Louis Railway, part of the New York Central Lines.

28. Mattoon, Illinois, with a 1900 population of 9,622, is 134 miles from East St. Louis, Illinois.

29. The Young Men's Christian Association operated nearly 180 hotels that catered specifically to railroaders throughout the country; they were nearly always clean and inexpensive.

30. Charleston, Illinois, population 5,488 in 1900, is 144 miles from East St. Louis.

31. The Toledo, St. Louis & Western Railroad, the "Clover Leaf Route," was a 454 mile road that extended from Toledo, Ohio to St. Louis, Missouri. It joined the Nickel Plate Road in 1923.

32. Number 6 operated between St. Louis and Toledo and took about 13 hours to make this 454-mile run.

33. Located 132 miles from Frankfort, Delphos, Ohio, 1900 population of 4,517, was a busy interchange point on the Clover Leaf Route with the Northern Ohio Railway (New York Central Lines) and the Pennsylvania Railroad.

34. The "Clover Leaf Route" owned a large fleet of Rhode Island-built 4-6-0's. These dated from the late 1880s and early 1890s and were commonly assigned to fast freights prior to 1905.

35. Morris & Company, formed in 1903, operated packing plants in Chicago, East St. Louis, St. Joseph, Kansas City, Oklahoma City, and Omaha. Armour & Company purchased Morris in 1923.

36. See note IV:1.

37. Marion, Indiana, a rapidly growing city of 17,337 in 1900, is 52 miles east of Frankfort and 80 miles west of Delphos.

38. State railroad commissions usually required carriers to erect warning devices, "tell-tale ropes," in front of low-clearance objects like bridges or tunnels.

39. Number 111, a 4-6-0, built by Richmond in August 1900, was one of three such locomotives on the T.St.L.&W.

40. Kokomo, a thriving north-central Indiana town of 10,609 residents in 1900, was 25 miles and four stations east of Frankfort.

41. The exploding track torpedo prompted the engineer (hogger) to "answer the flag" with two short blasts of the whistle.

42. Van Buren, Indiana, located 62 miles from Frankfort and the first station east of Marion, claimed a population of 965 in 1900.

43. Thayer, Missouri, with a 1900 population of 1,276 in 1900, is 138 miles southeast of Springfield, Missouri, on the Frisco's Springfield to Memphis line.

44. While the Frisco's Springfield to Thayer line may have been called the "Leaky Roof" Division, the Kansas City, Clinton & Springfield Railway, which connected Kansas City, Missouri, with Springfield and subsequently part of the Frisco System, was commonly known as the "Leaky Roof."

45. Sterling, Missouri, an unincorporated village in 1900, was the first station west of Willow Springs, or 51 miles west of Thayer.

46. Willow Springs, Missouri, with a 1900 population of 1,078 is 47 miles west of Thayer and four miles east of Sterling.

47. Koshonong, a village of 213 residents in 1900, was two stations and 9 miles west of Thayer.

48. The D.&R.G. is the Denver & Rio Grande Railroad.

49. Rogersville, Missouri, an unincorporated village in 1900, is 17 miles east of Springfield, Missouri.

50. Cedar Gap, Missouri, population of 112 in 1910 (it was unincorporated in 1900), is 41 miles east of Springfield and 6 miles west of Mansfield, Missouri.

51. As Brown explains, "Hossing her over means that the engineer

throws the reverse lever in back motion or reverse." 1929 ed., xiv.

52. A wye is used for reversing locomotives and cars when no turntable is available. Specifically it consists of tracks that run from the mainline or "lead," thus forming a letter Y.

53. Mountain Grove, Missouri, with a 1900 population of 1,004, is 67 miles east of Springfield.

54. The blower valve controls a steam line to the smokestack which creates a draft in the firebox and so excites the fire when the locomotive is standing. The fireman then turns off the blower once the locomotive is in motion.

An injector feeds water from the locomotive's tender or tank into the boiler.

55. The "Tom and Jerry" drink, one that appeared in England during the early nineteenth century, consists of eggs, sugar, brandy, rum, and milk.

56. The Terminal Railroad Association of St. Louis, opened in 1889, served carriers that entered St. Louis and used the city's Union Station. As a company advertisement said in 1906: "Operating St. Louis Bridge and Union Station, St. Louis and East St. Louis Terminals."

57. Eads Bridge, which spans the Mississippi River between East St. Louis and St. Louis, opened to traffic on July 4, 1874.

58. Relay stations were part of the network of telegraphic communications. Some were manual operations; telegraphers copied messages and then re-sent them to their destinations. In others the "relay" was accomplished automatically through switchboard connections. Early on, glass batteries, recharged by adding acid, provided the electricity. Eventually power came from outside sources.

59. Semaphore fixed signals are part of a system of electric or manual signal blocks. See also note VIII:39.

60. One of the nation's most popular and memorable fairs, the Louisiana Purchase Exposition of 1904, is better known as the St. Louis World's Fair.

61. St. Louis Union Station, opened on September 1, 1894, and located at 1820 Market Street, west of the city's commercial heart, was a massive structure designed by Theodore C. Link and Edward A. Cameron. In recent years developers have restored and redeveloped the structure as a festive marketplace with specialty shops, restaurants, entertainment and a hotel. It no longer serves rail travelers.

Chapter VI

1. Wichita, Kansas, with 24,671 residents in 1900, had become by 1904 an important railroad center: the Atchison, Topeka & Santa Fe; Chicago, Rock Island & Pacific; Frisco; Kansas City, Mexico & Orient; and Missouri Pacific railroads served this bustling trading and manufacturing center.

2. Neodesha, Kansas, with a 1900 population of 1,772, is 104 miles east of Wichita.

3. The Missouri Pacific Railway, controlled by the Jay Gould family, operated in conjunction with the St. Louis, Iron Mountain & Southern Railway an extensive system west and southwest of St. Louis.

4. Cheney, Kansas, population of 429 in 1900, is 26 miles west of Wichita on the 80-mile Pratt branch.

5. Flooding was extensive throughout Kansas in early July 1904. Reported the *New York Times* of July 8, 1904: "Wichita is flooded worse than ever before in its history. The dikes at several places along the Little River gave way before the rush of water which poured down Waco Avenue, one of the principal residence streets, in a raging torrent, becoming waist deep."

6. Carry Anna Moore Nation (1846–1911) received considerable notoriety in the spring of 1900 when she wrecked the bar of Wichita's fashionable Hotel Carey and other nearby saloons.

7. This paragraph appears in the earlier version, 1929 ed., pp. 270–71.

8. Decatur, Illinois, population 20,754 in 1900, and location of the Wabash System's shops, is 113 miles northeast of St. Louis, Missouri.

9. The Wabash, like the Missouri Pacific, a Gould property, extended from Kansas City and St. Louis to Chicago, Detroit and Buffalo with various appendages.

10. Danville, Illinois, with 16,354 residents in 1900, is 187 miles northeast of St. Louis and 74 miles east of Decatur, Illinois.

11. Blue Mound, Illinois, with a 1900 population of 714, was the first station and 14 miles west of Decatur.

12. Wabash's Number 9 was a Buffalo-to-Kansas City passenger and mail train and, at this time, almost always operated in two sections.

13. Bement, Illinois, with a 1900 population of 1,484, was a principal junction on the Wabash, 20 miles east of Decatur.

14. Wabash's Number 4, a Kansas City-to-Buffalo passenger train, was also known as the "Continental Limited," rather than the "Buffalo Limited."

15. Wabash locomotive #640, a 4-6-0, was built by Baldwin in August 1904 and scrapped in December 1933.

16. Brown mentions in the 1929 edition that "When an engineer sets the airbrakes in emergency, we say he bigholed her, or give them the works." 1929 ed., xiv.

17. Helen Gould (1870–1938) was the third of six children of Jay and Helen Gould. "Nellie" devoted her adult life to philanthropy and religious activities.

18. George Jay Gould (1864–1923), son of railroad magnate Jay Gould, reigned as Crown Prince of the Gould railroad empire, which included the Wabash. Generally, he was a poor railroad manager.

19. Sadorus, Illinois, a village of 340 in 1900, is 33 miles east of Decatur.

20. Trains Number 11 and 14, the "Banner Blue Limited," operated with parlor and observation cars and other first-class rolling stock. Number 11 left Chicago at 11:30 A.M. and arrived in St. Louis at 7:30 P.M.; Number 14 left St. Louis at 11: 30 A.M. and arrived in Chicago at 7:32 P.M.

21. The running times were about two hours longer than Brown recalled; the distance is 286 miles. Still, it is likely that the "Banner Blue" reached speeds in excess of 60 m.p.h.

22. The Wabash 600-class locomotives which Brown refers, are likely the Class E, 4-4-2's or "Atlantics," built by Baldwin, Brooks and Richmond between 1898 and 1904.

23. Granite City, Illinois, population 3,122 in 1900, is eight miles from Union Station in St. Louis.

24. The Chicago, Milwaukee & St. Paul Railway's Chicago to Janesville, Wisconsin line was 99 miles long and continued on to Madison, Wisconsin, 140 miles from Chicago.

25. Brown refers to the mainline between Milwaukee and Chicago.

26. The general offices of the 9,350-mile Atchison, Topeka & Santa Fe were located in the Railway Exchange Building at the corner of Michigan Avenue and Jackson Street in Chicago's Loop.

27. Temple, Texas, population of 7,065 in 1900, was a division point on the Fort Worth to Galveston line of the Santa Fe's subsidiary, the Gulf, Colorado & Santa Fe Railway.

28. Cleburne, Texas, with a 1900 population of 7,493, is 99 miles north of Temple and the site of major locomotive and car shops.

29. Known as the Lampasas Branch, the Temple to San Angelo line is 227 miles in length. San Angelo, Texas, while unincorporated in 1900, reached a population of 10,321 by 1910. It would later see the arrival of the Kansas City, Mexico & Orient Railway.

30. Somerville, Texas, an unincorporated village, is 77 miles south of Temple and the junction with the Beaumont Line. There the Santa Fe operated a large switching yard and also a major tie-treating plant.

31. O.R.C. is the Order of Railway Conductors.

32. The Santa Fe operated only passenger trains, 5, 17, and 19-15 between Temple and Somerville in 1906. Brown probably rode Number 5, which arrived in Somerville at 3:57 P.M.

33. The Fred Harvey Company, named after founder Frederick "Fred" Henry Harvey (1835–1901), developed, in the 1880s, a chain of eating establishments called Harvey Houses along the Santa Fe System that provided travelers and residents alike with good food and good service.

34. The so-called "Beaumont Line" ran eastward from Somerville, Texas, with a 10-mile branch from Bragg to Saratoga and a 21-mile branch from Silsbee to Beaumont, and then it turned northward to Center, 271 miles from Somerville. Later it reached Longview and Ero, Texas, the latter 43 miles from Center.

35. "Squirrel whiskey" is a home-brew drink.

36. Waitresses employed by the Fred Harvey Company were commonly called "Harvey Girls" and came mostly from New England and the Middle West. The "girls" agreed to refrain from marriage for one year, and those who remained with the firm might move from one Harvey House to another. Thus they became female "boomers."

37. The Texas Rangers, the country's oldest state law enforcement agency, dates from the 1820s. In the late nineteenth century the organization was known officially as the "Frontier Battalion of the Rangers."

38. The port city of Galveston, Texas, with a population of 37,789 in 1900, had been mostly rebuilt following the disastrous hurricane and flood of 1900. This storm killed one-sixth of Galveston's population and destroyed one-third of its property.

39. The *S.S. Denver* was a 5,000-ton steamship owned by the New York & Texas Steamship Company, the "Mallory Line." Headquartered in New York City, the Mallory Line operated a fleet of 11 vessels on three routes: New York to Galveston, 2,225 miles; New York to Mobile, Alabama, 1,920 miles; and New York to Brunswick, Georgia, 914 miles.

40. The Mallory Line sent the *S.S. Denver* or a sister ship from Galveston for the trip to Key West, Florida, at noon on Wednesday, and it arrived there on Saturday. The *S.S. Denver* then steamed from Key West to New York, arriving on Tuesday, a "delightful six days' voyage by sea."

41. The White Star Line operated six ships, including the *Majestic,* from Pier 48 on the North River at the foot of West 11th street in New York City to Liverpool, England.

Chapter VII

1. The New York Central was the only railroad to operate freight yards on the island of Manhattan.

2. The distance between Grand Central Station (42nd Street and 4th Avenue) and Albany is 142 miles.

3. New York Central freight "AR1" meant one destined for Albany and Rochester, New York.

4. "AN6" was a freight train that originated in Albany and was destined for New York City.

5. Poughkeepsie, New York, with a 1900 population of 24,029, is 73 miles north of New York City.

6. The New York Central, like other high-density roads, used operators, stationed in "block towers," to aid in train-control work. These employees operated semaphores and other signaling and switching devices.

7. The "Empire State Express," for example, left Grand Central Station at 8:30 A.M. and arrived in Albany at 11:10 A.M.

8. Croton-on-Hudson, population of 1,533 in 1900, is 34 miles north of New York City.

9. Tarrytown, New York, population 4,770 in 1900, is 9 miles south of Croton-on-Hudson.

10. Ossining, New York, with 7,939 residents in 1900, is 4 miles south of Croton-on-Hudson and 30 miles north of New York City.

11. The Lake Shore & Michigan Southern Railway, an affiliated New York Central Lines property, operated between Buffalo, Cleveland, Toledo, Detroit, and Chicago. It officially joined the New York Central in 1914.

12. Brown took a "Big Four" train from Cleveland to Indianapolis to Danville, Illinois.

13. Wellington, Illinois, with a 1910 population of 295 (unincorporated in 1900), is 29 miles north of Danville and 94 miles south of Chicago.

14. C.&E.I. train Number 4 was a northbound passenger that ran between Evansville, Indiana, and Chicago.

15. Dolton yards were approximately 20 miles south of Chicago.

16. Chicago Heights, Illinois, population of 5,100 in 1900, is 27 miles south of Chicago.

17. Brazil, Indiana, in the heart of the Indiana coal country, claimed a 1900 population of 7,786. The Brazil Division of the C.&E.I. extended from Momence Junction, near Chicago, southward to Brazil, a distance of 131 miles.

18. Villa Grove, Illinois, population of 1,828 in 1910 (it was unincorporated in 1900) was a junction on the C.&E.I., 165 miles southwest of Chicago.

19. Rossville Junction, Illinois, 105 miles south of Chicago, and 18 miles north of Danville, was the beginning point of the 36-mile "Rossville and Sidell Branch," which connected with Sidell on the Danville-Villa Grove-St. Louis Line.

20. Whiting, Indiana, with a 1900 population of 3,983, is in the heart of the greater Chicago manufacturing and refining area.

21. The Chicago-based Elgin, Joliet & Eastern Railway, the "Chicago Outer Belt Line," interchanged with the C.&E.I. at Chicago Heights.

22. A Trojan coupler was the brand-name for one of the many "Janney-type" or knuckle couplers used during the late nineteenth century. It was manufactured by the Trojan Coupler Company of Troy, New York. Brakemen did not like Trojan couplers because they had a side rather than a more convenient overhead release.

23. Coaler was a station on the C.&E.I. in the Chicago terminal area.

24. "Yard snakes" is a reference to members of the Switchmen's Union of North America. This brotherhood used "S" for its symbol, and hence, perhaps, the "Snake" nickname. Also switchmen "snaked" cars throughout railroad freight yards.

25. The Grape Creek mines were located approximately five miles from Danville.

26. The Panic of 1907 brought about a brief interruption to the unrivaled prosperity that the country had enjoyed since the turn of the century.

27. Hot boxes are overheated journals or bearings and were a frequent

cause of delays and wrecks before the widespread use of ball bearings on rolling stock.

28. These previous two paragraphs appear in Brown's initial version. 1929 ed., pp. 333–34.

29. Rossville, Illinois, with a 1900 population of 1,435, is 18 miles north of Danville.

30. Alvin, Illinois, population 319 in 1910, is six miles south of Rossville and 12 miles north of Danville. The Illinois Central, unlike the C.&E.I., called its station Alvan.

31. The Illinois Central Branch that passed through Alvin (or Alvan), Illinois, linked West Lebanon, Indiana, with LeRoy, Illinois, a distance of 74 miles.

32. Railroads regularly gave their employees and those of "foreign" lines trip passes. They allowed riders free coach passage on most trains for a restricted period of time. Annual passes for travel commonly went to officials, especially from foreign roads.

33. The Chicago, Rock Island & Pacific, the "Rock Island," operated a 1,083 mile mainline from Chicago to Denver via Omaha and Lincoln, Nebraska.

34. The distance between Denver and Ogden, Utah, via Cheyenne, on the Union Pacific is 591 miles.

35. The trip from Ogden to San Francisco and then to El Paso, Texas was over the Southern Pacific for 2,078 miles. In the first version Brown writes, "the third [leg] from Ogden to El Paso, Texas via Frisco, and Los Angeles [is] over the Southern Pacific. . . ." 1929 ed., p. 341.

36. The El Paso & Southwestern System operated the 272 miles between El Paso and Santa Rosa, New Mexico. Technically, the El Paso & Northwestern Railroad controlled trackage between El Paso and Carrizozo, New Mexico, and the El Paso & Rock Island Railway from Carrizozo to Santa Rosa.

37. The Rock Island operated the 1,193 miles between Tucumcari, New Mexico, and Chicago, via Kansas City, the popular "Golden State Route." The Chicago, Rock Island & El Paso, affiliated with the El Paso & Southwestern, controlled the 59 miles between Santa Rosa and Tucumcari.

38. On this side trip, Brown rode the Oregon Short Line the 37 miles from Ogden to Salt Lake City, the Utah capital with a 1910 population of 92,777.

39. The Denver & Rio Grande Railroad, "the Scenic Line of the World" and a Gould property, operated a 742-mile mainline from Denver to Salt Lake City.

40. Helper, Utah, population 816 in 1910, is 115 miles east of Salt Lake City.

41. Thistle, Utah, an unincorporated village, is 65 miles from Salt Lake City.

42. Tucker, Utah, unincorporated in 1910, is 18 miles east of Thistle.

43. The station at Soldier Summit is seven miles east of Tucker.

44. The grade at Soldier Summit, Utah, was a steep four percent, but in 1913 the company reduced it to two percent, thus allowing one steam locomotive to handle a freight train over the divide instead of requiring three.

45. Mountain railroads often built snowsheds over their tracks to prevent a line's closing during heavy snows. This was referred to as "railroading in a barn."

46. The engineer applied sand, stored in the locomotive's sand-dome.

47. The Western Pacific operated its first passenger train between Oakland, California, and Salt Lake City, Utah, on August 21, 1910. The trip covered 914 miles.

48. Colton, Utah, is seven miles east of Soldier Summit station.

49. Colton is 18 miles west of Helper.

50. Number #723 is not a Western Pacific number. The road's earliest locomotives carried numbers 1 through 65, 71 through 106, 121 through 127, and 151 through 162. Number 723 may have come from another Gould-controlled line.

51. Saltair Beach, 14 miles west of Salt Lake City, was connected to the Utah capital by the Salt Lake & Los Angeles Railway. This little pike became the Salt Lake, Garfield & Western Railroad in 1916, and was later electrified.

52. The Tabernacle, completed in 1865, seats 6,500 people and has one of the largest domed roofs without center support in the world.

53. The Mormons started construction of their massive Salt Lake City Temple in the late 1850s; church members dedicated it in April 1893.

Chapter VIII

1. Brown arrived in Reno, Nevada, which had a 1910 population of 10,867, on a Southern Pacific train.

2. Brown has slightly exaggerated the length of these snow sheds. They had reached their maximum length of 37 miles in the nineteenth century. But as equipment and techniques for fighting snow became more successful, the length of sheds declined. By 1925, 21 miles remained; by 1940, only 8 miles. And in 1984, 12,000 feet of track were protected.

3. Truckee, California, unincorporated in 1910, is 35 miles west of Reno and 14 miles east of Summit.

4. Los Angeles's three principal railroads in 1909 were the Atchison, Topeka & Santa Fe (Santa Fe); San Pedro, Los Angeles & Salt Lake (later part of the Union Pacific); and the Southern Pacific.

Brown's career with the Santa Fe ha appeared in article form. See H. Roger Grant, ed., "Working for the Santa Fe: Memoirs of 'Brownie the Boomer,' 1909–1911," *Railroad History* 161 (Autumn 1989):35–65.

5. San Bernardino, California, population 12,779 in 1910, is 60 miles east of Los Angeles.

6. Barstow, California, unincorporated in 1910, is 141 miles northeast of Los Angeles. In Barstow the San Francisco line joins the Los Angeles to Chicago mainline.

7. Needles, California, unincorporated in 1910, is 169 miles east of Barstow, and was a Santa Fe division point.

8. This paragraph appears in Brown's first version. 1929 ed., pp. 361–62.

9. The 900 class locomotives of the Santa Fe were 2-10-2's and not 2-8-2's, or "Mikes." Baldwin built 86 of these locomotives in 1903 and 1904. Since this was the first order to be placed with a locomotive builder with this wheel arrangement, 2-10-2's became known as the Santa Fe-type.

10. A tandem compound-type engine has on each side a high- and a low-pressure cylinder set end-to-end with pistons mounted on one rod.

11. Santa Fe's 1600 class locomotives, 2-10-2's, were built by Baldwin between 1905 and 1907. The 74 locomotives of this class were originally four-cylinder tandem compounds but were later changed to simple engines.

12. Topock, California, unincorporated in 1910, was the first station east of Needles, a distance of 12 miles.

13. Number 9, the "California Fast Mail," operated daily between Chicago and Los Angeles and San Francisco. It, however, carried more than mail and express cars; the consist included a Pullman drawing-room sleeper between Chicago and Los Angeles and tourist sleepers between Chicago and San Diego, as well as other types of passenger equipment.

14. The "blow out cocks," located at each end of the cylinders and operated manually, force out water that has condensed in the cylinders. Locomotives also have "big blowout cocks," placed immediately ahead of engine cab, that are used to get rid of dirty or foaming water. After servicing at the enginehouse, locomotives were "blown down" before a trip. And on arrival for service, if work was required on the boiler or firebox, they were blown down to hurry cooling.

15. Seligman, Arizona, unincorporated in 1910, is 149 miles east of Needles and is at the western end of the Mountain Time zone.

16. Kingman, Arizona, unincorporated in 1910, is 62 miles northeast of Needles and 87 miles west of Seligman.

17. Hackberry, Arizona, unincorporated in 1910, was the first station east of Kingman, a distance of 27 miles.

18. Peach Springs, Arizona, unincorporated in 1910, is 50 miles east of Kingman and 23 miles east of Hackberry.

19. The Santa Fe had a station at the hamlet of Nelson, Arizona, which was 11 miles east of Peach Springs.

20. Number 10, the "Chicago Fast Mail," was a daily Los Angeles-to-Chicago passenger train.

21. Santa Fe's #940, a 2-10-2, was built by Baldwin in 1903.

22. Bakersfield, Fresno, and Oakland were leading California cities on the Santa Fe, with 1910 populations of 12,727; 24,892; and 150,174 respectively.

23. The Santa Fe, like other railroads, especially in the West, provided employees with various social facilities, including recreational halls. The company wanted to keep workers content, particularly in isolated areas, and they also sought to create suitable alternatives for saloons, brothels, and other "wicked" spots. Remarked S. E. Busser, Superintendent of Reading Rooms, "Give a man a bath, a book, and an entertainment that appeals to his mind and hopes by music and knowledge, and you have enlarged, extended and adorned his life; and, as he becomes more faithful to himself, he is more valuable to the company." By 1909 the Santa Fe had invested approximately $250,000 in its Needles facilities. See "A Memorable Evening," *Santa Fe Magazine,* 1(February 1907):81–82.

24. The Fred Harvey Company operated on the Santa Fe and briefly on the Frisco as well. In the early 1930s, however, it opened a restaurant in Terminal Tower in Cleveland, Ohio, its only off-line facility.

25. Goffs, California, unincorporated in 1910, is 31 miles and the first station west of Needles. Goffs was the junction with the Barnwell branch, which extended 45 miles northward to Ivanpah with an extension to Searchlight, Nevada.

26. The Santa Fe's Number 4, the crack "California Limited," operated between Los Angeles and Chicago.

27. The Santa Fe became a leader in the railroad hospital movement; its first ones were in LaJunta, Colorado, and Las Vegas, New Mexico. By 1916 the company-sponsored Atchison Railroad Employees Association operated seven medical facilities systemwide, including one in Los Angeles.

28. The Santa Fe's employee facilities in Needles proved costly to operate. The bill approached $75,000 annually and included a payroll for 46 staff members.

29. The fight between Jack Johnson (1878–1946), an African-American heavyweight boxer, and James J. "Jim" Jeffries (1875–1953), the "White Hope," took place before a crowd of 16,000. Johnson knocked out Jeffries in the fifteenth round.

30. Number 8, the "Chicago Express," ran daily between San Francisco and Chicago.

31. Santa Fe #1275, a 4-6-2, 1270 Class locomotive, was built by Baldwin in 1909. This type of locomotive was known commonly as a Pacific.

32. The Santa Fe 1270-Class, 4-6-2's or Pacifics, originally carried 170 pounds of steam and sported smokebox superheaters. The road owned 20 of this particular class.

A superheater on a steam locomotive boosts its power and reduces radiation loss in the cylinder without adding much to the locomotive's cost and weight. "Of all the improvements to the locomotive during the early

1900's none ranks higher than the superheater," wrote one contemporary authority. "Its remarkable effect on locomotive efficiency and power provided a reprieve when further development seemed at an end." Angus Sinclair, *Development of the Locomotive Engine* (New York: Sinclair Publishing Company, 1907), 665.

33. Yucca, Arizona, is 38 miles and two stations east of Needles.

34. When Brown "dropped some oil on the guides," he lubricated the guide bars that support the crossheads, a movable block that supports the piston rod outside the cylinder.

And in another lubrication process, he forced grease into the locomotive's bearings.

35. The scheduled time for Number 3, the "California Limited," was four hours and five minutes.

36. A revolution broke out in Mexico in 1910, against Porfirio Diaz, dictator for the previous 35 years. This revolution obtained slight sympathy from the American government.

37. The Presidio, a federal army post, dates from the 1770s, when the Spanish constructed a fortification for the San Francisco Bay area.

38. Steam locomotives contain reservoirs of oil in the cab, which lubricate various moving parts. Although this process is semiautomatic, a fireman must check and at times refill these reservoirs.

39. Automatic electric block signals have fixed signals along a route of track that is divided into sections or "blocks." These blocks are spaced so that trains will run at safe distances: trains activate the signals when their wheels short circuit the electric current.

40. Santa Fe's 1010, a 2-6-2, 1000 Class locomotive, was built by Baldwin in 1901. The company owned 14 of this particular model of "Prairie"-type locomotive, and altogether it operated nearly 150 2-6-2s.

41. Walter Scott, better known as "Death Valley Scotty," an eccentric prospector and miner, paid the Santa Fe $5,500 to take him from Los Angeles to Chicago in record time. The three-car train, "the Coyote Special," left on Sunday, June 9, 1905, and arrived at Dearborn Station on Tuesday, the 11th, in the record time of 44 hours and 54 minutes for this 2,265-mile trip.

Brown is mistaken about the 1010 pulling the "Coyote Special" from Barstow to Needles. Rather, this locomotive, a Baldwin-built Prairie (2-6-2), hauled Scott's train from Needles to Seligman. The engineer on that leg was F. W. Jackson. T. E. [Tom] Gallagher used another 2-6-2, #1005, to handle the special between Barstow and Needles.

Chapter IX

1. Santa Fe locomotive #1657, a 2-10-2, was built by Baldwin in 1907.

2. Bagdad, California, an unincorporated hamlet, is 91 miles west of Needles.

3. Daggett, California, unincorporated in 1910, is 9 miles east of Barstow. The San Pedro, Los Angeles & Salt Lake Railroad met the Santa Fe at Daggett and operated over its trackage to San Bernardino, a distance of 91 miles.

4. The locomotive firemen's union, in the vanguard of labor-mediation work, operated its own adjustment board. It regularly solved disputes relating to promotion of firemen to locomotive engineers. Generally, firemen were promoted on the basis of length of service, practice runs under the direction of the locomotive engineer, and examinations on locomotive machinery and operations. They also had to win endorsement of the Road Foreman of Engines, which included supervised trips. As one railroad official remembers, "There were opportunities for all kinds of discrimination."

5. Where Brown got the capital to buy the Star Restaurant is a mystery. Probably this operation was low-budget, and he could have been buying it on a long-term contract.

6. The Brotherhood of Locomotive Firemen and Enginemen was the firemen's union. Founded in 1873 as a mutual benefit society, it was not until the 1880s that a young fireman, Eugene V. Debs, energized the organization. Soon it became an active trade union, and in 1968 it merged with several brotherhoods to become the United Transportation Union.

7. The Pacific Electric Railway, the largest electric interurban in the country, connected most communities in the greater Los Angeles area. One route, the South Pasadena line, linked Los Angeles with Pasadena, the latter with a 1910 population of 30,291. The company's big red cars became their unofficial logo.

8. The employment agency, Hummel Brothers & Company, was located at 116-118 East Second Avenue, between Main and Los Angeles Streets in downtown Los Angeles.

9 Sacramento, the California capital, claimed a population of 44,946 in 1910. It was 561 rail miles from Los Angeles.

10. Wadsworth, Nevada, unincorporated in 1910, was a village several miles from Fernley on the Southern Pacific's Oakland to Ogden "Overland Route" line.

11. At this time the Southern Pacific was constructing a branch that extended in a northwesterly direction; it reached Susanville and Westwood, California, the latter 135 miles from Fernley, Nevada, in 1913. In the 1920s the company pushed this line into Oregon.

12. The eccentric straps and blade (the latter slang for rod) are parts of a locomotive's valve gears.

13. The previous two paragraphs appear in the earlier version. 1929 ed., pp. 424–25.

14. The unincorporated village of Bay Point, California, is 31 miles east of Oakland.

15. The Oakland, Antioch & Eastern was an electric interurban that

began at Bay Point, California, and a connection with the Santa Fe was built through the Ignacio Valley in 1910. The road reached Walnut Creek in 1911 and then it headed toward Sacramento. Through service between San Francisco (via the Key System) and Sacramento, a distance of 93 miles, began on April 3, 1913. Some additional construction work continued for several months. The Oakland, Antioch & Eastern later became part of the Sacramento Northern.

16. Pittsburg, California, unincorporated in 1910, is eight miles east of Bay Point on the then newly opened Oakland, Antioch & Eastern.

17. Wheatland, California, population of 481 in 1910, is 39 miles north of Sacramento on the Southern Pacific's Sacramento-Portland line.

18. Brown's description of operations on the Durst Brothers Ranch is remarkably positive. One historian recounted less attractive conditions there in August 1913: "Twenty-three hundred hop pickers in 105 degree heat were camped in filthy tents, with eight small toilets and no garbage disposal. No water was available in the fields. . . . Pay was at the rate of ninety cents per hundred pounds of hops picked. . . . The camp grocery store, with its ludicrous prices, paid half of the net profits to the owners." See Roger A. Bruns, *Knights of the Road: A Hobo History* (New York: Methuen, Inc., 1980), 144.

19. Richard "Blackie" Ford, an I.W.W. agitator, attempted to force the Durst Ranch to provide better working conditions.

20. The I.W.W. or the Industrial Workers of the World, "Wobblies," the most important radical union of the early twentieth century, was launched in 1905. The class-conflict orientation of this organization is revealed clearly in the preamble to its constitution: "The working class and the employing class have nothing in common. Between these two classes a struggle must go on until all the toilers come together . . . and take hold of that which they produce by their labor through an economic organization of the working class, without affiliation with any political party." Until it fizzled in the 1920s, the I.W.W. sought to create the "One Big Union."

21. The Durst Ranch was located in Yuba County, southeast of Marysville, California, a county-seat town of 5,430 residents in 1910.

22. The melee led to the deaths of two law-enforcement officials and two hop pickers, one of whom was a boy.

23. The Panama-Pacific International Exposition, which commemorated the completion of the Panama Canal, was held in San Francisco in 1915; it attracted nearly 20 million visitors.

24. During this time the Southern Pacific owned two stations in San Francisco: the Ferry Building where ferryboats left for the Oakland Pier terminal and one at 3rd and Townsend. This particular structure was moved to 4th and Townsend in 1914, and a new structure was built in its place for the Panama-Pacific Exposition of 1915.

25. San Luis Obispo, California, with a 1910 population of 5,157 and

a Southern Pacific crew-change point, is 252 miles south of San Francisco.

26. Portland, Oregon, claimed 207,214 residents in 1910 and was the northern terminus of the Southern Pacific.

27. Seattle, Washington, population 237,194 in 1910, had just received connections to a third transcontinental railroad, the Chicago, Milwaukee & St. Paul. The last spike on this Chicago to Puget Sound road was driven on May 14, 1909, four miles west of Garrison, Montana.

28. Butte, Montana, with a population of 39,165 in 1910, was a copper mining center and division point on the newly completed Chicago, Milwaukee & St. Paul. Butte, via the St. Paul, was 672 miles east of Seattle.

29. Superior, Wyoming, unincorporated in 1910 and located on a seven-mile stub line from Thayer Junction, never enjoyed regularly scheduled passenger service.

30. The approximate distance from the accident site to Rock Springs was 25 miles.

31. Brown likely received several thousand dollars cash from both the brotherhoods and the Union Pacific Railroad. Records that would reveal specific figures are unavailable, except for his $1,000 claim from the firemen's union. While these settlements might have carried Brown for a few years, it was necessary for him to find another job, which he did.

32. Brown rented initially but in the mid-1920s bought a house at 1418 McBride Avenue. He remained there through 1932. The Los Angeles City Directory for 1933 and subsequent years fails to list him at any local address.

Index

[255]

Buffalo, New York, 147–48
Buffalo Bill's Wild West Show, 18
Burlington, Iowa, 43
Butte, Montana, 213

Carter, Wyoming, 77–78
Cedar Gap, Missouri, 103–5
Charleston, Illinois, 95
Cheney, Kansas, 122
Cheyenne, Wyoming, 36, 44
Chicago, Illinois, 17–18, 34, 87, 129–30, 156–57
Chicago Heights, Illinois, 149–50
Chicago, Burlington & Quincy Railroad, 18, 33, 43
Chicago, Indianapolis & Louisville Railway, 90
Chicago, Milwaukee & St. Paul Railway, 18–19, 33–34, 130, 213, 218
Chicago, Rock Island & Pacific Railroad, 160
Chicago & Alton Railroad, 42
Chicago & Eastern Illinois Railroad, 17, 34, 36, 87, 89, 148–60
Chicago & North Western Railway, ix–x, 36, 86
Chicago Great Western Railroad, x
Cleburne, Texas, 131
Cleveland, Cincinnati, Chicago & St. Louis Railway, 15, 95
Cleveland, Ohio, 148, 218
Clover Leaf Route. See Toledo, St. Louis & Western Railroad
Coaler, Illinois, 154
Cody, William F. "Buffalo Bill," 18
Colton, Utah, 165–66
Coolidge, Kansas, 41
Crawfordsville, Indiana, 5
Creston, Wyoming, 56
Croton-on-Hudson, New York, 145
Crow Indian Reservation, Montana, 28

Custer, Montana, 28

Daggert, California, 197
Danville, Illinois, 148, 150–51, 154–57
Decatur, Illinois, 124, 127–29
Delphos, Ohio, 96–97, 101
Denver, Colorado, 37, 160
Denver & Rio Grande Railroad, 161–69
Dickinson, North Dakota, 31
Dixon, Missouri, 91, 94
Dodge City, Kansas, 41
Dolton Yards, Illinois, 149, 151
Durst Brothers Company, 209–10

Eades Bridge, 106
East Lafayette, Indiana, 90
East St. Louis, Illinois, 95, 106–7, 129
Elgin, Joliet & Eastern Railway, 153
El Paso & Northwestern Railroad, 160
Evanston, Wyoming, 67, 70–73, 77–79, 85–86, 161

Fargo North Dakota, 20, 22, 32
Ferris Wheel Park (Chicago), 18
Firemen's Adjustment Board, 197–98
"Flop-houses," 17–19, 33–34
Ford, Richard "Blackie," 210
Forsythe, Montana, 30
Fort Steele, Wyoming, 62
Frankfort, Indiana, 90, 96–99
Fresno, California, 179
Frisco Railway. See St. Louis & San Francisco Railroad

Galveston, Texas, 139

[256]